COLLINS
WORDPOWER

Word Check
Graham King

HarperCollins*Publishers*

HarperCollins*Publishers*
Westerhill Road, Bishopbriggs, Glasgow G64

www.**fire**and**water**.com

First published 2000

Reprint 10 9 8 7 6 5 4 3 2 1 0

Cartoons by Hunt Emerson. Hunt Emerson's website is at
www.largecow.demon.co.uk

HarperCollins Publishers would like to thank Bob Coole for reading and
commenting on the text of this book.

ISBN 0 00 472378 3

A catalogue record for this book is available from the British Library

Typeset by Davidson Pre-Press Graphics Ltd, Glasgow G3

Printed and bound in Great Britain by
Caledonian International Book Manufacturing Ltd, Glasgow

To dearest Lyn,
who as my wife
is a practised
WORK CHECK

Acknowledgements

The majority of the word definitions in *Word Check* are taken from the major dictionaries: *Collins English Dictionary*, *Oxford English Dictionary*, the *Chambers Dictionary*, *Cassell's English Dictionary*, *Webster's New 20th Century Dictionary*, *Funk & Wagnalls Standard College Dictionary*, *Chambers Science and Technology Dictionary*, *The Encyclopaedia Britannica*.

Acknowledgements are also made to the help supplied by the *New Fowler's Modern English Usage*, edited by R.W. Burchfield, Eric Partridge's *Usage and Abusage*, Sir Ernest Gowers' *The Complete Plain Words*, Stephen Murray-Smith's *Right Words*, David Crystal's *The Cambridge Encyclopaedia of The English Language* and Philip Howard's *The State of the Language*.

Of valuable practical help have been the style guides of the British press and also the newspapers of New York and Chicago, and the *Columbia Guide to Standard American English*.

Graham King (1930-1999)

Graham King was born in Adelaide on October 16, 1930.
He trained as a cartographer and draughtsman before joining
Rupert Murdoch's burgeoning media empire in the 1960s, where
he became one of Murdoch's leading marketing figures during the
hard-fought Australian newspaper circulation wars of that decade.
Graham King moved to London in 1969, where his marketing
strategy transformed the *Sun* newspaper into the United
Kingdom's bestselling tabloid; subsequently, after 1986, he
successfully promoted the reconstruction of *The Sunday Times* as
a large multi-section newspaper.

A poet, watercolourist, landscape gardener and book
collector, Graham King also wrote a biography of Zola, *Garden of
Zola* (1978) and several thrillers such as *Killtest* (1978). Other
works include the novel *The Pandora Valley* (1973), a semi-
autobiographical account of the hardships endured by the
Australian unemployed and their families set in the 1930s.

In the early 1990s, inspired by the unreadability and
impracticality of many of the guides to English usage in
bookshops, Graham King developed the concept of a series of
reference guides called The One-Hour Wordpower series:
accessible, friendly guides designed to guide the reader through
the maze of English usage. He later expanded and revised the texts
to create an innovative series of English usage guides that would
break new ground in their accessibility and usefulness. The new
range of reference books became the Collins Wordpower series

(see page 185), the first four titles being published in March 2000, the second four in May 2000. Graham King died in May 1999, shortly after completing the Collins Wordpower series.

Browse Articles

Introduction

A dictionary will tell you what words mean and a computer's spellcheck will show you how to spell words, but neither is much help when it comes to *using* words. Especially words that look alike, that are spelt the same, or are pronounced the same. These words are called *confusables*.

Many of us know about Mrs Malaprop's mistakes but we are all guilty of dropping verbal bricks from time to time. Like using **livid** for red when it means the bluish hue of a bruise. Or **practice** when we mean **practise**; **nauseous** when we mean **nauseated**; **parameter** for **perimeter**; **alibi** for **excuse**; **disinterested** for **uninterested** – to name just a few of the thousands of word-traps that are lying in wait for us. *Collins Wordpower WORD CHECK* is designed to help you avoid these pitfalls – not to mention the embarrassment caused by misusing and misspelling words.

Do you know the difference between **celibate** and **chaste**? **Bulimia** and **anorexia**? **Empathy** and **sympathy**? **Farther** and **further**? **Swinging** and **swingeing**? **Voodoo** and **hoodoo**? *Collins Wordpower WORD CHECK* will tell you and peel back the mysteries of using **it**, **its** and **it's**; **who** and **whom**; **round** and **around**; **lay**, **laid**, **lain** and **lie**; **shall**, **should**, **will** and **would**. It will also gently warn you about over-used and fashionable words such as **meaningful**, **empower**, **ongoing**, **situation**, **syndrome**, **quantum leap** and **debrief**.

Using words incorrectly can transform what you say and write into garbage and gobbledegook. Conversely, the ability to communicate with clarity, elegance and vivacity is little short of magic. But like all magic it has to be practised and this comes down to using words correctly. That's why you will find this book an invaluable guide through the minefield of those thousands of words, phrases and grammatical mischief-makers that we are never quite sure about.

1

A

a, an

Use *a* before words beginning with consonants *(a book, a cup, a video)* and *an* before words beginning with vowels: *an apple, an ice cream, an omelette, an undertaker.* There are some exceptions: the word *one,* because of the way it is pronounced (wun), demands an *a (a one-horse town)* as do certain words beginning with the long *u* (pronounced yew): *a ukelele, a uniform, a used car.* Words beginning with a soft *h* need *an (an heiress, an honest man)* but words that sound the *h* don't: *a horse, a hat, a hooter.* For cooks and gardeners, in British English it's *a herb,* whereas in the US it's *an herb.*

abjure, adjure

While not words you use every day, they are useful to know. You often see them in newspapers: *Elsewhere governments under threat of sanctions merely adjured their subjects to tighten their belts.* **Abjure** means formally and solemnly to renounce something, usually on oath. **Adjure** is (equally solemnly) to charge someone with a serious responsibility: *He abjured his former way of life and adjured his family to protect him from further temptations.*

abnegate, abrogate, arrogate

To **abnegate** is to deny oneself; **abnegation** is self-denial. To **abrogate** is to repeal or abolish something: *The abrogation of the despised emergency laws was a cause for national celebration.* **Arrogate** means to claim or seize without right; note the close tie with *arrogant.*

abnormal, subnormal

Note the significant difference: **abnormal** means 'not normal, departing from the norm or average'; an **abnormality** is an irregularity. Subnormal means 'below normal' and is often applied to individuals to indicate low intelligence.

about. See **round, around, about**

above. See **over, above**

abridged. See **unabridged**

abstruse, obtuse

A concept that's **abstruse** is one that's hard to understand – fairly similar to *obscure,* meaning 'unclear'. **Obtuse** derives from *dull* and means 'slow, stupid and insensitive': *The obtuseness of her pupils kept Miss Hayworth in a constant state of dismay.*

abuse, misuse, disabuse

Abuse and **misuse** have roughly the same range of meanings: 'to maltreat, insult, or damage someone or something'. **Misuse** is the milder expression *(he misused his talents)* while **abuse** continues to become more condemnatory, as with *child abuse* and *drug abuse* with their moral and legal overtones. But **disabuse** has just one specific meaning which is 'to rid a person of a mistaken idea': *She lost no time disabusing the girls of the notion that life at St Agatha's was going to be one big party.*

accede, agree

Accede, meaning 'to agree or give consent to', has become a pompous word now mostly confined to legal and regal circles. Use plain **agree to**, consent to, or allow.

accent, ascent, assent

The word **accent** (pronounced AX-sent) has to do with emphasis, usually with some aspect of speech and its pronunciation; **ascent** (pronounced a-SENT) is the act of moving or climbing upwards. Assent (also pronounced a-SENT) means 'to express agreement' or, as a noun, 'an agreeing'. A royal assent is the Crown's formal agreeing to an Act already passed through the Houses of Parliament.

accent, dialect

An **accent** is a variation of pronunciation from the standard language; a **dialect** also strays from standard pronunciation but in addition can use different vocabulary and grammar.

accept, except

To **accept** is to receive something or to agree with something; **except** means 'to exclude, omit, leave out, reject'.

accidental, incidental

An accidental **happening** occurs unexpectedly and unintentionally. Something **incidental** happens in relation to something else of greater importance *One incidental result of the calamitous floods was a renewed friendliness among neighbours.*

accidie, anomie

Strange words that we increasingly see in books and newspapers. **Accidie** (AK-sih-dih), or spiritual sloth, was one of the seven deadly sins; its modern meaning is embodied in the apathetic query 'what's the point?' **Anomie** is the erosion or distancing of a person or a society from laws, morals and acceptable social standards. A country suffering from **anomie** is out of touch with civilised social and moral behaviour.

according to. See *pace*, according to, notwithstanding

accountable, responsible

There seems to be no good reason to regard these words other than as synonyms, although **accountable** sounds more serious. See also **cause, responsible.**

acetic. See **aesthetic, acetic, ascetic**

acknowledgement

The *e* before *-ment is* now usually dropped in American English, but either spelling is generally accepted.

acoustics

Acoustics is plural: *He thought the acoustics of the new opera house were wonderful.* But there is a singular exception: *Acoustics is his favourite subject.*

acquire. See **get, acquire, obtain, secure**

activate, motivate

Activate is sometimes wrongly used to mean 'motivate'. You **activate** things *(He activated the fuse)* but **motivate** people. However, **motivate** is an overused vogue word for *encourage.*

actor, actress, authoress, poetess, sculptress, etc.

Actor was used for both sexes before the introduction of **actress**, but today there is a general return to **actor**. There is, for example, no Actress's Equity in the UK, nor a Screen Actress's Guild in the US. The move to non-feminine labels is happening to **authoress** (author), **poetess** (poet) and **sculptress** (sculptor). An aviatrix is now, simply, a pilot. The reason for all this is that feminists felt that the old labels perpetuated the notion that the male form is the norm and the female a secondary or inferior exception. However, to insist that *hero* should replace *heroine, heir* replace *heiress, waiter* replace *waitress* and for *god* to replace *goddess* is perhaps going too far.

actually, virtually, really

Actually scored a high place in the *Sunday Telegraph's* 1995 Collection of Irritating Words, and is certainly grossly overused. **Actually** and **really** mean 'in fact': *Did he actually call me that?* is legitimate usage; *Well, actually, I wouldn't mind a drink* is not. If **actually** doesn't change or add to the meaning of a sentence, then forget it! **Virtually** means 'in effect, mostly, for all practical purposes'.

acute. See **chronic, acute**

A.D. See **B.C., A.D.**

adapt, adopt

To **adapt** means 'to change or adjust something to suit different conditions'; to **adopt** is to take over something or someone as one's own: *In time they adapted their eating habits to the tropical climate; Once he understood what it was all about he adopted the idea with enthusiasm.*

adapter, adaptor

An **adapter** (and, interchangeably, **adaptor**) is someone who adapts something for another purpose: *As an adapter of plays for children she is undoubtedly the best.* But the electrical fitting that you plug into a socket is always an **adaptor**.

adjacent, adjoining, contiguous

If two things are **adjacent**, they are close to each other. If they are **adjoining**, they are joined or touching: *My room adjoins hers; Marie's house is adjacent.* **Contiguous** means sharing a common boundary.

adjudge, adjudicate

To **adjudge** is to decide, but more usually to decide *judicially* in a court of law. To **adjudicate** is a serious although less formal process of giving a decision.

adjure. See **abjure, adjure**

administer, minister

In the sense of treating and tending to, both words have similar meanings but are used differently: *The nurse **administered** what emergency first aid she could; Over the course of the next few months she patiently **ministered** to their medical needs.* Note that in this context **minister** is always followed by *to*.

admit

There is nothing wrong with *Thief admits committing four burglaries in West London*. But what we increasingly see is *Customs Officer admits to* filing false claims. If you substitute *acknowledges* for *admits*, would you write *acknowledges to*? In this sense the *to* after *admits* is redundant.

adopted, adoptive

A child is **adopted**; those who adopt the child are the **adoptive** parents.

advantage, benefit

An **advantage** is a situation that favours success; a **benefit** is a form of help that is earned, paid for, or given.

adventitious, adventurous

Adventitious is seen less nowadays than **fortuitous or serendipitous;** they all mean 'happening by chance'. **Adventurous** means 'daring, enterprising, bold and audacious'.

adversary, opponent

Both are interchangeable, a fine difference being that **adversary** has a hostile and antagonistic ring to it, while **opponent** has sportier, friendlier connotations.

adverse, averse

They look and sound similar but are used in very different ways. **Adverse** means 'hostile and damaging': *The adverse conditions wrecked their holiday.* **Averse** indicates disinclination and reluctance: *She is averse to handing out favours.* Note that *averse* is followed by *to.*

advice, advise, advisedly

The first two are easy. If you give counsel to or **advise** someone, you are giving them helpful information or **advice**. **Advisedly** is the tricky word: it has nothing to do with being advised or receiving advice. It means to take your *own* counsel. In a looser sense, it can mean 'prudently and cautiously': *The King made the decision, advisedly, no doubt with the intention of dividing the troublesome clans.*

adviser, advisor

Both mean 'someone who advises' (*Brett hired a financial adviser*) and both spellings are acceptable. But remember that the adjective is **advisory**.

aeroplane, airplane, aircraft

British English has it as **aeroplane**; American English as **airplane**, with **plane** common to both. However, the industry on both sides of the Atlantic usually calls them **aircraft**, which has the advantage of being singular *and* plural.

aesthetic, ascetic, acetic

Aesthetic (usually **esthetic** in American English) relates to the appreciation of beauty in art and nature above material considerations; an **aesthete/esthete** is one who has a highly developed appreciation of artistic beauty. An **ascetic** is a person who rejects worldly comforts in favour of self-denial, often for religious reasons. **Acetic**, from acetic acid, the main component of vinegar, is sometimes used as an adjective for sour and bitter. Pronounce them as *es-THET-ik, ah-SET-ik, ah-SEE-tik*.

affect, effect

These two words are super-confusables! To **affect** is to cause or influence something to happen: *Smoking can adversely affect your health.* An **effect** is a result: *One effect of smoking can be lung cancer.* Other meanings are close but not quite the same: *The burglar effected entry by the bathroom window; The third movement of the symphony always affected him greatly.* Remember that:

* **affect** – cause – usually a verb
* **effect** – result – usually a noun

Confusable Quiz: Affect AND Effect

Can you always use **affect** and **effect** correctly? Many newspapers can't. Which of these quotations are right or wrong?

1. 'Despite a Cambridge education, Emma effects a horrible, almost estuary-like, cockney accent'. – *The Sunday Times*

2. 'Inquiry into affects of new woodland village'. – Headline, *Kentish Gazette*

3. '... and its existence put under the control of competitors who can effect every participant's market share by their own price rises or poor performance'. – *The Times*

4. '... the cause of the fire, why it spread so fast, the affect of the firefighters' response, will all be investigated' – *The Independent*

5. 'She said drinking water without boiling it could cause stomach upsets, and that affects on the young and elderly could be serious' – *The Times*

Answer: All are wrong

---

affecting, affection, affectation

A troublesome trio. An **affecting** play is one that touches the deeper emotions; **affection** describes the act or state of fondness and attachment; while an **affectation** is a pretence.

7

affinity with, affinity for

If you respect the definition of *affinity* as a relationship involving a natural inclination towards someone or something, you will use **affinity with**. But recently *affinity* has become a loose synonym for 'liking' in which case users will logically opt for **affinity for**.

Afrikaans, Afrikaners

The language of South Africa is **Afrikaans;** the people are **Afrikaners.**

affront, effrontery

These are easily confused but are used in different ways. An **affront** is a deliberate, contemptuous insult. Effrontery means 'barefaced insolence, audacious impudence': *The effrontery of the performers was an affront to every decent family present.*

after, afterwards, afterward

He ran after the thief is used here to mean to pursue or seek. But **after**, like **afterwards** (**afterward** in the US), can also mean merely following, or later in time: *After the escape the detective resumed his investigations…* or: *Afterwards/Afterward the detective resumed his investigations.*

ageing, aging

Both spellings are acceptable, with **aging** more common.

ago, before, back, past

Most dictionaries define **ago** as 'in the past', so it is correct to write: *The O'Briens left these shores over a century ago.* In such a context, **ago** is preferable to the other choices, *a century before,* and *a century past* beg the question, 'Before or past what?' while *a century back* is idiomatic. A common mistake is to couple **ago** with **since**: *It was over a century ago since the O'Briens left,* where *since* is clearly redundant. The correct version would be: *It was over a century ago that the O'Briens left.* Or, without **ago**: *It was over a century since the O'Briens left.*

Agenda and Other Problem Plurals

The agenda were agreed by all present… In the light of the findings the original data were urgently reviewed… She agreed reluctantly that the criteria for her criticism were faulty… These sentences may sound strange to our ears but technically, perhaps pedantically, they are all correct. **Agenda** and **data** are examples of Greek- and Latin-derived words where, having all but abandoned the singular forms (**agendum, datum**) we tend to use the plural forms to serve the needs of both. There also exist a couple of genuinely 'missing singulars'; **trivia** exists

8

only in the plural, and you will find the singular for **erotica** only in the
original Greek: *erotikos*.

Here are some more common singular/plural confusables:

Singular	Plural
bacterium	*bacteria*
criterion	*criteria*
graffito	*graffiti*
medium	*media*
minutia	*minutiae*
phenomenon	*phenomena*
species	*species*
spectrum	*spectra*
stratum	*strata*

Don't get caught on **kudos,** however; it is singular, pure and simple.
And while you're thinking about all this, are such words as **acoustics** and
politics singular or plural? (They are both plural nouns functioning as
singular, but **politics** takes singular and plural tense with equal regularity. See
acoustics, politics.)

---

aggravate, exasperate

Aggravate means to make a condition worse. It does not mean to annoy –
except in everyday speech where its use annoys the purists! If you want to
exasperate someone, try teasing, irritating or provoking them, which could
aggravate their ill-temper.

AGGRAVATE, EXASPERATE

agnostic See **atheist**

agree with, agree to, agree about, agree on
One usually **agrees with** a person but **agrees to** a proposition or an idea: *I agreed with him about using the car but couldn't agree to his taking it for a whole week.* Other combinations include: *We eventually agreed on a deal,* and *This is the deal we've agreed upon.* Sometimes the preposition is omitted altogether: *We agreed the deal on Thursday.*

How Changing a Letter Can Change the Meaning!

A changed letter or word can make a lot of difference, and most of us make Malapropian slips from time to time:

* *He's in the hospital's expensive care ward*

* *When it comes to marriage, Western people believe in the principle of monotony.*

* *She went off in high dungeon.*

* *He was proud to have at last entered the portholes of fame.*

* *Although he's very old he still retains all his facilities.*

* *Superman was supposed to have possessed X-rated vision.*

---

aid, abet; aid and abet
Both **aid** and **abet** have a common meaning: 'to assist, help or encourage'. **Abet** is now virtually confined to 'encouraging a criminal act', while **aid and abet** is little more than legal tautology.

AIDS, HIV
AIDS is the acronym for Acquired Immune Deficiency Syndrome and is a medical condition, not a disease. **HIV** is Human Immunodeficiency Virus and, again, is not a disease. People who are *HIV-positive* may suffer and die from *AIDS-related* diseases.

akimbo
Akimbo describes a position of a person's arms: hands on hips with the elbows pointing outwards. To describe a man 'standing at ease, legs akimbo', as a well-known novelist recently did, is to describe an osteopathic impossibility.

alibi, excuse
Increasingly, **alibi** is being used as a synonym for **excuse**, to the extent that

many grammarians worry that we shall be left with no word for the true meaning of alibi. *The Government is using French intransigence as an alibi for its own slow progress on free trade agreements* is wrong. An **alibi** is the defence that an accused person could not have committed a crime because he or she was elsewhere at the time. Ignore dictionaries that suggest **excuse** as an informal meaning of alibi; excuses are explanations to cover some fault or shortcoming; they can be true or false and come in a thousand guises.

allege, allegedly

Both are useful warning qualifiers to make it clear that something is not yet proved: *The alleged bribe was in the form of an envelope full of banknotes stuffed into his pocket.*

allegory, fable, myth, parable, legend

An **allegory** is a play, poem or picture in which the characters symbolise a deeper moral message. A **fable** is a short story, usually improbable, usually with a moral, and usually with animals as characters. A **parable** is a short and simple story which illustrates some religious or moral principle. The original **myths** used gods and superhuman characters to explain natural phenomena and social customs; today the word is used mostly to describe a baseless popular belief. A **legend** is a traditional story, popularly thought to be true or based on fact: the Arthurian legends are an example. But **legend** is now extensively and incorrectly used to describe an enduring feat, or someone whose notoriety has spread and persisted – *the legendary baseballer Babe Ruth* – even though Ruth did exist in fact. The cliche *He was a legend in his own lifetime* is incorrect.

allergy, aversion

An **allergy** is an oversensitive reaction by the body to some substance; hay fever is an **allergic** reaction to pollen. But allergy is not a synonym for **aversion**. We sometimes read, '*The man is allergic to any form of hard work*, whereas what is meant is, *The man has an aversion (i.e. dislike) for hard work.*

almost. See most, almost

all ready, already

All ready, meaning 'prepared and ready for some proposed action', is clear enough, but **already** can present problems. **Already** means 'by a certain time' or 'before some specified time', but other shades of meaning abound. Sentences like: *You want me to leave already?* have a certain Jewish flavour, meaning, *Are you telling me to leave?* Other expressions include: *We're already in plenty of trouble; I've already done the work; The deliveries are already running ten* *minutes late.* You can see that *already* is a sort of all-purpose word that vaguely expresses or emphasises a time relationship.

all right, alright

If we accept **already, altogether** and **almost,** why not **alright**? Although it carries with it the whiff of grammatical illegitimacy it is and has been in common use for a century, as in: *I got the exam questions all right and overall I think I did alright.*

allude, elude, elide

Allude means 'to refer to something indirectly'; **elude** (think of *elusive*) means 'to escape by cunning and skill'. **Elide** means 'to omit or ignore'.

Alsatian, German Shepherd

Both are correct when referring to the dog; the latter used more commonly only in the US.

altar, alter

Discussing the refurbishment of the church, the builder said to the bishop: *I'm sorry, but I can't alter the altar.*

alternate, alternative

Alternate means 'one after the other', 'to take turns', or 'to substitute' An **alternative** is a choice between two or more options. The same applies to **alternately** and **alternatively:** *You can work alternately, that is on alternate days, or alternatively you might prefer to work one week on and one week off.* **Alternative** cannot be used without relating it to a prior option. *The non-alcoholic beer is to be marketed as a party alternative* is nonsense: alternative to what? *The non-alcoholic beer is to be marketed as an alternative to the range of alcoholic drinks consumed at parties* is sobering but clear.

although, though

Both are generally interchangeable but **though** is considered to be more colloquial. **Though** means 'despite the fact that… ; **although** means 'even though'. It's largely a matter of which looks and sounds right. *Although it was a mongrel I bought the dog anyway; I bought the dog even though it was a mongrel.* **Though** can also be used to end a sentence as an afterthought: *I happen to like mongrels, though.* Avoid *tho* and *altho.*

all together, altogether

All together is a grouping phrase meaning 'gathered in the same place at the same time'. **Altogether** means 'completely, entirely, totally': *When you put the facts all together you will realise that you are altogether wrong.*

alumnus, alumna, alumnae, alumni

An **alumnus** is a male graduate of a college or university (plural **alumni**) while an **alumna** is a female graduate (plural **alumnae**). Collectively they are *alumni.*

amateur, novice, tyro

An **amateur,** as opposed to a professional, indulges in an activity as a pastime. A **novice** is a beginner, while a **tyro**, a word used less frequently, is an awkward, raw beginner.

ambiguous, ambivalent

The two are not synonyms. **Ambiguous** is used to refer to a confusing situation which has two or more meanings or interpretations. To be **ambivalent** is to be confused by two contradictory or conflicting thoughts or emotions.

Ambition vs Policy

If there is a tendency to use the word **policy** where **ambition** would be the correct term, then London journalist Peter Barnard is doing a sterling job trying to halt it. Here he is in *The Times* berating Prime Minister John Major:

> *Whereas Major used to give the impression that he did not know the answers to some questions, he is now obliged to give the impression that there is nothing for which he does not have a solution.*
>
> *This sad development involves speaking when silence would be better, and in speaking, abusing the English language. Thus we have Major saying that the government has a policy called low inflation. Low inflation is not a policy, it is an ambition. As a young man I wanted to sleep with Catherine Deneuve, but that was an ambition, not a policy. Low inflation is Major's Catherine Deneuve.*

---

ameliorate. See **improve, ameliorate**

amend, emend

In relation to a text, **amend** means 'to correct, improve, change or revise it', while **emend** means 'to correct it by removing errors'. **Amend** is nowadays acceptable to describe both tasks.

America, American

Through common usage, the United States of America has more or less grabbed **America** for its own, much to the annoyance of its northern and southern neighbours. Strictly speaking, **America** refers to the two continents. Do **Americans** include native Indians and Nicaraguans along with the citizens of Brooklyn and the Bronx? If you wish to be both clear and fair, use **The United States of America**, the **United States**, or the **US**. Where the term **US citizen** is cumbersome and there is little risk of confusion, use **American**: *The world record is held by an American.*

amiable, amicable

Both words imply friendliness but with this difference: **amiable** generally applies to people and living things (*I always remembered him as an amiable sort of fellow*) while **amicable** can also be used to describe inanimate relationships: *They quickly reached an amicable agreement.*

amid, amidst

Use **amid**; **amidst** is considered rather flowery.

amok, amock, amuck

To run **amok** is to charge about in a murderous frenzy. **Amock** and **amuck** are misspellings.

among, amongst, between

Use **between** to connect two persons, objects or ideas: *There is little difference between the two of them; she couldn't tell the difference between either of them.* **Among** is used in connection with *several* things: *There is little difference among all five candidates; He shared the reward among his friends.* It's worth remembering that when describing a choice, **between** is followed by *and* and not *or*: *It's a matter of choosing between Jane and George* – not *Jane or George*. And keep an open mind about situations where several things are considered individually: *He divided the reward equally between the five of us.* **Amongst**, while still in general use, is regarded as a bit old-hat.

amoral, immoral

Amoral means 'unconcerned with morals', 'an unmoral person', 'someone without a moral code'. To be **immoral** is to offend against an established moral code.

amuse, bemuse

To **amuse** someone is to divert and entertain them and to make them smile or laugh: *The baby's antics never failed to amuse the family.* **Bemuse**, however, is to

14

confuse and bewilder: *She could see that the guests were totally bemused the moment they walked into the gallery.*

analysis, synthesis

Analysis means 'to take apart, to examine, to reduce something to its elements'. Synthesis means the opposite: 'to combine, to build something from various elements'.

anemone, anenome

Perhaps because it is easier to pronounce this way, the latter is often used as the spelling, but it is incorrect.

anaesthetic, analgesic

An **anaesthetic** (American English = **anesthetic**) produces a loss of physical feeling, an **analgesic** reduces sensitivity to pain: *He was given a general anaesthetic for the operation; Paracetamol is a widely used analgesic.*

angry. See mad, angry

annex, annexe

Two common confusables worth separating by their different spelling. To **annex** is to attach or to take possession of something: *The government lost no time announcing the annexation of the adjoining territory.* An **annexe** (but often **annex** in the US) is an addition or extension: *The new annexe will provide accommodation for another sixty students; The lawyer said she would annex the extra paragraphs to the will.*

anniversary, birthday, jubilee

A small point, perhaps, but humans and animals celebrate their birth with **birthdays**, while everything else has **anniversaries**. A **jubilee** used to be a 25th or 50th anniversary but is now used to describe any important periodical celebration.

anomie. See accidie, anomie

anorexia. See bulimia, anorexia

answer. See reaction, answer

antagonist. See protagonist, antagonist

ante-, anti

When using words beginning with these prefixes it may help to remember that **ante** = *before*; **anti** = *against.*

>Before – *antebellum, antecedent, antedate, antediluvian, antenatal*
>Against – *antibody, antifreeze, antimacassar, antinuclear*

anticipate, expect, hope

The traditional meaning of **anticipate** is foresee, or to think of beforehand, or forestall: *The captain anticipated the cyclone and put into the nearest harbour.* It is now general usage to use **anticipate** for **expect**, which really means 'to look forward to something that is certain or fairly likely to happen': I *now expect you to arrive early every Monday; We can expect some rain over the next day or two.* Admiral Nelson exhorted his men with *England expects every man will do his duty,* rather than *England hopes… ;* **hope** is an altogether more wish-oriented word implying no certain outcome: *I hope the neighbour's party won't be too noisy.*

anxious, eager

She was anxious to get home is probably a shortening of *She was anxious (about the dangers of walking alone in the dark) and eager to get home.* **Anxious** implies a degree of worry, fear or apprehension, while to be **eager** is to be impatient, keen, enthusiastic.

anybody, anyone, any one

The first two are interchangeable and, strictly speaking, singular: *If anybody/anyone is there, will he please answer the doorbell?* is correct. However, with objections to *he,* and with the questioner not knowing the gender of the person on the other side of the door, it is now acceptable to use the plural forms *they* or *their: Will they please answer the doorbell?* The same principles apply to **somebody/someone**. **Any one** is used when single persons or objects are being described: *The first prize could go to any one of the entries.*

anymore, any more

Anymore is preferred in the US; **any more** in the UK, but both mean 'not now': *Marilyn doesn't work here anymore/any more. Any more* is correct when referring to quantity: *I don't want any more porridge.*

anyplace, anywhere

Anywhere means any unspecified place. **Anyplace** is the American English version.

apartment. See flat, condominium, apartment

apparent, evident

Apparent means 'seeming to appear, or appearing to exist', but dictionaries also define the word as meaning 'readily seen or understood' which creates a mighty confusable! **Evident** means 'conclusive, obvious, clear to one's understanding'. We often hear something like *It's fairly evident that the home team will lose,* which is confusing until you delete the 'fairly'. Good alternatives are **clear** and **unclear**: *It was clear that the home team would lose; At halftime it was still unclear whether the home team would lose, as expected.*

apposite, apt

Both mean 'appropriate', or 'ideal for the occasion or purpose'. **Apposite** perhaps carries a little more literary weight.

appraise, apprise, assess, evaluate

To **appraise** is to estimate the worth of somebody or something; to **assess** is to estimate the value of something, for example, property for tax purposes; to **evaluate** is to determine the numerical or monetary value of something. **Apprise** is the odd man out, it means 'to inform': *After the desserts were served the waiter quietly apprised him of the size of the bill.*

appreciate. See understand, appreciate, comprehend

approve. See condone, approve, allow

a priori, prima facie

The Latin term *a priori*, which is sometimes misapplied, defines reasoning deductively, from cause to effect, which, without supportive observation, leads to a conclusion. *A priori* reasoning can, of course, lead to a wrong conclusion. *A priori* is sometimes confused with *prima facie*, which means using available but not necessarily complete or tested evidence to arrive at a conclusion: *His* a priori *view was that there was sufficient evidence to convict the man; The fact that the notes were found in the student's locker was* prima facie *evidence of his cheating.* Note that both should normally appear in italics.

arbitrate, mediate

These words represent quite distinct methods of settling a dispute. An **arbitrator** hears evidence from both sides before handing down a decision, which is binding; an **arbitrary decision** is one over which the disputants have little or no say. A **mediator** is much more involved in negotiating (or 'arm-twisting') with the parties in dispute and aims more for a compromise solution.

Argentina, Argentine

Argentina is the country although old hands may still refer to it as **The Argentine;** more to the point, **argentine** refers to silver or something with silvery qualities. There's a lot of argy-bargy (which is from the Scottish, incidentally) about whether its citizens should be called **Argentinians or Argentines.** Purists prefer the latter although the former is perfectly acceptable. As one wit has pointed out: "Would Evita have been so successful if the composer had scored 'Don't whine for me, Argentine'?"

around. See **round, around, about**

arouse. See **rouse, arouse**

arthritis, rheumatism, lumbago, sciatica

Arthritis is painful inflammation of the joints, **rheumatism** is a similarly painful joint disorder but can extend to muscle and connective tissue; **rheumatoid arthritis** is a chronic condition often characterised by swollen joints. **Lumbago** is backache, usually in the lower lumbar region, while **sciatica** is neuralgic pain in the thigh and leg, caused by inflammation of the sciatic nerve.

artist, artiste

A painter or public performer is an **artist;** although the inflated term **artiste** still survives, it is best avoided.

Art Nouveau, Art Deco

Both define styles of decorative art and architecture. **Art Nouveau** is a highly stylised form based on natural vegetation, especially leaves and flowers; it arose in the 1890s and extended well into the 20th century. **Art Deco** evolved in the 1920s and is a style primarily based on geometric and symmetrical forms.

ascent. See **accent, ascent**

ascertain, find out

Jim, find out how many people are waiting out there, will you? Jim, ascertain how many people are waiting out there, will you? Which would you prefer to use? If you can substitute **ascertain** for **find out** without appearing pompous, feel free to do so.

ascetic. See **aesthetic, esthetic, ascetic, acetic**

ascribe. See **prescribe, ascribe**

ass. See **donkey, ass, burro, mule**

assume, presume

One meaning of **assume** is quite unambiguous: 'to undertake something', as in: *He rather arrogantly assumed the role of team leader.* The other meaning – 'to suppose, to take for granted, to conclude on the basis of existing evidence', is often confused with **presume**, which means 'to take for granted without any proof or reasoning': *Knowing Jennifer was a close friend of Margaret's, she naturally assumed she'd be going to the party; He presumed for some reason that Fred was an insurance salesman, but he was wrong.*

assurance, insurance

Assurance is life insurance in the form of a policy that ensures an eventual financial benefit. **Insurance** is a guarantee of payment only if there is damage to person, property or financial expectation through some unexpected event.

assure, ensure, insure, promise

To **assure** somebody is to give them confidence or reason to be sure about something: *James assured Helen that everything would be fine.* To **ensure** is to make sure or certain: *He went around the house to ensure that all the doors were locked.* To **insure** is to protect against risk or loss. To **promise** is to undertake or pledge something in the future, but is increasingly and wrongly being used as a synonym for *assure: Mark promised his mother that he had done his homework.* Mark might correctly promise his mother that he would *do* his homework, but could not possibly promise that he had *done* it!

astonishing. See incredible, astonishing

astronaut, cosmonaut

American space travellers are **astronauts**; the Russians have **cosmonauts**. Why? The Americans plumped for the Latin *astrum*, which means star (although the Greek *astro* also translates as star), while the Russians, with their Greek-derived Cyrillic alphabet, took their cue from *Kosmos*, or universe. **Astronaut** seems likely to prevail.

as well as, besides

As well as means 'and not only', and links two things: *As well as the funfair they went to the theatre.* **Besides** means 'in addition to': *Besides gardening, they love classical music.* See also beside.

at your earliest convenience, soon

Dump the first – it doesn't mean what it says and always seems impolite. Replace it with more concise and specific directions: **soon, promptly, shortly, immediately, speedily, without delay, in reasonable time.**

atheist, agnostic

An **atheist** believes that there is no God or gods; an **agnostic** insists that it is impossible to know whether God exists or not. *'I'm still an athiest, thank God'*, *said the film director Luis Buñuel.*

auger, augur

American author Bill Bryson quotes the British *Guardian: 'The results do not auger well for the President in the forthcoming mid-term elections'.* What the *Guardian* is saying is that *results do not drill well for the President...* an **auger** is a tool for boring holes in wood or earth. **Augur** means foresee or presage: *the results do not augur well for the President*, or a suitable substitute: *the results do not bode well for the President*.

authentic, genuine

Authentic is usually applied to something that is produced by someone, about which there is no doubt; it is the opposite of *counterfeit: The expert agreed that the painting was an authentic Titian*. **Genuine** has a wider range of meanings and is generally used to imply some innate or original quality: *The handbag was made of genuine Italian leather; She seemed genuinely apologetic*.

authoritarian, authoritative

An **authoritarian** dominates or rules by fear, demanding obedience and submission. An **authoritative** person (or text) commands respect through being accepted as true and reliable: *Her work is regarded as the authoritative text on Hardy's poetry*.

autobiography

If you should ever commit your life story to print, don't refer to it as *my autobiography;* it's tautological. Anyone else can say *It's Bill's autobiography* but if you need to refer to your masterpiece you say or write, *It's an autobiography*.

avenge. See revenge, avenge

average, ordinary

To say that someone lives in an *average* home is fairly meaningless; the person probably lives in an **ordinary** home. Perfectionists insist that **average** should only be used in its mathematical sense. If five individuals for example, the average age of 5, 11, 14, 20 and 25, 18, 15, their average age is calculated as the total of all the ages (75) divided by the number of individuals in the group. Generally, however, **average** is used to mean 'usual' or 'typical': *As far as till takings went it was an average day; On average the business takes about £800 a week*.

averse to, averse from

Etymologically, **averse from** has a sound case, but usage now favours **averse to:** *She was not averse to his offer; She had an unreasonable aversion to open windows*.

aversion. See allergy, aversion

avocation. See vocation, avocation

await, wait

The two forms are used differently although in the end they amount to much the same thing. *We await the judge's decision; we await news of the survivors.* In other words, one *awaits* something. But, *We wait for the judge 's decision; We wait to hear about the survivors; We wait until early morning for the news.* **Await** sounds a bit formal for everyday use.

awful

This commonly-used word can confuse: *This is an awful wine! This is an awfully good wine!* **Awful** has become an all-purpose intensifier, although more in conversation than in writing, and many writers avoid it.

axiom, axiomatic

An **axiom** is not an absolute or self-evident truth but a generally accepted statement, law or principle. Likewise **axiomatic** does not refer to an absolute or self-evident truth but to something resembling an axiom, a self-evident statement or some universally accepted principle that is not necessarily absolutely true.

B

back, behind, backward, backwards

Back is a true all-purpose word describing a position at the rear, away from you, reversed or returning, and, with its other meanings, is used in an amazing number of ways (**quarterback, backchat, backslider, back off, back down, back up**). American English relates *back* and *front* in a logical way: *He hid **in back** of the house; he appeared **in front** of the house;* whereas British English insists on *He hid **behind*** (or *at the back of*) *the house.* **Backward** is an adjective: *He was a backward child; It was a backward step;* but it can also be used adverbially, like **backwards**: *They all fell over backward/backwards.*

back. See ago, before, back, past

back again

When she complained, he gave her the book back again is fairly common. *Again is* clearly redundant: *When she complained he gave her back the book.*

bacteria, virus, bug

Bacteria is the plural of **bacterium** but is now generally used as the singular form. They are single-celled micro-organisms (also called *germs* or *microbes)* and can be observed through an optical microscope. A **virus** is a sub-microscopic nucleic acid entity, with a protein coating, that replicates only within plant and animal cells. Most people give up and call them all **bugs**.

bail, bale

Today's liberal acceptance of interchangeable spellings has added to the confusion that these two words have always caused. The money paid into a court to release a person charged with an offence and forfeited if that person absconds, is always spelled **bail**. A **bundle** of hay, wool, paper or other material is always spelled **bale**. But do you **bale out** or **bail out** the water in a swamped dinghy? If you respect the Old French origin of bucket (*baille*), you will use bail; otherwise either will do. More perplexing is whether you **bale out** or **bail out** of a doomed aircraft; or usually you **bail** someone out of trouble following the idea of releasing someone from trouble, while you **bale out** of a doomed aircraft, following the figurative idea of dropping a **bale** from the plane. Either spelling is now acceptable. The two wooden spindles placed on top of cricket stumps are spelt **bails**; the mystery is, why?

baited, bated

Bated means restrained or diminished; **bait** is a lure to catch something: *He stood by the stream with bated breath while his wife baited the hook.*

balcony, circle, dress circle, gallery, stalls

In most theatres, the **stalls** are at floor level, with the **circle**, usually divided into **dress circle** and **upper circle,** on the next level. Above the circle is the **balcony**, with the **gallery** at the very top.

baleful, baneful

Baleful is sometimes used incorrectly to mean 'miserable or gloomy': *'As one who has never denied his youthful homosexual encounters, what did he think the age [of consent] should be? He looks baleful. 'I think I'm in favour of 18, I'm rather ashamed to say.'* (Interview with poet Sir Stephen Spender in *The Times*). The modern meaning of **baleful** is 'menacing, malign or destructive'. **Baneful** is little used today, but means 'poisonous or harmful'.

balk, baulk

The former spelling is the modern version and predominant in American English; either is acceptable to mean 'to suddenly refuse or be reluctant to do something': *The horse baulked at the first hurdle.*

balmy. See barmy, balmy

barbaric, barbarous

Both adjectives mean 'primitive, uncivilised, brutal and cruel' and are synonymous.

barbecue, barbeque

Barbecue derives directly from the Spanish-Caribbean *barbacoa*, a fire surmounted by a grid of sticks on which to cook, and is the correct spelling.

Barbeque may have originated from the common American abbreviation, *BBQ*.

BARBECUE, BARBEQUE

baring, barring, bearing

These three derive from *bare, bar* and *bear,* meaning respectively: 'to uncover', 'to obstruct', and 'to carry'.

barmy, balmy

Occasionally confused. **Balmy**, usually applied to describing weather, means 'mild, pleasant and soothing'. Barmy is a British slang word meaning 'mentally not quite all there': *Everyone thought the boss was a bit barmy.*

base, basis

Base has a wide range of meanings, defining a foundation, a support or a fundamental element in a structure. Both **base** and **basis** can mean the same, but are used differently. **Base** is usually applied to literal description (**base** of a pyramid, a skull, a compound) while **basis** finds more figurative or abstract uses (**basis** of an agreement; **basis** of a solution to the problem).

base, bass

Whatever confusion there is between these two probably derives from the fact that the musical **bass** (voice range, musical instrument) is also pronounced *bayss.*

bated. See **baited, bated**

bath, bathe

Bath can be used as a verb (*She baths twice a day*) but nowadays is usually used as a noun (*She takes a bath twice a day*). **Bathe**, meaning 'to wash', is used as the verb: *She bathes twice a day.*

bathos, pathos, bathetic, pathetic

Apart from its precise meaning of 'an undignified descent from the sublime to the commonplace', **bathos** is also loosely used to convey pompous insincerity, excessive sentimentality and a really low point – the pits. **Pathos** is the quality of drama capable of arousing deep feelings of pity and compassion. The adjectives **pathetic** and **bathetic**, however, are today often contemptuously used to indicate utter worthlessness, so be careful.

A.D, B.C.

A.D. comes before the date, and **B.C.** after: *Emperor Augustus died in A.D. 14; The archaeological discoveries were dated between 400 – 250 B.C.* **B.C.** and **A.D.** often appear without points, i.e., **BC** and **AD**.

Beatles, beetles

The six-legged variety of crawly is actually spelt *beetle*.

because, since, on account of, owing to, due to

Some delicate decision-making here! **Because** means 'for the reason'; **because of** roughly translates as 'by reason of': *He had to buy a new car because his other one packed up; He had to return his new car because of a faulty gear box.* **On account of** is used to qualify a phrase: *He can't drive the car on account of the faulty gear box.* The correct use of **since** is to imply a time lapse: *He's been cycling to work since his car broke down.* **Owing to, on account of** and **because of** are for all practical purposes synonymous. **Due to** invites grammatical error; it means 'caused by' and should logically link the result with the cause: *His lack of success with girls was due to his not having a car.* Grammarians warn against using **due to** as a substitute for **because** but long usage has now established them as synonymous.

beetles. See **Beatles, beetles**

begging the question, beg the question

The term is commonly misused to mean 'evading the question' or 'avoiding the point of the argument'. It really means 'assuming as true some point has not yet been proved': *That God exists, because there are stars, begs the question.*

begin, commence, inaugurate, initiate, start

Although all have much the same meaning, they are used differently. **Initiate**

and **inaugurate** are rather formal and are mostly used to describe the
origination of some significant undertaking, like a building project or a peace
accord. **Commence** is interchangeable with **begin**, except that it is a shade
more formal, while **start** implies a certain urgency: *Drivers – start your engines!*

belabour, labour

Occasionally **belaboured** is used as a synonym for **laboured**, which it isn't.
Belabour can mean 'physically to beat someone or something', or 'to attack
verbally': *He belaboured his opponent with his poor political record*

believe, feel, think

The usage of these words follows this logic: You **believe** with faith, you **feel**
with your senses, and you **think** with your mind: *At first I believed he was telling
the truth but felt he was hiding something, and now I think he was lying all the time.*
Think about **feel** before using it. *I feel I should leave now*, or usages similar to
this example are common enough. But... feel? In most cases the user means
think, having worked out that a train must be caught, or that the party is
becoming boring anyway. On the other hand if the person is at a party and
realises that he or she is a bit under the weather, **feel** would no doubt be
appropriate. **Feel** is becoming an overused, if harmless, synonym for **think** –
which it isn't.

bellwether, harbinger

Often seen in the financial pages of newspapers, **bellwether** is sometimes
used wrongly in place of **harbinger**, which is someone or something that
foretells of an approaching event. A **bellwether**, on the other hand, is
traditionally a sheep with a bell hanging from its neck, which was used to lead
the flock. The modern meaning is therefore something which others follow
blindly, like sheep, or a trend-setter: *The share issue proved to be a mesmerising
bellwether which predictably resulted in the usual sacrificial slaughter of incautious
punters* is correct (and adroit) modern usage.

bemuse. See **amuse, bemuse**

beneath, below, under, over

Beneath and **below** mean 'lower than' and are the opposite of **above**. **Under**
(and **underneath**) is the opposite of **over** and both suggest a sense of
position and proximity: *His exam marks were well below* (not under) *mine; She slid
eagerly under* (not below) *the blankets.* As you can see, the differences are
extremely subtle.

benefit. See **advantage, benefit**

bereft, bereaved

Both words have the broad meaning of loss, of being deprived, but while **bereft** is used in a general sense (*She was suddenly and tragically bereft of sustenance, of hope, of all human dignity ...*), **bereaved** is reserved for a loss brought about by death.

beside, besides

Beside means 'next to', or 'by the side of'. **Besides** means 'in addition to', or 'moreover': *She asked me to sit beside her; besides, there were no other available seats.*

best, better

Better applies to a choice of two entities (*Of the two entries Mr Peacock's was the better*) and **Best** is used when the choice is wider: *Of the fifteen entries, Mr Peacock's was easily the best.*

between. See among, amongst, between

biannual, biennial, bimonthly, biweekly

The only unambiguous words in this lot are **biennial**, which as gardeners know means 'once every two years' and **biannual**, which means 'twice a year'. Unfortunately **bimonthly** and **biweekly** can mean twice a month or once every two months, and twice a week or once every two weeks. To make yourself clear, do not use either – spell it out in full.

Bible, bible, biblical

When referring to the Old and New Testaments, use a capital *B*, but use a lower case *b* in the context of, for example, *His book on stamp collecting is regarded as the bible of philately*. The word **biblical** uses a lower case *b*.

billiards. See snooker, pool, billiards

billion

Fifty years ago, the British billion equalled a 'million million', and that the American billion was a 'thousand million'. Now the British billion, too has become a 'thousand million'. A trillion is 1,000,000,000,000,000,000 (a million million million)... for now!

birthday. See anniversary, birthday, jubilee

black, negro, coloured, non-white

Tread warily and sensitively through this linguistic minefield. **Black** has emerged as the most acceptable term to define most dark-skinned ethnic groups (although not all Asians); the other terms are usually only acceptable in an historical sense for example, when writing dialogue set in a time-period when such usage was commonplace. Also extend sensitivity to the use of idioms such as *black sheep* and applications like the verb *to black,* meaning to boycott: *Chief police officers decided unanimously yesterday, after studying a paper highlighting the huge number of timewasting callouts, to black people whose alarms kept going off (The Times)* is, on a quick reading, potentially provocative.

blame

I blame that stupid chair for this bruise on my leg is incorrect – blame cannot be attributed to inanimate objects for misfortune: they can't accept it was their fault or feel remorse. **Blame** should not be followed by *on,* as it so often is: *They blamed the disaster on me.* A correct version would be *They blamed me for the disaster.*

blanch, blench

Strange word, **blanch**. Although in cookery books it can mean 'to plunge vegetables briefly into boiling water to preserve their colour', it usually means 'to *remove* colour. to lighten and whiten' Thus, if someone received a shock, they might **blanch** or go pale: *She shuddered, and blanched at the thought.* **Blench** is also strange: from an older meaning of 'to deceive' it now means to 'flinch from in fear'. Many dictionaries unhelpfully list both meanings under both words.

blaze, blazon

Apart from its use to describe fire and light, to **blaze** means to mark or open up a path or territory: *He helped blaze a new trail across the Rockies.* Occasionally we see the word **blazoned** wrongly substituted for **blazed**. To **blazon** means to 'boldly proclaim something to all and sundry' and, in heraldry, 'to draw up heraldic arms'.

blench. See **blanch, blench**

bloc, block

Bloc is used rather than **block** to describe a group of individuals, organisations or nations united in a common cause. A good example is the former *communist bloc.*

blond, blonde

If the subject is a male, use **blond,** if female, use **blonde.** Even less known (and observed) is the male version of **brunette** – is **brunet.**

boar, boor, bore, Boer

Although a dictionary soon sorts them out, this quartet is commonly confused: a **boar** is a male pig; a **boor** is a rude, insensitive, uncivilised person; a **bore** is a tiresome, garrulous and fiendishly uninteresting person, and the **Boers** were the original white, mostly Dutch, settlers in South Africa.

bogey, bogie, bogy

A **bogey** in golf is a score of one stroke over par for a particular hole on a course. A **bogie** is a set of wheels, usually 4 or 6, on locomotives or railway carriages; a **bogy** (as in bogyman) is an evil spirit, but confusingly, can be spelled bogey/bogeyman. Finally, a bogy (one spelling only) can be something unmentionable ejected from the nose.

bona fide, bona fides

Bona fide, which looks like the singular of *bona fides*, actually isn't. It's the adjectival form: *He judged it to be a bona fide complaint*, meaning a genuine one. *Bona fides* is the noun and it is singular: *He hoped his bona fides was sufficiently convincing to allow him entry*.

born, borne, bourne

Born is used exclusively in relation to birth: *She was born on September 3; He was born of an English mother and a Turkish father*. **Borne** can be used similarly (*The mother had borne the baby over the full term*) but has wider applications: *The pain he had borne was beyond belief; These facts should be borne in mind*. **Bourne** is an old English word for stream that survives in countless place names such as Littlebourne, Bishopsbourne, etc.

both, each, either

Both embraces two things. **Each** refers separately to one of two or more things: *Both buckets had holes in them; Each of the three buckets was riddled with holes*. Be careful not to mix singular and plural: *Each of the volunteers has a job to do* is all singular and correct. *The volunteers each have a job to do* is also correct; in this case a plural verb (*have*) must follow the plural *volunteers*. The fairly common use of **either**, as in *Two large trees stood on either side of the house*, can be confusing. A clearer version might be: *A large tree stood on each side of the house*.

bowdlerise

Bowdlerise is sometimes wrongly used to mean to 'cut and mutilate a text' when it really means 'to remove words or passages considered to be offensive or obscene': *Their edition of The Family Shakespeare had been thoroughly bowdlerised.*

Boy Scouts. See **Scouts**

brand new, bran new

Believe it or not, confusion exists: *A bran-new population, in a bran-new town, in a bran-new quarter of the city* (*The Guardian, 1991*). What is intended, of course, is **brand-new**, meaning absolutely new.

bravery, bravado, bravura, courage, heroism

Bravery is the readiness to face danger or pain; **bravado** is the ostentatious pretence of bravery; **bravura** is a display of daring brilliance, often in an artistic performance. **Courage** is the quality required to meet confrontation or danger with firm resolve – a quality most of us would like to possess at times of stress or challenge. Heroism implies an act of selflessness that transcends normal human behaviour.

breach, breech

To **breach** is to break or violate, as in a breach (break or gap) in a wall; a breach (violation) of the peace. **Breech** (remember that breeches is the garment that covers the posterior!) refers to the rear of anything, as in *breech birth* (a baby born feet-first), *breech-loading gun* (loaded from behind).

BRITAIN

Britain and Great Britain are synonymous; both mean the union of England, Scotland and Wales. The United Kingdom (full title: The United Kingdom of Great Britain and Northern Ireland, abbreviated to the UK) comprises England, Scotland, Wales and Northern Ireland plus various islands. The British Isles loosely include the UK, the Republic of Ireland, and the dependencies of the Isle of Man and the Channel Islands. UK citizens are known as British, Britons, Britishers or Brits.

---

broach, brooch

To **broach** is to open up: *He eventually broached the delicate subject of marriage.* A **brooch** is jewellery, usually fixed to the clothing with a pin.

Broken Up, Boken Down and Other Phrasal Verbs

Take a typical verb: **break**. Its primary meaning is to separate, or damage. Now see how, by simply tacking on an adverb or preposition, we can create a string of new meanings: **break down, break up, break with, break in, break out, break off, break through, break away from, break even**.

These are known as phrasal verbs, and we use them constantly: **turn off, turn up, turn down, turn out, turn on; give in, give up, give back, give ground; look out, look after, look up, look over, look back, look forward to...** there are thousands of these versatile verbs.

The trouble is, we like them so much that we invent ones which are meaningless. Take, for example, **slow down** and **slow up**; *down* and *up* add nothing to the original meaning of **slow** but the expressions are now so ingrained in the language as to be irremovable. Others include **check out, eat up, sell off, cut back, phone up** and **meet with**.

brownie points

Go up in your kids' estimation. Earn some brownie points. A gold star even. (ad for EuroDisney, 1994). The original **brownie points**, named after an unpopular superintendent, were introduced in the early 1900s on the Canadian Pacific Railway as demerits for breaking regulations.

buffet

Buffet (pronounced as spelt) means to batter: *The ship was buffetted by gales all across the Bay of Biscay.* A **buffet** (pronounced boo-fay) is a counter from which refreshments are served or an informal meal where guests help themselves.

bumf, bumph

The correct spelling is **bumf**, an abbreviation of 'bum-fodder' (i.e. toilet paper), and refers to useless, time-wasting documents and paperwork.

buccaneer. See **pirate, buccaneer, corsair, privateer**

bulimia, anorexia

Both are psychological eating disorders. With **bulimia**, sufferers compulsively overeat to the point of obesity, then force themselves to vomit (*bulimia nervosa*). With **anorexia**, the sufferer looses all appetite for food to the point of serious wasting – and even death.

bulls and bears

These stock market terms can be confusing. The **bulls** buy shares when they think the price will rise, to sell them later at a profit. If enough bulls buy, the market becomes buoyant and is called a **bull market**. **Bears** sell shares when they expect the market to go down, hoping to buy them back later at a much lower price. Too much selling activity may drive all share prices down and this may cause a **bear market**.

burgeon, burgeoning

The words are frequently used to indicate rapid and luxuriant growth or increase, but the primary meaning is to bud or sprout, to *begin* growing.

burglar, burgle, burglarise; burglary, robbery, stealing, theft

Stealing is taking or appropriating something belonging to someone else without their permission. **Burglary** is entering premises with intent to steal or commit a felony. A **burglar** does the breaking-in to **burgle**. **Burglarise** is not a real word. **Robbery** is stealing that involves violence or the threat of it. **Theft** is synonymous with stealing.

burned, burnt

The two are virtually interchangeable except: *The bushfires burned for several days* rather than *The bushfires burnt for several days*. A rough rule is **burned** when the burning is continuing; **burnt** when everything is ashes.

burro. See donkey, ass, burro, mule

bursar. See registrar, bursar, bursary

bust, burst

Do you bust a balloon, or burst it? Careful users will **burst** a balloon and use **bust** only in informal contexts: *Joe's firm went bust; That nightclub is busted at least twice a year; It was quite a bust-up.*

C

cabalistic, cabbalistic

Cabalistic is the adjectival form of **cabal**, a group of plotters or intriguers, or the plot itself, and consequently meaning 'someone by nature a secretive conspirator'. **Cabbalistic** derives from **cabbala**, an ancient Jewish mystical tradition based on an interpretation of the New Testament – so the adjective means 'mystically secretive'.

cache, cachet

A **cache** is a hidden store of treasure, food, documents, etc. A **cachet** is a stamp or seal of approval. The pronunciations are respectively *kash* and *kah-SHAY*.

caddie, caddy

A **caddie** is someone who carries the bag of golf clubs for a player, now often replaced by a **caddie-cart** or **caddie-car**. A **caddy** is a small container for storing tea.

café, cafe, caff

General usage in British now drops the accent and pronounces it *KAF-ay* – despite some inroads by the Cockney affectation *kaff*. American English retains the French pronunciation: *kaf-AY*.

calendar, calender

A **calendar** is a table showing the succession of years, months and days and any phenomena connected with it (phases of the moon, holidays, schedules, etc.). A **calender** is a pair or series of rollers through which cloth or paper is pressed.

callous, callus

Callous denotes insensitivity in people: *He had a callous attitude towards his animals*. A **callus** is a hard patch of skin.

can, may, might

Can and **may** each have two meanings. The first relates to probability: *I can now go to the party* (now that I've finished my chores); I may go to the party (if I feel well enough), where *can* indicates a far more positive and likely outcome than *may*. The second relates to permission, and in this context any difference between **can** and **may** is almost extinct: *Yes, John, you can go to the party; Yes, John, you may go to the party*. Though often used interchangably, **May** and **might**, however, do imply different degrees of possibility. Of the two, **may** is far more positive: *Yes, you may have given me the book* implies a reasonable likelihood that I was given the book. Well, you might have given me the book implies the possibility that I was given the book, but I doubt it. Also remember to use **may** in the present and future tense, i.e. when the result is still unkown; **might** in the past: *The boss may leave for New York tomorrow; The boss might have left for New York last night.*

candelabra, chandelier

These two are sometimes confused. **Candelabra** (singular = *candelabrum*) are branched candle holders; a **chandelier** is an ornamental hanging light.

cant, hypocrisy

Often used wrongly as synonyms. **Cant** describes a wide span of verbiage from pious platitudes through repetitious, meaningless stock phrases to jargon. **Hypocrisy** is the act of a person purporting to hold beliefs or standards not manifested in that person's actual behaviour.

canvas, canvass

Canvas is a heavy cloth; **to canvass** is to solicit – votes, opinions or sales orders for double glazing. But note: *His collection included several canvasses* (plural) *by Hockney; He regularly canvasses the downtown areas*.

capital, capitol

The **capitol** is the legislative building, while the **capital** is the city in which the legislature is situated. The Capitol in Washington DC always has a capital *C*.

capsize

British English uses the **-ise** suffix as apposed to the American English usage **-ize**: **regularise, supervise, personalise, privatise**. One exception is, of course, **capsize**.

cardigan. See **sweater, jersey, jumper, pullover, etc.**

cardinal. See **crucial, cardinal**

carat, caret, karat
A **carat** (spelt **karat** in the US and Canada) is the unit of weight for diamonds and precious stones, and also indicates the amount of gold in an alloy. A **caret** is the small inverted *v* editorial mark used to show that inserted material is required.

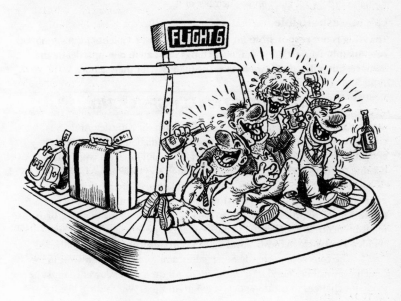

CAROUSAL, CAROUSEL

carousal, carousel
A **carousal** is a boisterous, well-lubricated drinking party; a **carousel** is a rotating fairground ride, and also that revolving conveyor at airports on which you vainly search for your luggage. Pronounced *kuh-ROW-suhl* and *kar-ruh-SEL*.

cash. See **money, monies, funds, cash**

caster, castor
Caster is very fine, ground white sugar, a sweetener; **castor oil** is a purgative. The swivelling little wheels on the legs of furniture can be spelt as either **casters** or **castors**.

casual, causal

A confusing pair of near-opposites. **Casual** denotes something unplanned, happening by chance, relaxed, unconcerned: *Theirs was merely a brief, casual affair*. **Causal** is the relationship between an affect and its cause: *The causal agent for the environmental damage was undoubtedly the build-up of nitrates*.

catholic, Catholic

With a small *c*, **catholic** means 'wide-ranging, comprehensive, near-universal': *She had catholic tastes in music*. With a capital *C*, it is the shortened form for the Roman Catholic religion, and a member of it.

cause, responsible

Thick fog is not **responsible** for motorway pileups; a violent storm cannot be **responsible** for death and damage. Things can **cause** pile-ups, death and damage, but only people can bear **responsibility** for their actions.

CATACHRESTICALLY SPEAKING...

One of the bête noires of the late novelist Sir Kingsley Amis was **catachresis**, or the incorrect use of words. Any dictionary misguidedly allowing the admission of new meanings that would make a word ambiguous became the object of Amis's wrath, a fearsome spectacle indeed.

Some of the catachreses Amis particularly deplored included: **aggravate** to mean 'irritate'; **epithet** to mean 'a term of abuse'; **dilemma** to mean 'a problem'; **fulsome** to mean 'lavish'; **pristine** to mean clean; **brutalise** to mean 'maltreat'; **infamous** to mean 'quaint'; **peremptory** to mean 'sudden'; **quixotic** to mean 'absurd', and **schizophrenic** to mean 'divided'.

The correct or currently accepted meanings of these and scores more catachreses will be found in *WORDCHECK*. All the same, allowance must be made for changes in meaning over a length of time. Whether we like it or not, alternative meanings of words must be recognised through sheer weight of usage; **pristine** to mean 'perfect' or 'perfectly clean' is an example of accepted modern usage. Another example is **consummate** which Sir Kingsley might have reasonably used in the sense of 'to make complete, or to bring to perfection'. Yet during this century, *consummate* was for a time one of his hated catachreses; its primary meaning, as typically recorded in the 1901 *Chambers' Twentieth Century Dictionary*, was 'to raise to the highest point'. That original definition now seems to be completely lost.

---

cavalry, Calvary

Cavalry are mounted soldiers, on horses, camels or wheels; **Calvary** is the mount near Jerusalem where Christ was crucified.

ceiling, maximum

Ceiling is a figurative term used to express a limit or maximum, but is often used incorrectly, as in: *The committee agreed that under the circumstances the ceiling would be appropriately increased*. A ceiling can be raised or lowered but not increased.

Celsius. See centigrade, Celsius

celibate, chaste

To be **chaste** is to be pure, modest and sexually faithful. To be **celibate** is to abstain from marriage (and sexual intercourse) altogether, as do members of many religious orders.

cement, concrete

Cement is a bonding agent which comes in many forms and can be used to join a variety of materials. **Concrete** is the product of a bond between cement (the powdered grey variety of calcined limestone) and aggregates such as sand and gravel.

censer, censor, censure

A **censer** is the container in which incense is burned during religious ceremonies. A **censor** is a person who, usually by authority, suppresses matter – written, drawn or otherwise expressed – on moral or political grounds. To **censure** is to reprimand severely.

centre, middle

Geometrically, the **centre** of something is a focal point, precise and measurable; the **middle** of something is a more general, approximate term.

centering, centring

Centring means 'placing in the centre'; **centering** is a temporary structure used to support an archway during construction. Confusion can arise because of the American-English spelling of centring = centering.

centigrade, Celsius

The **centigrade** temperature scale (0 degrees = freezing point of water; 100 degrees = boiling point of water) was invented by the Swede Anders **Celsius** in 1742; the scale is now commonly called Celsius but both mean the same. In the *Fahrenheit* scale, water freezes at 32 degrees and boils at 212 degrees.

certainty, certitude

Certainty means 'being certain, without doubt': *The coach relaxed in the certainty of victory*. **Certitude** is a synonym but suggests additionally the feeling of satisfaction in being so certain: *The bishop was now thoroughly convinced and almost rejoiced in his certitude*.

chafe, chaff

To **chafe** is to irritate or make sore by rubbing; to **chaff** is to tease light-heartedly.

chairman, chairwoman, chairperson, chair

Depending upon your committment to political correctness, you can safely use **chairman, chairwoman** or **chairperson** as appropriate. **Madam Chairman** is not uncommon in Britain but there remain many who resist calling a person a **chair**: *Will those with questions please now address them to the chair?*

chaotic, inchoate

These two are wonderful confusables. **Chaotic** needs little explanation: totally disordered, confused and seemingly out of control. Perhaps because in appearance it sits between incoherent and chaotic, inchoate appears to be related to these words, but isn't. It means 'just beginning, undeveloped, incomplete': *The inchoate nature of the plans made it difficult for the committee to visualise the sculptor's ambitious project.*

character. See trait, character

chart. See trace, chart

charted, chartered

If an area of land or sea is **charted**, it has been explored, surveyed and mapped. It might have been done by a **chartered** surveyor, that is, a surveyor who has passed the examinations of the Institute of Chartered Surveyors – which in turn has been granted a charter to confer such privileges. The same applies to chartered accountants and numerous other professions. In quite another sense, a **chartered** bus, train, aircraft, etc., is one which has been hired for an occasion.

chary. See wary, chary

chemist, druggist, pharmacist

If you want medicine, you go to a **chemist** in the UK, and a **druggist** in the US. In both, you should meet the **pharmacist** who is qualified to prepare and dispense drugs and medicines. But there are also many varieties of professional chemist: analytical, agricultural, organic, molecular, to name a few.

chequered, checkered

The former is the UK spelling; the latter is standard in American English.

childish, childlike

Childish is usually used in a disparaging way to describe someone who is acting 'like a child': *Every now and then Mrs Hounslow would throw a childish tantrum.* **Childlike** is a much kinder term, expressing some aspect of the charm of childhood: *Even as an adult, Emma still retained a childlike trust in others.*

choose, pick

These are synonymous, **pick** being the more idiomatic, as in *take your pick*. *Make a choice* means the same thing but would be considered more elegant.

chords, cords

A **chord** is a group of musical notes played simultaneously. Cords are various kinds of string. Vocal cords are the vibrating folds at the back of the larynx. *They feared that Miss Caparello's vocal chords might have been damaged by the accident* is incorrect.

Christian name, first name, given name, forename

Strictly speaking, only Christians can have **Christian names.** The other terms – **forenames/ given names/ first names** – distinguish from someone's surname.

chronic, acute

Acute means 'sharp and quick', whereas **chronic** means almost the opposite, 'long lasting and recurring': *The acute pains he suffered were symptoms of a chronic illness.*

chutney. See **ketchup, sauce, chutney, pickle**

circumspect. See **discreet, circumspect, prudent**

cite. See **quote, cite**

city, town, village, hamlet

It is no longer easy to define these terms precisely. The largest of these communities is a **city** which, in the UK, was once defined as a town which included a cathedral within its boundaries – not necessarily so any more. A **town** is smaller than a city but larger than a **village**. A village in the UK might consist of a dozen to several hundred homes; a **hamlet**, smallest of all, might include as few as two or three dwellings, probably without a church.

claim, allege, assert, maintain

Just four of a group of words that are often used synonymously and wrongly. To **claim** is to demand or assert a right: *He came to England to claim the crown*. It is, however, frequently used wrongly as a synonym for *declare, assert, protest and allege: It was claimed in the High Court yesterday'*. To **allege** is to assert without proof, and as it nowadays implies guilt (as in the satirical news quiz, *Have I Got News For you*), it should be used with caution: *the alleged bribe; the alleged crime.* **Assert** has a stronger emphasis than said and means to declare positively. The primary meanings of **maintain** are to 'hold, preserve and sustain', so it is a supportive word: *In the face of the allegations, she steadfastly maintained her innocence.*

classic, Classics, classical

Classic has by modern usage almost been stripped of any meaning. From TV comedy programmes, horse races, old cars to soft drinks, anything can be a '**classic**'. **Classics** in the plural and upper-case is the study of ancient Greek and Latin: She read Classics at Oxford. Classical describes the highest attainments of an era (e.g. Greek and Roman) or of literature and art. Classical music is usually chamber or orchestral in nature and is distinct from jazz, folk music or rock.

clean, cleanse

As verbs, **clean** and **cleanse** both mean 'to clean', but the latter additionally implies to 'clean thoroughly and to purify': *His mother used to insist that merely cleaning the face did not cleanse the soul.*

climatic, climactic, climacteric

Climatic relates to weather conditions: *The climatic conditions were extremely trying and sometimes unbearable* disposes of that one. **Climactic** relates to a climax, a high point (*After the thunderous applause it was agreed that it was the climactic speech of his career*), while a **climacteric** is a critical period of change (usually physical) in human life, for example, puberty or the menopause.

climb down, climb-down

Inch by heart-stopping inch he climbed down the treacherous ravine. Isn't there a contradiction here? Those who respect the meaning of climb as 'to ascend' may prefer *he descended into the treacherous ravine*. But although **climb down** is now an ingrained phrasal verb (as is **climb up**, where the *up* is redundant) it has acquired a second meaning which is 'a retreat from a position': *By withdrawing her libel action the Duchess suffered a humiliating climb-down.*

coat, jacket

Today's usage accepts that an **overcoat** is a **coat** and the upper half of a suit a **jacket**.

collaborate, cooperate

To **collaborate** is to work jointly with someone, usually on some specific project. To **cooperate** is to work with someone or be willing to help or contribute. Curiously, if you *cooperate* with the enemy, you are a *collaborator*.

collectable, collectible

Usage is divided. Perhaps the best idea is to follow the big international auction houses, such as Christie's and Sotheby's, which tend to use **collectable** and **collectables**.

collision, collusion

A **collision** is the impact of two moving objects or forces; **collusion** is a conspiracy to deceive: *They were forever colluding against the rightful owners of the land*.

colony, protectorate, dependency

A **colony** is a territory annexed by another power; once numbering more than a hundred, only a few of these now survive. These include former British Crown Colonies, now termed **dependencies**, which have their own legislatures – Cayman Islands, the Falklands, Ascension and Hong Kong (until 1997) are examples. A **protectorate** is a territory administered and defended by a stronger state but whose inhabitants are not granted citizenship of that state.

Colosseum, coliseum, Coliseum

The **Colosseum** is the original (now ruined) amphitheatre in Rome, built in A.D.75–80. A **coliseum** now describes any major amphitheatre or stadium, while the **Coliseum** is the landmark theatre of that name in London.

come, cum

Occasionally, we see a combination such as *an office-come-den*, or *she was a secretary come childminder*. These are incorrect as the connecting preposition is cum (Latin = with) which is used to connect two nouns: *He showed us into an office-cum-den; She complained she'd become a secretary-cum-childminder*.

comet, meteor

A **comet** is a celestial body of vaporised debris that orbits the Sun and from which streams a luminous tail; Halley's comet, for example, completes an orbit every 75 years. A **meteor** is a meteorite that enters the earth's atmosphere with a one-off display of luminosity.

comic, comical

Comic is something that is intended to be funny; a **comical** situation may be hilarious but unintentional; however, the difference between the two words

41

today is almost erased. Where tragedy, real or theatrical, is shared with the humour, the terms are *tragicomic* and *tragicomical*.

commensurate, consummate

Commensurate means 'corresponding or roughly proportionate in size, amount or degree': *The guidelines he laid down were commensurate with the laws of the previous administration*. **Consummate** has two meanings: 'highly skilled and accomplished' and 'to complete': *With consummate ease and considerable enthusiasm, the couple consummated their marriage on the Orient Express between Innsbruck and Venice*.

Common Market. See European Union, European Community

commonly, customarily, frequently, generally, habitually, ordinarily, usually

Commonly, **generally**, **ordinarily** and **usually** are virtually synonymous, meaning 'normally as expected'. **Customarily** differs by only a fine degree, meaning 'according to established practice'. **Frequently** means 'often', while **habitually** implies frequency as the result of habit.

compare to, compare with

The convention has been to use **compared to** to express dissimilarities to make a point (*She often compared her boyfriend's intelligence to two thick planks; or, more poetically, Shall I compare thee to a summer's day?*) and **compared with** to note the differences between two similar things or classes: *You can't really compare Caruso's voice with Pavarotti's; Compared with Australia's, New Zealand's Sauvignons are much more refined*.

compatriot. See expatriate, compatriot

compel, impel

If you are **compelled** to do something, it is due to some outside force or pressure that you can't resist, and over which you have little or no control. But if you are **impelled** to do something, the decision is yours, despite the pressure, the urging and all the reasons.

complacent, complaisant

Spelt differently, but pronounced similarly, a **complacent** person is self-satisfied and smug; a **complaisant** person is always rather eager to please others and will do anything to oblige.

complement, compliment, supplement

A **complement** is that which makes something complete: *The hospital finally* *achieved its full complement of nursing staff; She complemented the dish with a swirl of cream.* A **compliment** is an expression of praise or approval, and a **supplement** is an addition to something already complete: *He complimented her on the meal; The doctor supplemented her diet with a course of vitamins and minerals.*

completion. See fruition, completion

complicated, complex

As adjectives, these are for all practical purposes synonyms, although **complex** tends to be used in more scientific contexts and **complicated** to express something difficult to understand: *The substance turned out to be a complex mixture of rare herbs and spices; Mary felt the affair was becoming absurdly complicated and washed her hands of the matter.* As a noun, **complex** come into fashion to describe a group of units: *The team went to inspect the new sports complex.*

comply, conform

These are synonyms, but **comply** is followed by **with** (*He always complied with the regulations*) and **conform** by **to**: *The quality of the cloth conformed to the standards laid down by the EU.*

compose, comprise, constitute, include

Comprise means 'consists of' and describes all the parts that make up the whole: *The house comprised five bedrooms, four reception rooms and the usual offices.* The meanings of **compose** and **constitute** are the same, but don't necessary imply completeness: *The pudding is composed of some unusual ingredients; She hardly dared list the ingredients that constituted the pudding.* Use **include** when only part or parts of the whole are indicated: *The ingredients included Chinese walnuts and cherry brandy.*

comprehend. See understand, appreciate, comprehend

compulsive, compulsory

Compulsive means 'being subject to some degree of inner compulsion, either psychological, moral or physical': *Ray was a compulsive gambler; The new TV crime series makes for compulsive viewing.* **Compulsory** means 'obligatory by law, regulation or some other force': Car registration is compulsory. In both cases, there is an implied inability to resist.

concave, convex

Concave means 'curving inwards' (think of a cave); **convex** means curving outwards (think how vexed you are when you develop a bulge!)

concede, accede

Accede indicates willing agreement; **concede** implies grudging agreement, or 'giving way': *After an hour he conceded the argument to his opponent; The chess team acceded enthusiastically to the idea of a return match.*

concrete. See **cement, concrete**

condominium. See **flat, condominium, apartment**

Condone, Approve, Allow

In her bestselling book on sex, *The Hite Report*, the American author Shere Hite fell for a common misconception: *Heterosexual intercourse… is the only form of sexual pleasure condoned in our society*. It is doubtful if Ms Hite meant that heterosexual intercourse was overlooked or forgiven or excused, for that is what **condone** means – it is not a substitute for *allowed* or *approved*. Nor is it a synonym for *disapprove*: *My position is that I neither condone nor condemn fox hunting*.

---

confident. See **optimistic, confident**

confident, confidant

To be **confident** is to be assured, certain of yourself, without doubts. A **confidant** (pron. *kon-fih-DANT*) is a trusted friend to whom you confide your closest secrets. If the friend is female, use the feminine **confidante**.

conform. See **comply, conform**

congenial. See **genial, congenial, congenital**

conjugal, connubial

These are virtual synonyms. Because its most frequent usage is in the phrase *conjugal rights* – which, legally, denotes the rights to sexual relations with a spouse – **conjugal** tends to relate more to the responsibilities of marriage, while **connubial** ('connubial bliss') rather hints at the joys of the union.

connote. See **denote, connote**

conscience, conscious, conscientious

A **conscience** is a person's sense of what is right and wrong. **Conscious** implies self-awareness, being aware of one's mental and physical state. To be **conscientious** is to act according to one's conscience or to a code of principles.

consecutive, successive

Consecutive means 'following without an interval or break', while
successive means 'following in order but without emphasion the intervals':
After winning three consecutive Derbys, he went on to claim six successive Derby wins
over 12 years.

consensus, consensus of opinion

A **consensus** (not **concensus**) is widespread agreement or general opinion.
Consensus of opinion is a very common waste of words.

consequent, consequential

Consequent means 'following as an effect or direct result'. **Consequential** in
this context also means 'following as a result' but usually indirectly: *It was*
obvious that thirty years down the mines had something to do with his lung problems
and consequent death; His behaviour had been scandalous so his consequential
abandonment by the party came as no surprise. In quite another sense,
consequential can mean 'significant, important' and 'self-important'.

consequently, subsequently

Often confused. **Consequently** (see above) means 'following as a direct
result'; **subsequently** simply means 'occurring after'.

conservative, Conservative

With a small *c*, it means 'opposed to change', 'moderate, cautious and
conventional'; with a capital *C*, it denotes a member or supporter of a
Conservative political party.

consists of, consists in

These are used differently. **Consists of** means 'comprises, formed of, made up
of': *He knew the committee consisted of some pretty unusual characters.* **Consists in**
means 'to have its existence in': *Her entire life seemed to consist in those three daily*
visits to her church.

constitute. See compose, comprise, constitute, include

constrain, restraint

Both are forms of restriction but one is often self-imposed and the other arises
through outside forces. A **constraint** is something that prevents one from
pursuing some action: *Her knowledge of Sir Percy's crime acted as a constraint to her*
speaking freely on the matter. **Restraint** is self-control, the ability to check or
moderate one's actions, passions or impulses.

consulate, embassy, legation

A nation establishes only one **embassy** in another country to represent its diplomatic and economic interests, usually in the capital or key city, whereas **consulates** can be found in centres where there is a need for them. A **legation** is a diplomatic mission typically headed by a government minister. The key figure in an embassy is the *ambassador* (although in the British Commonwealth it is usually a *High Commissioner*) and in a consulate, the *consul*. A *chargé d'affaires* is, in the absence of an ambassador or minister, the temporary head of a diplomatic mission.

consultant, specialist

In medical language, patients are referred to a **specialist**; a **consultant** is a specialist consulted by doctors on behalf of their patients. However, the term *consultant* is now freely applied to almost every avenue and level of medical specialisation.

contagious. See **infectious, contagious**

contemporary

Contemporary means 'living at the same time, belonging to the same period, existing in the present time'. Modern usage also extends its meaning to 'up-to-date, modern'.

contemptuous, contemptible

To be **contemptuous** means 'to be scornful, arrogant, sneering and insulting': *She was always contemptuous of my plans to make money.* The object of her scorn could very well be **contemptible** and deserving of contempt: *His ridiculous efforts to make a fortune were contemptible.*

contiguous. See **adjacent, adjoining, contiguous**

continual, continuous

Continual means 'repeated at short intervals'; **continuous** means 'uninterrupted': *I've just suffered continual interruptions; I can't possibly work with that continuous racket blaring from next door!*

contrary

Two meanings and two pronunciations. **Contrary** (pronounced KON-truh-ree) means to be opposed, opposite: *He invariably held views contrary to everyone else's.* **Contrary** (pronounced kon-TRAIR-ee) means obstinate, perverse: *If you remember, Janet was always a contrary child.*

contrast to, contrast with, in contrast with

Usage has rendered these interchangeable. **In contrast** was usually followed by **with** but even that convention has been dropped and **in contrast to** makes no difference to the meaning: *The progress made in Manchester is in stark contrast to the situation in Liverpool.*

Contradictory Words

When you **dust** an object, do you clean it of dust, or sprinkle fine powder on it? Why does a **seeded** bun have seeds baked in it, while **seeded** raisins have the seeds taken out? Does a child know the difference between **getting up** from the meal table, or **getting down** from the table? These two-way words and terms are understandably the source of much confusion. Try looking up **ravel** and **unravel** in a dictionary; they can both mean the same. And **parboil**, a model of imprecision, means to 'boil thoroughly' – and also 'to boil partially'.

converse, inverse, obverse, reverse

This quartet all mean 'opposite' in some sense. **Inverse** is used in mathematics and **obverse** when refering to the faces of a coin or medal. **Converse** (pronounced KON-vers) and **conversely** (which is used loosely as 'on the other hand') denote a reversal of meaning: *Every journalist knows that dog bites man, and its converse, man bites dog; Every journalist knows that dog bites man, and, conversely, that man bites dog.* Note also that to **converse** (pronounced kon-VERS) means to have a conversation. **Reverse** is rarely misunderstood: *He maintains that a high-fibre diet makes you fat; the reverse is true.*

convict, impeach

To **impeach** is to bring a charge or accusation against someone and is often a first step in trying to remove an official from office. To **convict** (pronounced kon-VICT) is (for a court) to find a person guilty of an offence against the law. A **convict** (pronounced KON-vict) is is one who has been found guilty of a crime, or someone who has been gaoled.

convince, persuade, induce

Convince implies proving something to somebody by argument, by an exposition of the facts: *After hearing John's version he was convinced that Emily was in the wrong.* **Persuade** is a stronger word, meaning 'to urge, encourage, influence and convince a person to the stage where he or she is won over to a point of view or course of action': *After a series of tense discussions they finally persuaded her to stay the night.* **Induce** is a near synonym except that it implies that in return for being persuaded there may be some reward or penalty: *The promise of peace of mind was the factor that really induced William to agree.*

cooperative. See flat, condominium, apartment, cooperative

copy. See replica, copy, facsimile

coral, corral

Coral consists of the skeletons of marine creatures which form reefs; a **corral** is an enclosure for horses and cattle.

core

Very much a vogue word that modern usage has rendered into a vague word: *core values, core executives, core missions, soft-core, hard-core*... use carefully if you must use at all.

corporal, corporeal

In the army, a corporal is *a non-commissioned officer*, senior to a private and junior to a sergeant; in the navy, a petty officer under a master-at-arms. **Corporal** also means 'relating to the body', as in *corporal punishment*, that is, punishment of the body, such as flogging. Similarly, Corporeal refers to the material or physical side of nature as opposed to the spiritual.

corps, corpse, copse

A seemingly simple trio but often confused. A **corps** (pron. *kor*) consists of two or more army divisions; a **corpse** is of course a dead body; a **copse** is a thicket of trees or bushes.

correspond to, correspond with

If you **correspond with** someone, you exchange letters with them. **Correspond to** means 'to be in harmony with', or 'to tally with': *Your version of the affair corresponds to that of Matilda's.*

correspondent, co-respondent

Don't be confused between **correspondent** (one who writes or exchanges letters with another) and **co-respondent** (someone cited as 'the other party' in divorce proceedings).

corsair. See pirate, buccaneer, corsair, privateer

cosmetic. See superficial, cosmetic

cosmonaut. See **astronaut, cosmonaut**

council, counsel, councillor, counselor

A **council** is a body of people, usually elected, for the purpose of advising, guiding or administrating; a **councillor** is a member of a council. A **counsel** is an individual qualified in some way to give advice or guidance, especially in law: *The barrister eventually agreed to act as counsel for the defence.* A **counsellor** (counselor in American English) is the same as a *counsel,* but the term, with **counselling,** is now fairly widely applied to anyone advising on some aspect of social services or personal problems.

couple, pair

A **couple** is two things that are united or joined together, as in a couple of drinks, or a married couple. A **pair** is two things of a kind that are mutually dependent, as in a **pair** of scissors (joined) and a **pair** of gloves (not joined). Both words are singular – *a pair of gloves was found* – except when the parts are treated individually: *The couple decided to go their separate ways; The pair were considered to be very odd characters indeed.*

Is a Couple One or Two?

A **couple** is, as everyone knows, two people. The word looks like and seems like a collective noun, and should therefore, in theory, be singular: *The couple with the display of roses was judged to be the winners of the section.* But look at this example: *The young couple was injured when their motorcycle ran out of control and hit the tree.* There's trouble here: it looks and sounds fine but we're using singular (*was*) and plural (*their*) in the same breath. Here's another dilemma: *Mr Cartwright told the judge that the couple had separated and was living separately.* Here the singular is used (*was*) but it sounds faintly ridiculous. The answer is to treat **couple** in both cases as a plural noun, which today's usage regards as perfectly acceptable.

---

courage. See **bravery, bravado, bravura, courage, heroism**

covert, overt

Covert means 'concealed, secret, disguised'; **overt** is the opposite: 'open to view, public and free for all to see'.

crape. See **crepe, crape**

crapulous

In a review of a biography of the poet Dylan Thomas and his wife Caitlin, the reviewer regarded the tone of much of the account as 'crapulous'. This was not intended as an insult to the biographer. Those familiar with the fact that the couple (note the plural, see 'Is it a Couple One or Two?' above) were ferocious drinkers for most of their lives would have had a clue: **crapulous** means given to extreme intemperance and has nothing to do with bodily functions.

crass, silly, stupid, gross

Of these terms of abuse, **silly** is the mildest, with **stupid** close behind; in fact both are often applied to oneself – Oh, silly me; How stupid of me! – whereas one would hardly label oneself as *crass* or *gross*. To be **crass** is to be ignorant and insensitive and, idiomatically, extremely thick. **Gross** is all of these with an overlay of repulsiveness, coarseness and vulgarity. Save it for someone special.

credible, creditable, credulous

Credible means 'believable'; **creditable** means 'deserving credit or praise'; **credulous** is the naive willingness to believe in something.

crepe, crape

Crepe, the thin crinkly fabric or paper, is the traditional spelling. Also the spelling for the orange-flavoured pancake flambéed in brandy. Note the first 'e' has a circumflex: **crêpe suzette**. **Crape** is generally understood to be a heavier fabric than crepe and used extensively for mourning clothes.

crescendo

Towards the end of the piece the orchestra rose to a crescendo is a commonly heard expression, but it is wrong. **Crescendo** means 'getting louder'. An orchestra can play a *crescendo passage*, but can't rise to one.

criterion, criteria

Although **criteria** is today generally used in both singular and plural senses, it is worth keeping them separated, if only to display your superior knowledge: *The committee had always insisted that the criterion for efficient book-keeping was scrupulous honesty; Harvey had never quite understood the criteria used to value Peruvian Railway stocks.*

crotch, crutch, crux

One of the more hilarious Malapropisms on record is *I'm not going to rest until I get to the crutch of the matter!* The word intended, of course, was **crux**, meaning 'the essential or fundamental point (of a problem)'. The **crotch** is the genital area of the human body and also, in tailoring, the inner join of the legs of a pair of trousers. **Crutch** is also sometimes used in this sense but more correctly defines a support, or an aid to standing or walking, its original meaning.

crucial, cardinal

If something is **crucial** it is decisive: *There is no doubt that O'Brien's brilliant tackling will be crucial to our winning the match.* If something is **cardinal**, it is fundamental: *The coach claimed that O'Brien's inclusion in the team was of cardinal importance if it was to win.* And remember the **cardinal virtues**: justice, prudence, temperence and fortitude, to which are sometimes added faith, hope and charity to make up the Seven Virtues.

Cry, see **weep, cry**

cultured, cultivated

In the sense of 'refined, educated, exhibiting good taste', these are now accepted as synonyms.

curb, kerb

Curb means 'to check or restrain'. In the UK, a **kerb** is the edge of a pavement; in the US, a **curb**.

currant, current

A **currant** is a small, dark dried grape. **Current** has two meanings: 'a flow (of electricity, water, air, etc.)'; and 'existing in the present time': *It is difficult to keep up with current events.*

cyclone, hurricane, tornado, typhoon, waterspout

Hurricanes are violent gales with winds of above around 745 miles an hour and are found in the Atlantic and eastern Pacific oceans; a **cyclone** is a hurricane, the winds of which blow spirally towards a centre region of low barometric pressure, found in the Indian Oceans. **Typhoons** are hurricanes, found in the western Pacific and Southeast Asia. **Tornados** (and, lately, twisters) are hurricane speed winds that rotate, creating funnel or cylindrical shapes over land. A **waterspout** is a tornado, occurring over water.

cynical, sceptical

A **cynic** is someone who believes there is little good in anyone or anything; a **sceptic** (skeptic in American English) is a doubter who has a problem believing anything without ample proof.

Cyprus, cypress

Cyprus is the former British island colony, now split into Greek and Turkish territories, situated in the Mediterranean; a **cypress** is a coniferous tree.

Czar, Tsar

Although *czar* looks more 'Russian' the preference (initially by *The Times* and Oxford) is nowadays decidedly for *tsar,* even though that means *tsaritsa,* replacing the more romantic-sounding *czarina.*

D

dais, lectern, podium, rostrum

A **rostrum** is a raised platform, and a **dais** (pron. *day-iss*) is a rostrum upon which several people can sit or stand. A **podium** is a platform for a single speaker. A lectern is the stand on which the speaker's notes are placed.

darkly, darkling

Both mean the same when referring to darkness, but **darkling** has the additional meaning of 'obscure'.

data, datum

Data is the plural form of **datum**: *Data Affirm Higher Cancer Risk For Female Spouse of a Smoker* (headline, *NY Times*) is correct: **data** is the plural form of **datum**. But the tendency to use **data** as a singular word, particularly in the computer industry, is now so widespread. as to render the practice acceptable.

The Death Watch

Watch out for the family of death words, as they can spring some surprises. **Deadly** can mean 'fatal', 'poisonous', 'relentless' or even merely 'deadly boring'; while **deathly** means 'like death': *Her face was deathly pale.* **Deathless** means 'immortal' but its use today is almost always satirical, as in 'deathless prose'. **Deceased** is a formal and perhaps euphemistic word for dead: *The deceased will be buried tomorrow at 2 p.m.* Interestingly, animals are dead, never deceased.

---

debar, disbar

Debar means 'to exclude or shut out'; **disbar** means 'to expel', usually a barrister from a law court.

debate

Dole will debate Clinton on Tuesday is incorrect usage. You may **have a debate**, **be engaged in a debate**, or **debate a subject**: *Senator Dole will debate the issues with President Clinton on Tuesday.*

deceitful, deceptive

To be **deceitful** is to deliberately to mislead or cheat. **Deceptive** describes the effect of a misleading circumstance: *The bright sunshine proved to be deceptive, for it was really quite cold.*

decent, descent, dissent

Decent means 'good, respectable, morally upright'; **descent** is a movement downwards; **dissent** is disagreement. Note also the spelling of the opposites, *descent/ascent* and *assent/dissent*.

decimate

Decimate, strictly, means to 'kill or destroy one in ten'. However usage has extended its meaning to indicate great destruction and even total annihilation: *He said the blast had cost the firm £150,000 in damage and loss of trade. 'Basically this has decimated us,' he added.*

decry, descry

To **decry** is to disparage or condemn; to **descry** something is to detect or discover it by careful looking: *He decried the use of force in getting the prisoners to cooperate; Then, suddenly, out of the darkness, the lookout descried the vague shape of a conning tower.* Descry is a word hardly ever used today.

deduce, deduct, adduce

The confusion between the first two probably arises because their nouns are spelt the same: *deduction*. But **deduce** means 'to arrive at a conclusion through reasoning', while **deduct** means ' to subtract or take away'. To **adduce** is to present something as an example of evidence or proof: *The hypnotist adduced a series of demonstrations, to the amusement of the audience.*

defective, deficient, defected

Defective means that something is faulty; **deficient** means that something is missing. A notice seen recently on London's Underground advised passengers that *Due to a defected train at Charing Cross there are delays on the Bakerloo Line.* The word the notice was looking for is **defective**. Someone who has **defected** has deserted their country or allegiance to join an opposing interest.

defer, delay

There is a subtle difference here: **defer** implies a decision to postpone; while

delay carries overtones of slowing up a process, of hindering, procrastination: *The final decision was deferred until January; The difficulties with the new computer design will delay completion of the production line.*

definite, definitive

These are not synonymous. **Definite** means 'explicit, exact, clearly defined': *About her views on examination standards she was most definite.* However the word is also widely used to mean 'unquestionably': *Looking at the advance results, I'd say the Berkeley team will definitely win.* **Definitive** means not only 'precise and explicit', but also 'conclusive, absolutely final, the last word': *It took him many years but Professor Abrams produced the definitive essay on the phi-phenomenon.*

defuse, diffuse

Defuse means 'to remove a device or some circumstance likely to cause an explosion or an explosive situation'. **Diffuse** means 'to spread': *Unrest was diffusing among the crowd, and he knew he had to defuse what was becoming an ugly situation.*

deleterious, harmful

These are synonymous, but the trend is to use the simpler and better understood harmful.

delusion. See illusion, allusion, delusion

denigration, denegation

Denigration is the disparaging or belittling of someone; **denegation** is the denial or refusal of a request.

denote, connote

Denote means 'to indicate', or 'to designate': *The arrival of that whisper of a breeze around four o'clock always denoted a cool evening.* **Connote** means 'to suggest or imply an association or an idea': *In Joe's mind a Turkish bath invariably connotes something sinful in all that steam.*

dependant, dependent

The difference here is that **dependant** is a noun and dependent an adjective; a **dependant** is someone **dependent** upon someone or something form of physical, moral or financial support: *It was well-known that the captain had half a dozen dependants in various ports; The young man was unfortunately dependent on drugs.*

dependency. See colony, dependency, protectorate

deplete. See exhaust, deplete, reduce

depository, repository

A **depository** is more correctly a warehouse used for storage, while a **repository** is generally some place of indeterminate size used for storing or displaying things. *He used the old chest as a repository for his medal collection; Leonardo's notebook was the repository of many of the world's most brilliant ideas; The British Museum is one of the greatest repositories of Egyptian artifacts in the world.*

deprecate, depreciate

Often confused but easily separated. To **deprecate** is to disapprove or belittle: *She never missed an opportunity to deprecate his efforts.* **Depreciate** means 'to reduce or lessen': *The pound depreciated alarmingly during the 1970s.* Confusion may arise when **depreciate** is used to devalue something by criticism: *His harsh comments were cleverly calculated to depreciate all their hard work on the project.*

derby, Derby

A **derby** is a bowler hat; **Derby** is the county town ('capital') of Derbyshire in England, and more famously, the classic horse race, named after the Earl of Derby, the race held annually at Epsom Downs in Surrey, and also a kind of porcelain made at Derby.

derby, Derby

derision, derisive, derisory, desultory

Derision (noun) is the act of mocking or derision; **derisive** (adjective) means 'mocking and scornful': *Henry's knockout in the first round was met with derisive laughter.* To be **derisory** (adjective) is to be the object of derision and ridicule: *The men regarded the management's latest offer as utterly derisory.* The look-alike

56

word **desultory** is sometimes seen in a context that seems to indicate that it was meant to mean *derisory* – but not so! *Such a massive sum is not only an insult to those victims of crime awarded desultory amounts, it also fails to acknowledge that the woman takes some responsibility for such brainless abuse.* (Lesley White in *The Sunday Times*, 17.5.98). Here the writer uses *desultory* to mean *irresponsibly haphazard*.

deserts, desserts

Often confused. Note the correct spelling of the word in the well-known phrase *He got his just deserts*, meaning 'he got what he deserved'. A **desert** is an arid, usually sandy region; **dessert** is the sweet or pudding course of a meal.

desiccated.

Desiccate (note the tricky spelling) means 'to dry or dehydrate' – **desiccated** coconut caused the problem because many people assumed that dessicated meant 'chopped up'. *An hour or two in that sun is enough to desiccate anyone.*

desire, want, need

Of this trio, **need** expresses the strongest requirement and urgency. **Want** implies a less urgent craving, while **desire** involves a degree of wishful thinking: *He desired an easier life, wanted a house to live in, but meanwhile needed the price of a square meal.*

despatch, dispatch

Dispatch, meaning to 'send or to do something promptly', is the more common spelling, meaning to send or to do something promptly: *The postmistress promised to dispatch the parcel immediately; He accomplished the tasks with admirable dispatch.*

detract, distract

To **detract** is to 'take away from,' or diminish: *Her rudeness detracted from the otherwise good impression we'd made of her*. To *distract* is to divert someone's attention away from what they're doing: *It is unlawful to distract the driver while the vehicle is in motion.*

device, devise

Device is a noun, and is something designed and made for a specific purpose: *The electric potato peeler was one of the most intriguing devices she'd ever seen*. **Devise** is a verb which means 'to plan, work out or create something': *The inventor had spent three years devising the electric potato peeler.*

devil's advocate

A **devil's advocate** is not so much a person who defends an unpopular cause or point of view but rather someone who deliberately and constructively sets out to uncover faults and flaws in an argument: *It became obvious that because of his engineering knowledge Benny was acting as devil's advocate in the heated discussion.*

diagnosis, prognosis

A **diagnosis** is an identification of or an opinion about a problem or disease, while a **prognosis** is a prediction about the outcome: *When the initial diagnosis was confirmed Dr Metcalfe remained very cagey about the prognosis.*

diametric, opposite, opposed

Many of us use the terms **diametrically opposed** and **diametrically opposite** without knowing quite what they mean. **Diametrically** means 'completely, directly and irreconcilably opposite', so the terms are redundancies. The simpler **opposite** and **opposed** should serve for most purposes (or even *violently opposed*).

dice, die

Although **die** is the correct singular for the plural **dice** (*the die is cast*), nobody in their right minds today would say to his fellow Ludo player, *Hey, Bill, hurry up and throw that die!*

different. See disparate, different

differ from, differ with

To **differ from** suggests a contrast: *Male views usually differ from those of females.* To **differ with** someone is to disagree: *I differed with Frank on just about every point he put forward.*

different from, different to, different than

Different to has been consistently frowned upon and **different from** is recommended instead. **Different than** is more widely used in American-English which avoids the clash.

dilate, dilatory

To **dilate** something is to expand it; to be **dilatory** is to waste time.

dilemma

A **dilemma** does not mean 'a problem', 'a puzzle' or 'a difficult situation', but a choice between two equal (and often undesirable) circumstances.

dinghy, dingy

A **dinghy** is a small boat; **dingy** means 'grimy, soiled, shabby and gloomy'.

Who's Coming to Dinner, Supper, Lunch or Tea?

Depending upon your background, your work and where you live in Britain, these terms can be very confusing. An invitation to **dinner** from strangers can be social dynamite! Many people eat **lunch** (or, formally, **luncheon**) at about 1 p.m. and their main meal, **dinner** (sometimes called **supper**), at 7-8 p.m. Others have **dinner** as a main meal between noon-1 p.m. and a lighter meal called tea between 5-6 p.m., with perhaps a light **supper** before bedtime. Yet other families will have a lunch snack before noon, dinner around 1 p.m., tea at about 4 p.m. and a substantial supper during early evening. **High tea** is a meal replete with meat or fish served late in the afternoon, while **afternoon tea** is a mid-afternoon snack of sandwiches or cake washed down with tea or coffee. And this by no means covers all the confusing gastronomic bizarreries of Britain.

directly

The traditional meaning of **directly** is 'immediately, at once': *She went to him directly she entered the room.* But a confusing secondary meaning is entering the usage scene, meaning 'soon, in a short while, when I'm ready': *Arthur shouted that he'd be down directly, and went on with his work.* Avoid confusion by sticking with the original usage. Also see *soon, presently*.

disabuse. See **abuse, disabuse, refute**

disc, disk

The two spellings have been slugging it out for a couple of centuries. Although today usage is still far from consistent, we tend to use **disc** to describe flat circular surfaces – *disc brakes, compact disc* – , and disk in connection with computers, as with *floppy disk and disk drive*. But usage is still far from consistent.

discomfit, discomfiture, discomfort, discomfiture

Discomfort means, as the word suggests, 'lack of comfort', pain or distress: *The operation was a success but left her vaguely discomforted.* To **discomfit** someone is to disconcert, frustrate or embarrass them; **discomfiture** is the noun: *There was national sympathy for the miners, who were obviously enjoying the discomfiture of the owners.*

discovered, invented

To **discover** something is to find it for the first time – even though that something is already existent: *Benjamin Franklin discovered the electrical properties of lightning; Jane was happy to discover her mother was sympathetic to her case.* To **invent** is to create something that never previously existed: *We will probably never know who invented the wheel; he invents absurd excuses to avoid attending Jane's parties*

discreet, discrete

Discreet means 'tactful, careful to avoid embarrassment'. **Discrete** means 'separate, unattached, distinct': *The lecturer emphasised that the two subjects were discrete; Her discreet behaviour ensured the two relationships remained discrete.*

discreet, circumspect, prudent

Most people use all three interchangeably, but there are shades of difference. To be **discreet** is to be tactful and sensitive, especially in order to avoid some potential embarrassment. To be **circumspect** or to act **circumspectly** is to combine discretion with caution, whatever the circumstance. **Prudent** has traditionally meant 'to be careful about one's affairs' and also 'to provide against the future', but with recent usage it has also come to mean 'wise': *When he saw the size of the man who'd just knocked the drink out of his hand, he felt it prudent not to make a fuss.*

discriminating, discriminatory

Although they derive from *discriminate*, they have two quite distinct meanings. To be **discriminating** is to have the ability to discern fine distinctions, especially in matters of taste. To be **discriminatory** is to be biased and prejudiced: *Eric held what many regarded as discriminatory views on the subject of women's rights.*

disinterested, uninterested

These are not synonyms. To be **disinterested** is to be impartial and free from bias; to be **uninterested** is to lack interest altogether, to be bored: *Although he was asked to contribute to the discussion as a disinterested party, he found himself completely uninterested in the proceedings.* Surprisingly, many grammarians and some dictionaries suggest that the difference in meaning between these two words is not worth maintaining in the face of usage, but this is yet another case of yielding to ambiguity and should be resisted.

disoriented, disorientated

Both words mean the same – 'to be confused', or 'to lose your bearings' – so opt for the shorter word.

disparate, different

Different means 'not the same' or 'partly or completely unlike something else'. **Disparate** means 'utterly different', with nothing whatsoever in common.

disparity, discrepancy

Both words indicate a 'difference'. **Disparity** highlights a dramatic inequality: *The disparity between the wages of men and women in the plant was hard to defend.* A

discrepancy is a difference that shouldn't exist at all: *The investigators soon uncovered some glaring discrepancies in the company's recent annual reports.*

dissatisfied, unsatisfied

To be **dissatisfied** is to be discontented, displeased, unhappy, disappointed. To be **unsatisfied** is to feel the lack or want of something: *Apart from his dissatisfaction with the menu, the miniscule portions ensured that he left the table quite unsatisfied.*

dissemble, disassemble

Confusingly, the opposite of assemble is not dissemble but disassemble, meaning to take apart: The entire machine could be assembled and disassembled in less than a day. Dissemble means 'to conceal by pretence': His evil intentions were dissembled by a pious demeanour.

dissociate, disassociate

Not only is **dissociate** the opposite of *associate* – meaning 'to break up an association between two parties' – but so is **disassociate**. The shorter word is preferred.

distinct, distinctive

Distinct means 'readily distinguished from', clear, precise, definite: *That dish had the distinct flavour of fermented cabbage.* **Distinctive** means 'possessing some obvious characteristic or distinguishing feature': *The badger is always easily identified by the distinctive stripes on its back.*

distinguish, differentiate

In the sense of detecting the difference between things, the two are synonymous, but **differentiate** has an additional shade of meaning, which is 'to discriminate': *The assistant then proceeded to differentiate between the genetic clusters using a code of coloured dyes.*

distract. See detract, distract

distrust, mistrust

Usage maintains a distinction between the two rather than a difference. To **distrust** someone is to suspect strongly that he or she is dishonest or untrustworthy. To **mistrust** is to have doubts, to be wary or sceptical. You can **mistrust** (but not **distrust**) your own feelings and judgement at times.

divers, diverse

Divers, meaning 'several, various and sundry' is an old-fashioned word that is little used now. **Diverse** means 'varied, assorted, of many and different kinds': *We will never cease to be astounded by the diverse creatures of the sea.* Or to use the noun form: *We will never cease to be astounded by the diversity of the creatures of the sea.*

do-able, doable, do able

I could cook my way through the River Cafe Cookbook for ever. Every recipe is seductively do-able. That was from *The Times* so **do-able** is presumably their style. Most dictionaries plump for **doable** although the American *Funk & Wagnalls* recommends the rather quaint **do-a-ble**. It's probably best to avoid using this word altogether.

Domesday, doomsday

Though similar in pronunciation, the **Domesday Book** is the survey of England made in 1086; **doomsday** is the biblical day of judgement.

dominate, domineer

To **dominate** is to control or rule over; to **domineer** is to tyrannise.

donate, give

In his *The Complete Plain Words*, Sir Ernest Gowers advises succinctly: 'Use give.' However, in the context of giving money or time to charity, or organs to medical science, **donate** is well understood.

donkey, ass, burro, mule

A **donkey** is a hardy, long-eared small horse which originated in Africa. An **ass** is the same animal although some strains may have originated in Asia, as is the **burro**, which is the Spanish/Mexican version. The odd one out here is the **mule** which is the sterile progeny of a male donkey and a female horse.

doubtful, dubious

Doubtful is preferred, unless you wish to suggest something underhand: *She was very doubtful about the arrangement, especially with so many dubious characters involved.*

doubtless, undoubtedly

By comparison with the more forceful and unequivocal **undoubtedly**, **doubtless** is rather passive, but both have their uses for discriminating writers.

douse, dowse

There seems no good reason why these should be interchangable as they are in some dictionaries. To **douse** is to saturate with fluid or water, as with **dousing** a fire, or **dousing** (plunging) something into water or some other liquid. **Dowsing** is what a diviner does with a forked twig or divining rod – locate underground water.

Draconian

Draconian has nothing to do with Dracula or blood as many people seem to believe. Meaning 'unduly harsh', the word derives from the ancient Greek lawmaker Draco, who around 600 BC introduced some new laws designed to smarten up the lax Athenian populace. These laws had the merit of simplicity – they awarded death for just about everything from treason and sacrilege to minor theft and even plain laziness. Draco met his own death in an ironically unintentional way. While attending the theatre one evening, Draco was recognised by the crowd who, in the traditional tribute to high officials, threw their capes and cloaks at him. Whether from loyal enthusiasm or for some other reason Draco was swamped by the respect shown and suffocated under the immense pile of discarded old clothing.

Draught, Draughts, Draughtsman, Draftsman

The spelling of **draught** is an English survivor – in the US the spelling **draft** is used and even the game of **draughts** is called **checkers**. and otherwise. In British English the following differences continue to be preserved:

draught: a current of air; a quantity of liquid; a dose of medicine; beer on draught; the depth of a loaded boat or ship; a draught-horse; draughting a plan or map.

draft: to compose a preliminary outline of an article, book or speech; to draw up a parliamentary bill; a banker's order for payment; to separate, usually sheep or cattle.

A person who draws maps or plans is a **draughtsman** or **draughtswoman**; the official who draws up parliamentary bills is the **government draftsman**.

awing room. See **living room, drawing room**

draws, drawers

Draws are small lotteries; **drawers** slide out from cabinets and tables. **Drawers** is also used as a comic alternative to underpants and knickers. All take plural verbs.

drowned

Check the difference between these two statements: *The unfortunate young man drowned in the weir; The unfortunate young man was drowned in the weir. The Times* insists that **drowned** means suffocation, usually accidentally, in water or other liquid; but **was drowned** indicates that another person caused the victim's death by holding the unfortunate's head under water. Few, if any, dictionaries discriminate.

druggist. See **chemist, druggist, pharmacist**

dryer, drier, drily, dryly

By using **dryer** for drying machines (spin dryer, hair dryer), the way is left
clear to use drier as the comparative adjective to mean 'more dry, lacking
moisture'. **Drily** not **dryly** is the correct spelling of the averb. But note: *dryish,
dryness*.

dual, duel

Dual means 'consisting of two', or 'double': a **dual carriageway**, **dual
brakes**. A **duel** is a contest or combat between two adversaries.

due to. See **because, since, on account of, due to, owing to**

dwarf, midget, pygmy

A **dwarf** is a human, animal or plant of stunted growth; in a human dwarf,
the head may be large and extremities disproportionately short. A **midget** is
an extremely small person, normally proportioned, while a **pygmy** (not *pigmy*)
is generally one of several tribes (including the Pygmy tribe), the members of
which are undersized by average human standards.

dyke, dike

In the context of female homosexuality, **dyke** (or **dike**), formerly an insulting
term for a lesbian, is now being reclaimed – although halfway respectable, use
with caution.

dysfunction, malfunction

In the meaning of 'failure to operate properly' due to some disturbance or
deterioration of a part or organ, both mean roughly the same. **Dysfunction**
tends to be used more to express some organic abnormality, while malfunction
seem more clearly associated with mechanical failure.

dyslexia, dysentery

Dyslexics aren't the only people who commit dyslexic mistakes. Everyone
transposes letters in a word every once in a while. But perhaps not quite in the
league of a *bona fide* dyslexic who, answering an RAF medical questionnaire for
officer recruits, mistook dysentery on the form for dentistry and wrote in the
appropriate box: 'One extraction and two fillings'.

each. See **both, each**

each other, one another

Many people try to preserve a difference between these, using **each other** for two things, and **one another** for more than two. Their usage has, however, become so intertwined that few of us now would appreciate the difference.

eager. See **anxious, eager**

earn, paid

Many people strongly object to such statements as like *The administrative head of the department earns £105,000 a year.* Perhaps not unreasonably they ask, 'does he really honestly *earn* that money?' and insist that such statements should read *The administrative head of the department is paid £105,000 a year.* A strong case exists for preserving the difference between something deserved or merited (**earned**), and an amount given in return for imprecise, perhaps even undeserved, services (**paid**).

earthly, earthy

The use of **earthly** can mean 'real, of the world, material' as opposed to 'heavenly', such as an earthly paradise is virtually confined; or can be used in a negative context such: *no earthly chance.* **Earthy** means 'characteristic of the earth', or 'course, crude': *This has an earthy taste; Bill's language can be pretty earthy at times.*

eatable, edible

Both are synonymous, perhaps with the distinction that eatable implies something more tasty than merely edible: The mushroomm, once thought to be poisonous, is edible although bitter; She was relieved when she found the dish to be quite eatable.

eclectic. See esoteric, eclectic, exotic

ecology, environment

Ecology is the study of the relationship between the environment and its inhabitants, human or otherwise. The environment defines the external habitat and all the conditions surrounding an individual or group, human or otherwise: *Having studied the ecology of the lichen family for many years Peter concluded that the tiny plant recently found in the Andes lived in the harshest environment imaginable.*

economic, economical, encomium

Economic relates to economics, the principles governing the production and consumption of goods and services and commercial activity: *The government's latest economic policy is founded on optimistic expectations.* To be **economical** is to be thrifty and not wasteful. An **encomium** is a formal eulogy.

educationalist, educationist, educator

There is still debate about these. **Educationalist**, the traditional form, is giving way to the simpler **educationist** but surely **educator** is the simplest and least pompous of all.

effect. See affect, effect

effective, effectual, efficacious, efficient

This quartet causes plenty of confusion. **Effective** means 'an action that produces the intended effect': *He found that the threat of detention was effective in keeping control.* **Effectual** (subtle, this one) means 'capable of producing the desired effect': *Detention and demerits were quite effectual in keeping the boys under control.* **Efficacious** means 'having the power to produce the intended effect', or 'the ability to apply a remedy': *He claimed the medicine was the most efficacious cure for sore throats; The efficacy of his so-called sore-throat medicine was in some doubt.* **Efficient** means 'competent': *He was an efficient judge, effective on the bench, with a style that was effectual in clearing up the backlog of cases; and above all, he believed in handing out the sort of sentences that were efficacious.* Watch out for an emerging new meaning for **efficient** in 'management-speak'; in company terms, being more efficient means getting fewer people to do more work. This technique is called 'efficiency savings'.

effectively, in effect

Effectively is sometimes wrongly used to mean 'almost, all but': *The* *management's tactics effectively routed the demonstrators and only the hard core remained.* **In effect** might be the more precise term here, meaning 'for all practical purposes': *In effect the demonstrators were routed and only the hard core remained.* **Virtually** is a useful synonym.

effete, effeminate

Although **effete** can be used unisexually, it is usually applied to weak, ineffectual, morally and intellectually decadent men. It can sometimes be used otherwise – in biology, for example, where it can refer to animals no longer capable of reproducing. To be **effeminate** is for a man to display unmanly or feminine characteristics.

effrontery. See affront, effrontery

egoist, egotism

Egoism is a person's undue preoccupation with his or her self, a display of obsessive self-interest. An **egotistical** person is also obsessively self-interested but reveals it to all with excessive boasting and a predominance of 'I' in conversations.

egregious. See gregarious, egregious

either, any

Either means 'one or other of two': *Either take it or leave it; There were two movies showing and I didn't like either of them.* **Any** refers to more than two: *There were four movies showing and I didn't care for any of them.* Both **either** and **neither** are singular: *Either you or I am lying.* Although gramatically correct this looks and sounds awkward, so reconstruct: *Either you are lying or I am.* Also remember the *either/or* and *neither/nor* rule.

elder, older, eldest, oldest

The use of these words is still governed by tradition. **Elder** and **eldest** are used primarily for human family relationships; you would not say: *Toby is the eldest horse in the stables,* but you might say *Mr French is the firm's elder partner.* **Older** is the comparative of **old**: *Esther is the older of the two sisters; I thought that Emily was the oldest member of the family but it turns out that Rebecca is the eldest* (or *elder*).

elemental, elementary, alimentary

Elemental relates to the primal forces of nature, things basic and fundamental: *She found herself transfixed by the elemental surges of the tide.* **Elementary** means 'basic and simple', and 'returning to first principles': *'As*

for the reason for Cargill's panic,' Holmes replied, *'it's elementary, my dear Watson.'*
Alimentary refers to food and eating; hence one's *alimentary canal*.

elide. See **allude, elude, elide**

elucidate, explain
Elucidate is merely a fancy word for **explain**.

elude. See **allude, elude, elide**

emaciate, emancipate
A guinea pig was found in an emancipated condition – Matlock Mercury, Derbyshire.
The word required is **emaciated**, meaning 'abnormally thin' . To **emancipate**
is to free from restriction, usually in a social context: *In most respects she regarded
herself as a truly emancipated woman, free to do do as she wanted.*

EMACIATE, EMANCIPATE

embassy. See **consulate, embassy, legation**

emigrant, immigrant
If John Smith leaves Britain to live in Australia, he's **emigrating** from Britain
and **immigrating** to Australia, where he becomes an **immigrant** or, as some
Australians have it, a **migrant**.

eminent, imminent
An **eminent** person is somebody of note, 'distinguished': *He was the most*

eminent neurosurgeon of his time. **Imminent** means 'impending, threatening, about to happen': *Everyone felt that war was imminent.* There is also a rarely-used word, **immanent**, which means 'inherent'.

emotional, emotive

To be **emotional** is to be affected, sometimes excessively, by emotion: *On the subject of her former partner David she invariably became emotional; The boy suffered from a variety of emotional problems.* **Emotive** means 'to arouse emotion': *Discussing missing husbands with their abandoned wives is understandably an emotive issue.*

empathy, sympathy

Sympathy means 'a sharing of emotions and feelings of compassion and pity with another, especially at a time of difficulty'. **Empathy** is a feeling of intimately understanding a person, 'the close identification with the thoughts and feelings of another': *In his latest portrait the artist revealed an unusual empathy with the sitter.*

empirical, imperial

Confusion between these two may arise from the similarity of *emperor* and *empire* to *empirical*, but there is no connection. **Empirical** means 'knowing by observation, facts and experience rather than from theory'. The word that relates to *empire* is **imperial**.

empowerment

Meaning 'to delegate or give power to someone', this has become widely used in the 1990s. Use with discretion, as its once precise meaning has been somewhat suffused.

encyclopaedia, encyclopedia

There is a tendency today to use **encyclopedia**, the American-English version, but many writers take care to retain the diphthong. The shortened cyclopedia is a sloppy term for the real thing.

endemic, epidemic, pandemic

Cholera has been endemic in parts of the Indian subcontinent for the past 200 years; it causes numerous epidemics and from time to time pandemics, when it spreads across the world – The Times 1994. **Endemic** means 'frequently found in a particular area'; **epidemic** means 'affecting many people at the same time'; while **pandemic** means 'affecting many people over a wide geographical area'.

enervate, energise

Enervate is often used wrongly; it means 'to drain and weaken': *The succession* *of hot, humid days left them irritable and enervated.* **Energise** means the opposite: *After three large glasses of chilled orange juice, Barry felt bouncy and energised.*

enjoin, join

To **join**, meaning 'to 'bring together', offers few problems. To **enjoin** is 'to 'order, urge or require': *The speaker enjoined the angry gathering to proceed quietly to their homes.*

The Enormity of it All

Examples of the misuse of **enormity** abound – often surprisingly committed by centres of grammatical awareness such as posh newspapers that should know better. Here are some recent examples:

1. *By then she [Sharon Stone] was 34 years old and had been around the block a few times, and thought she could handle the enormity of the experience. (This experience was uncrossing her legs in the movie Basic Instinct). – Sunday Telegraph 1995*

2. *As we topped the Mendip Hills on the Somerset Levels, the enormity of the distance we had walked struck home… – Daily Telegraph, 1995*

3. *At four o'clock yesterday morning, Brian Lara woke in his hotel room, sweating and shaking with nerves over the enormity of the day ahead. – The Times, 1994*

Enormity can often be loosely defined in dictionaries as 'vastness of size or extent' and it is entries like this that lead to confusion and ambiguity. **Enormity** describes the quality of extreme wickedness, something monstrous or offensively outrageous: *Even hardened policemen were shocked by the enormity of the crime.*

In the examples above what is probably meant is (1) *ramifications*, although the definition of 'offensively outrageous' is not a totally inappropriate fit, (2) *immensity* and (3) *challenge*.

enquire, inquire, enquiry, inquiry

The two can be used interchangeably: *The reporter enquired how the departmental inquiry was going.*

enrol, enroll

The 1992 brochure of Kingsbridge Community College in Devon invites students to '*enrole*' in a variety of courses – including A-Level English. There is no such word. The word the college wanted was **enrol**. **Enroll** is the American-English version.

ensue, ensure

Occasionally confused. **Ensue** means 'to follow subsequently, often as a consequence': *When the prizewinners were announced the usual babble and shouting ensued.* **Ensure** means 'to make certain': *Her powerful serve ensured her place on the tennis team.*

ensure. See assure, ensure, insure

envelop, envelope

Don't confuse these. To **envelop** (pron. *en-VEL-up*) something is to wrap it or cover it: *She screamed when she was suddenly enveloped by the poisonous green gas.* An **envelope** (pron. *EN-vel-lope*) is of course a flat wrapper or other container, usually of paper.

envious, enviable, envy, jealousy

Although one of the seven deadly sins, **envy** can range from being merely a casual longing for something to deep hatred and malice towards someone possessing something that one wants. **Enviable** means 'arousing envy, or to be worthy of envy': *George has got himself an enviable position in the firm.* To be **envious** is to feel or show envy; a near synonym is *to covet* which is to lust after the possession of something or someone. **Jealousy** is the expression of personal unease or resentment about a situation, often involving rivalry, the transfer of affection or love from one to another, or a suspected infidelity, and can surface as irrational behaviour and vindictiveness.

envisage, envision

These are near synonyms, but **envision** tends to imply future possibility rather than an image: *The minister envisioned a day when everyone, regardless of circumstance, would be adequately housed.* To **envisage** is to form a mental image of something in the future: *She envisaged her ideal home: a modernised thatched cottage with an old-fashioned garden and orchard.* Loose usage has tended to extend the meaning of *envisage* (and *envision*) to 'expect, feel, think': *The farmers envisaged/envisioned that next year's crop would be the biggest ever.* Not to be encouraged.

epidemic. See endemic, epidemic, pandemic

epigram, epigraph, epitaph

The playwright Dennis Potter's *The trouble with words is that you never know whose mouths they've been in* is an **epigram**: a pithy, witty slice of wisdom. An **epitaph**, is an inscription on a gravestone, as in this example commemorating the 17th-century architect Sir John Vanbrugh:

Under this stone, reader, survey
Dear Sir John Vanbrugh's house of clay.
Lie heavy on him, earth! for he
Laid many heavy loads on thee.

An **epigraph** is usually a thematic quotation appearing at the beginning of a book, but it can also be an inscription on a statue or building.

epithet

Careful users will observe this word's original meaning: an adjective or phrase expressing some attribute or quality characteristic of a person or thing. Richard the Lionheart, Chubby Checker, Gorgeous Gussy Moran, Babe Ruth are all epithets, none of them necessarily disparaging. Today many, if not most, people regard an **epithet** as abusive: *'Stupid bitch' and other epithets were shouted at her by passing lorry drivers.*

equable, equitable

Equable means 'unvarying and free from extremes' or, as applied to people, 'placid, even-tempered': *As the executive who fields all the complaints, Margaret has the ideal equable temperament.* **Equitable** means 'fair, impartial and just': *The insurance company arrived at an equitable settlement.*

equal to, equal with

These are used for quite different purposes. *He was glad to hear that they felt his skills were equal to the immense task ahead.* Here **equal to** is used to convey 'adequate, equivalent to'. **Equal with** means 'being identical, evenly balanced': *She felt that after her pay rise she was now about equal with the men in the firm.*

erotic. See **obscene, pornographic, erotic**

erupt, irrupt

To **erupt** is to burst out violently; to **irrupt** is to enter forcibly and violently. The same meanings apply to the nouns, **eruption** and **irruption**.

Eskimo, Inuit, Aleut

The use of **Eskimo** to describe the north Canadian or Greenland peoples has now been generally replaced by the specific tribal names, **Inuit** (sometimes *Innuit*, plural *Innu*) and **Aleut**.

esoteric, eclectic, exotic

Many writers find these hard to separate. Something **esoteric** is confined or restricted to a minority who understand it, such as obscure religious ritual, the peculiar attractions of trainspotting or, these days, Latin. Something **exotic** is strange, unusual and foreign, but it can also mean 'outrageous' and 'thrilling'. An **eclectic** person has the talent and taste to select the best of everything.

especially, specially

Especially means 'really exceptionally'; **specially** means 'out of the ordinary, individual, particular': *The dog was specially chosen for his alertness, but he is especially attentive at mealtimes.*

Esq.

If you insist on using this ancient abbreviation in your correspondence, don't make the mistake of preceding it by 'Mr'. Simply write *John Smith Esq.*

euphemism, euphuism

Euphuism looks like **euphemism** spelt incorrectly but it is a word that defines a high-flown, ornate and affected style of writing. A **euphemism** is a word or phrase substituted for one considered to be offensive, hurtful, unpleasant or embarrassing. *Bathroom* for *lavatory, perspiration* for *sweat, passed away* for *died, let go* for *sacked* or *dismissed, that time* for *menstruation, passing wind* for *fart* are all common euphemisms. Much politically correct and nondiscriminatory language is also euphemistic.

European Union, European Community, Common Market

Use the former and the abbreviation **EU** rather than **Common Market, EEC** or **EC**.

evacuate, vacate

Evacuate means 'to make empty' (e.g. the bowels) or 'to remove from': *The evacuation offrom the threatened town went smoothly.* **Vacate** means 'to give up occupancy': *The squatters vacated the premises with surprisingly little fuss.*

evade, elude, avoid

Avoid means 'to shun, to keep away from'. **Evade** and **elude** are similar and mean 'to avoid by cleverness or deception'. Knowing the difference between **avoidance** and **evasion** could keep you out of jail when paying your tax; **tax avoidance** (by good advice) is legal, while **tax evasion** (by dishonest means) is clearly illegal.

evaluate. See appraise, apprise, assess, evaluate

every day, everyday

As an adjective, **everyday** means ordinary, usual: *Sighting deer during their walks* *along the cliffs was now an everyday occurrence.* **Every day** means each day: *We saw deer wandering through the garden nearly every day.*

everyone, every one, everybody

There were ten apples and every one was rotten; There were ten people in the pub and everyone was drunk. Here **every one** is used to emphasise individual apples, and **everyone** the whole, as a group, but note that **everyone** and **every one** are both singular. Sir Roy Strong's book *The Story of Britain* is described on the cover as: *One man's quest to give to everyone the history of their country.* The publishers should have known better, although the practice of using the plural pronoun instead of, for example, *his/her* is now widespread. **Everybody** and **everyone** are interchangeable.

evidence, proof, testimony

Testimony is the statement of a witness; **evidence** is information presented to support an argument; **proof** is evidence that removes any doubt.

evident. See apparent, evident

evince, evoke

Both are used in relation to abstractions, such as emotions, images and visions. To evince is to 'to show, to make evident': *She evinced little surprise when confronted by her former enemy.* **Evoke** is a near synonym but perhaps a little more active in that it implies 'to summon up, to make clear': *In his speech he evoked the dream of freedom, independence and nationhood.*

exacerbate, exasperate, aggravate

All three mean 'to make worse' but are used in different ways. **Exacerbate** is customarily applied to things and conditions: *The almost-forgotten feud between the brothers was suddenly exacerbated by family interference.* **Exasperate** is used to express a worsening situation between individuals: *She finally exasperated me to the point of screaming!* **Aggravate**, which many people mistakenly believe to mean 'annoy', is a synonym for exacerbate but which may sometimes involve a degree of intent and persistence: *Elizabeth's constant sniping at Jack was cunningly calculated to aggravate the already tense situation.*

exact, extract

In the sense of 'demand, force or compel', these are synonymous: *After winning the lottery, Barney knew it would be only a matter of time before the family would be around to exact their share.* Perhaps **extract** implies a greater degree of removal by extortion than **exact**, but it is a matter of choice.

exasperate. See **aggravate, exasperate**

except, unless

Use **except** to express an omission and **unless** to make a condition: *I will work every day except Saturday unless you disagree.* The use of **except** as a synonym for **unless** is an archaism except perhaps in Northern Ireland: *Except [unless] you right now give me a categorical assurance that you believe my word on the constitutional position of Northern Ireland, I will not hold any conversation with you* – Ian Paisley MP, 1994.

except. See **accept, except**

exceptional, exceptionable

Exceptional means 'out of the ordinary, most unusual', but to be **exceptionable** is to be objectionable: *On the court, he was an exceptional tennis player, but in the clubhouse most found his behaviour quite exceptionable.*

excoriate, execrate

One old meaning of **excoriate** was to 'flay, or to strip the skin' from someone. Today's usage is less physical but no less severe: to denounce or scathingly condemn. To **execrate** is to loathe and detest: *In no uncertain words the President excoriated his former ally as a barbarian traitor; She positively execrated the memory of her late stepmother.*

exercise. See **exorcise, exercise**

exhaust, deplete, reduce

Exhaust means 'to drain, empty, remove and to deplete totally'. **Reduce**, in a similar context, means 'to make smaller in size, number or extent'. The odd man out is **deplete**, which, rather unhelpfully, can mean 'to use up or empty partially or completely'. If you intend to write *The local reservoirs were depleted well before the end of summer*, you are inviting confusion. Better to be specific and use *reduced* (partial depletion) or *exhausted* (total depletion).

exigency, exiguous

Two classic confusables, which is perhaps why we don't see them (or even need to use them) very often. An **exigency** is a state of great urgency that requires immediate attention. **Exiguous** means 'meagre, small': *The problem with the Somalis, apart from having to cope with natural and manmade exigencies, was simply their traditionally exiguous incomes.*

exorcise, exercise

Although there cannot be many writers unfamiliar with **exercise**, these two are sometimes muddled. A New South Wales government leaflet advises car buyers to demand the car's history from the vendor, *Otherwise, a finance company could exorcise its rights*. To **exorcise** is to attempt to dispel evil spirits from a person or place (or even a car!).

expatiate, expiate

To **expatiate** is to elaborate or enlarge upon a topic in speaking or writing: *The doctor expatiated on the dangers of bad dietary habits*. To **expiate** is to make amends or atone for some wrong: *In his desperate efforts to expiate his cruel treatment of his sisters, Joel moaned and tore his hair and banged his head upon the floor*.

expatriate, compatriot

An **expatriate** (often abbreviated to **expat**) is a resident of a foreign country: *All the American expatriates would gather every Friday in their club on the Nanking Road*. To **expatriate** is to expel a person from a country. A **compatriot** is a fellow countryman: *He found several compatriots among the British expatriates in Barcelona*.

expect. See anticipate, expect, hope

expeditious, expedient

Expeditious means 'speedy and efficient', while **expedient** expresses an action that is convenient for the purpose: *It was considered expedient to wind up the firm as expeditiously as possible*.

expert

Think before conferring this honour on anybody; it's overused and near-meaningless.

expertise, skill

Expertise is usually substituted as a posh word for **skill**, although you can differentiate between them if you wish. **Skill** suggests practical ability, as in a *surgeon's skill*, while **expertise** conveys (or should convey) the acquisition of specialised knowledge and experience to an exceptional degree.

explain. See elucidate, explain

explicit, implicit

To be **explicit** is to be absolutely clear and specific; something **implicit** is not directly expressed but implied or hinted at. Nevertheless, whatever is **implied** is usually or instinctively understood, or taken for granted: *The volunteers were only too keenly aware of the implicit dangers of the task ahead*.

extempore. See **impromptu, extempore**

extinct, extant

Similar looking, but opposites. Something **extinct** no longer exists; something **extant** is still, or thought to be, in existence or surviving: *Everyone knows that the trilobite is extinct, but its distant cousin the woodlouse is still extant throughout the world.*

extract. See **exact, extract**

extraneous, extrinsic, intrinsic

Extraneous means 'external, coming from without' or, in another sense, 'irrelevant, unrelated or not essential': *At the enquiry the business about the missing personal effects was considered to be an extraneous issue.* **Extrinsic** has a subtly similar meaning but is applied in the sense of not being an inherent or essential part of something: *The auctioneer played up the extrinsic contribution of the necklace's previous alleged royal owners to its fame and value.* Its opposite, **intrinsic**, meaning 'an essential part of something', is more common.

F

facility, faculty

Of the various meanings the one that causes most confusion concerns ability. By **facility** we usually mean 'having the ability to do something with apparent ease': *She had the charming facility to make people relax*. By **faculty** or **faculties** we mean 'natural or inherent powers' (that is, sight, hearing, taste, intuition, intelligence, etc.): *The task they set him was going to challenge all his faculties to the hilt*.

facsimile. See **replica, copy, facsimile**

facts, true facts, factitious

Facts are verified or observable truths, events that have actually happened, or things that have existed or are real. The phrase **true facts** is tautological. Something **factitious**, on the other hand, is false or artificial: *She claimed that most of Deborah's teachers had been seduced by her academic achievements, which turned out to be factitious.*

faint, feint

Faint means 'weak, feeble, indistinct' as an adjective, and also 'to lose consciousness' as a verb. A **feint** is a feigned or pretended attack intended to mislead: *The Missouri Kid feinted with his left and then belted Navarro on the chin with a terrific right.*

Extract the Extract, and Other Lookalikes

A family of words exists that frequently cause people to pause: words which are spelt the same but are pronounced or accented differently where there is one pronunciation for the noun and another for the verb. An example is **extract**. The **extract** of cod liver oil you may have known in your childhood is pronounced *EX-trakt*, while the process of **extracting** it from the poor cod is pronounced *ex-TRAKT*.

Here are some other fairly common words where the nouns and verbs look alike but are pronounced differently (noun first, then the verb): **abstract** (AB-strakt; ab-STRAKT); **accent** (AK-sent, ak-SENT); **attribute** (AT-trib-yoot, at-TRIB-yoot); **combat** (KOM-bat, kom-BAT); **compound** (KOM-pound, kom-POUND); **compress** (KOM-press, kom-PRESS); **conduct** (KON-duct, kon-DUCT); **consort** (KON-sort, kon-SORT); **contest** (KON-test, kon-TEST); **contract** (KON-trakt, kon-TRAKT); **convert** (KON-vert, kon-VERT); **convict** (KON-vikt, kon-VIKT); **defect** (DE-fekt, de-FEKT); **digest** (DY-jest, dih-JEST); **discharge** (DIS-charj, dis-CHARJ); **escort** (ES-kort, es-KORT); **ferment** (FER-ment,fer-MENT); **object** (OB-jekt, ob-JEKT); **pervert** (PER-vert, per-VERT); **present** (PRES-ent, preh-SENT); **project** (PRO-jekt, pro-JEKT); **rebel** (REH-bel, reh-BEL); **refuse** (REH-fyoos, reh-FYOOS); **suspect** (SUS-pekt, sus-PEKT).

fair, fayre

Does the current ubiquity of **fayre**, to denote a country or charity fair or fête, indicate a desire to return the word to its Old Saxon root – *fagr* or *fagar*? This doesn't wash because the etymology of **fair**, the holiday or entertainment, derives from the Old French *feire*, or festival. More likely **fayre** is a symptom of 'Ye Olde Syndrome', or the quest for the quaint. Be sensible and use **fair**.

fallacy, misconception

A **fallacy** is not an 'erroneous belief' but a faulty opinion or argument based on inaccurate facts or false reasoning. An erroneous belief is a **misconception**.

familiar with, familiar to

Familiar with indicates 'having a good knowledge of': *James was familiar with the type of engine and had it going in no time*. **Familiar to** implies a lesser degree of familiarity: *As she entered the church Ethel realised that many of the faces in the congregation were familiar to her*.

famously

As in *Canute was the king who famously commanded the tide to turn*, **famously** is an overrated and overused adverb. Use with caution, if at all.

farther, further

Farther is used exclusively to express distance, either literally (*He guessed that*

Bristol was farther from London than Bath), or figuratively (*Fred's claims could not be farther from the truth*). **Further** means 'in addition': *She was seriously thinking about further education.*

fatal, fated, fateful

The primary meaning of **fatal** means 'causing or resulting in death'; fated means 'doomed'. **Fateful** is the most loaded of this group, suggesting all kinds of ominous portents beyond anyone's control, including death, disaster and ruin: *From that fateful encounter sprang a legacy of hate that engulfed the two neighbouring states.*

fauna. See flora and fauna

faze. See phase, faz

feel. See believe, feel, think

ferment, foment

He [*Englishman Hugh Ryman*] *fomented his ultra-ripe grapes in oak barrels* ... (Oz Clarke in the *Daily Telegraph*, 3.5.97). Strange way to make wine! **Fermenting** rather than **fomenting** might be a better way to brew a better vintage. In the sense of 'causing or stirring up trouble' these are synonyms. Otherwise, to **ferment** is the chemical process of fermentation, of converting, for example, grapes into wine; while to **forment** is to apply moist heat to the body to reduce pain.

fervent, fervid, fervour

Fervour is an intense feeling, a passion, from which springs **fervent**, meaning 'to be keenly enthusiastic, ardent and passionate'. **Fervid** is synonymous but tends to be used to suggest a heightened, more passionate, even incandescent fervour for which the little-used **perfervid** is really the correct word.

feud. See vendetta, feud

few, little, less, fewer

It is not unusual to see on the label of a dietary product an assertion that it is **less** fattening, **less** expensive and has **less** calories. Two correct out of three; what is meant is **fewer** calories. The rule is simple: use **few** and **fewer** with numbers and when what is being described can be counted, and **less** when describing something abstract or uncountable: *In my last driving test I made fewer mistakes than ever before; Although I made fewer mistakes my instructor seemed less* *pleased with my performance*. Use **little** to indicate 'not much': *Although I have little spare time, I do have a few minutes to spare now.*

fiancée, fiancéee

The first is masculine, the second, with the double *ee*, is feminine. Conscientious writers will retain the accent.

fictional, fictitious

Something **fictional** relates to a fiction, a work of the imagination – a novel, play or movie: *He referred to the fictional account of his grandfather's life in 'The Moon and Sixpence'*. Something **fictitious** is untrue or not genuine: *I'm tired of hearing her obviously fictitious excuses for being late each morning.*

filet, fillet

In British English, the noun **fillet** (pron. *FILL-it*) the noun means a strip of boneless meat or fish, while the verb **to fillet** means to 'remove the bone from meat or fish'. In American- English, the word is **filet** (pron. fil-LAY). The well-known dish **filet mignon** is pronounced fih-LAY MEEN-yohn wherever you are.

fill in, fill out

There's logic here. When you **fill in** something, you insert: *I filled in the gaps; I filled in the application form*. When you **fill out** something, you add or complete: *He filled out John's speech with some spicy anecdotes*. In American English, **fill out** is used universally.

find out. See **ascertain, find out**

finial, filial

A **finial** is an ornament on top of a spire, gable or piece of furniture. **Filial** relates to sons and daughters: *He expected, and received, daily displays of filial devotion.*

finish, finalise

These are not synonyms. **Finish** means to complete; to **finalise** (or finalize) is to 'settle something, to reach agreement' or 'to put something into a final form': *She finalised the amendments, but the agreement was far from finished.*

first, firstly

It's hardly worth getting into a stew over **firstly** as many grammarians do in objecting to **firstly, secondly, thirdly**, etc. Use this pattern if you wish, or even **firstly, second, third**, and so on. But shorter and neater (and avoiding ninety-ninthly) is the formula: **first, second, third**…

fish, fishes

Both are used as the plural form of **fish**, though **fishes** nowadays appears infrequently.

flagrant, blatant

Flagrant means 'shocking and outrageous'; **blatant** means 'glaringly obvious': *Mavis's flagrant disregard of her mother-in-law upset the whole party; Barrie's accusation was recognised by everyone as a blatant lie.*

flammable. See inflammable, flammable

flare, flair

These are sometimes confused. **Flare** expresses 'bursting with activity' – usually to do with fire and flame: *The sudden gust caused the fire to flare alarmingly; As they explored deeper into the cave they had to light flares; As the temperature rose, tempers flared among the miners.* **Flair** refers to a person's natural ability, talent, elegance and style: *Barbara always dressed with flair.*

flat, condominium, apartment, cooperative

While transatlantic usage is variable, a **flat** in the UK, and in other places like Australia, is an **apartment** in the US. A **condominium**, a more common description in the US than elsewhere, is a block of flats whose owners share costs and responsibilities for the upkeep of the building and its facilities. In the US **cooperative** is a block of apartments owned by a corporation in which the owners hold shares equivalent to the value of their individual apartments.

flaunt. See flout, flaunt

flautist, flutist

In Britain, a flute player is a **flautist; flutist** is the American English term.

flora and fauna

Unlike similar Latin nouns these aren't plural, but collective nouns. The plural forms, rarely used, are *floras* and *faunas*, even more rarely *florae* and *faunae*.

flotsam, jetsam, ligan

These all originate from ships, and are items that either float off (**flotsam**), are jettisoned or thrown off (**jetsam**), or sink to the bottom of the sea (**ligan** or **lagan**). The question is, how can you tell which is which when you find them?

flounder. See founder, flounder

flout, flaunt

Flout means to 'disregard, show contempt or to deliberately defy'; **flaunt** means 'to show off boastfully, to display ostentatiously': *In playing the overture the violinist flouted just about every one of the composer's directions; The dancer shamefully flaunted her smouldering sexuality.*

flu, flue

Flu is short for influenza; a **flue** is a chimney or pipe to carry off smoke or gas.

fob, foist

Usage seems to favour **foist** as meaning 'to pass off something fake or inferior as genuine and valuable', or 'to impose an unwanted item or task onto someone': *That supervisor deliberately foisted this lousy job on me.* **Fob** means to 'put off by evasion' and is usually followed by **off**: *She won't fob me off with that weak excuse again.*

foetus, fetus

Foetus (and **foetal**) is the traditional, scientific spelling and remains prevalent in British English; the American English spelling is **fetus** (and **fetal**).

forbear, forebear

As nouns, both mean the same: 'an ancestor'. **Forbear** (without the 'e') is also a verb meaning 'to refrain from': *She could hardly forbear crying out aloud when she heard Frank's voice.*

forceful, forcible, forced

Forcible and **forced** are near adjectival synonyms, the latter more common, to express the use of force: *The evidence indicated a forced entry.* **Forceful** means 'powerful and persuasive': *His advocacy during the trial was both thoughtful and forceful.*

forego, forgo

Forego means 'to precede, to go before'; **forgo** means 'to do without, or to give up something': *Betsy thought twice about forgoing her morning coffee.*

forensic

Many think that **forensic** is a medical term; in fact as an adjective **forensic** means 'legal'. **Forensic medicine** is medical science applied to the purposes of law.

forever, for ever

These are worth separating, with **forever** meaning 'continuously, at all times'

(*The two old dears were forever gossiping*), and **for ever** meaning 'eternally, always' (though in American English, it often appears as one word): *He swore he'd love me for ever* (or *for ever and ever!*).

foreword, forward

Forward conveys 'moving ahead, towards the front': *Every time he had the chance he moved a little bit forward*. A **foreword** is a preface or introduction to a book: *Max was paid £150 to write a new foreword to the book*.

formally, formerly

Pronounced the same, spelt differently, and often confused. **Formally** means 'in a formal, conventional or established manner': *For the wedding they all had to dress formally*. **Formerly** means 'in past or earlier times': *Formerly it was accepted that you'd dress for dinner*.

former, latter

The convention, still healthily maintained, is to use these only when referring to two people or things: *The doctor recommended brandy and lemon for his cold – with plenty of the former; There wasn't much between Harris's and Smith's quotes but Jill felt inclined to choose the latter.*

fortuitous, fortunate

Something that happens by chance or accident is **fortuitous**; if the result is a happy one it is also **fortunate**: *Our meeting at the supermarket was fortuitous but, fortunately, she remembered the money she owed me.*

forward and backward, backwards and forwards

As adjectives, forward and backward are not spelled with 's': *She had a very forward attitude*. Otherwise, with or without the 's', both are acceptable except in some selective usages. You would not say, for example, *Look forwards to a cosy evening by the fireside*. In most cases, your ear should tell you which sounds right.

founder, flounder

Flounder means 'to struggle helplessly': *After a series of interruptions, the speaker floundered for several minutes*. If you **founder**, however, you're in serious trouble; it means 'to sink': *The ill-fated ship foundered in only ten feet of water*.

Founding Fathers, Pilgrim Fathers

The **Founding Fathers** were members of the 1787 US Constitutional Convention. The **Pilgrim Fathers** were the Puritans who sailed on the *Mayflower* to New England in 1620.

fracture, break

There is no difference between a **broken** bone and a **fractured** bone. Medically, the preferred term is **fracture**.

fragile, frail

Although their meanings overlap, careful writers will use these differently. Both mean 'delicate and easily broken', but **fragile** is more aptly applied to things (*a fragile vase, fragile health*), while **frail**, implying physical weakness, feebleness and incapability, is best reserved for people: *Even in her frail state, she always managed the evening trip to the corner pub.*

franc

It is fair to assume that the single word **franc** denotes the French franc. But other countries, such as Belgium and Switzerland also have the franc – the country should be specified.

Frankenstein's monster

Many people think that **Frankenstein** is the monster. Not so. In Mary Shelley's 1818 novel, Baron Frankenstein *created* the monster that destroyed him. If you allude to something that destroys its creator, you can call it *Frankenstein's monster*.

frantic, frenetic

Someone **frantic** is to some degree, over-excited, hysterical and agitated. Frenetic is a close synonym but its roots from both Greek and Latin link it more to the mind and insanity; perhaps best reserved for conveying a wild, deranged frenzy or delirium.

The French are Capital

Although once some French suffixes were spelt with a lower-case **french** (*french fries, french polish, french polisher,* etc.), the accepted spellings today (for consistency, no doubt) all carry a capitalised **French**, *including French leave, bread, cricket, cuffs, doors, dressing, fried potatoes, horn, knickers, letter, mustard, polish, pleat, stick, toast, vermouth* and *windows.*

---

frequently. See **commonly, frequently, generally, usually**

freshman. See **sophomore, freshman**

frightened, scared, alarmed, afraid

Afraid has a certain permanance about it: *He was afraid of crossing roads.* To be **frightened** or **scared** is a more immediate or passing experience: *The children were frightened/scared by the loud bang.* **Alarm** is a fear or anxiety that can build : *Finding nobody, she began to be alarmed by the eerie silence.*

fruition, completion

Fruition conveys the enjoyment of fulfilment and success. **Completion** is the state of being finished, complete: *The completion of the project signalled the fruition of his life's work.*

Unfamiliar Facts About Fulsome

Els, of South Africa, who drew fulsome praise after playing a round with an esteemed countryman, Gary Player ... – The Times, 1994

Listening to the fulsome praise heaped upon her by the President the champion glowed with visible pride ... – New York Daily News, 1991

Someone should have tipped off the golfer and the poor girl; today's meaning of **fulsome** is 'embarrassingly insincere, excessive, distasteful and nauseating'.

Fulsome is often misused to mean generous and lavish but perhaps, reviewing its etymology over the past 800 years, this is not surprising. In the 13th century it did mean 'full and copious', but by the 14th had come to imply 'fat and overgrown'. By the 15th, the word was even less attractive (gross, satiated) and in 1604 a dictionary records that it meant 'morally foul and obscene'. The present usage has remained fairly constant since the end of the 17th century, except perhaps for this extraordinary example of misuse: *The fruit of a tree is the female part of the flower, fertilised and grown to ripeness. Nothing describes this more explicitly than a pear, with its shape like fulsome hips. – The Observer, 1995.*

---

funds. See **money, monies, funds, cash**

Fujiyama, Mt Fuji

The famous Japanese peak is either **Fujiyama** or **Mt Fuji**, not Mt Fujiyama.

furnish, furbish

Furnish means to 'provide, equip, supply, fit out': *By agreement the room was furnished with only top quality cupboards and appliances.* To **furbish** is to 'polish or restore to brightness'.

fustian, fusty

Fustian is used mostly in the literary sense of being pretentious, pompous and bombastic. **Fusty** means 'smelling damp and mouldy' and, thus figuratively, being stale and old-fashioned.

futility, fatuity, futurity

Futility means 'total lack of purpose, point and success'. **Fatuity** is 'complacency, inanity, smug stupidity'. **Futurity** is the odd one out and is a fancy word for 'the future'.

G

gaff, gaffe

A **gaff** is a fishing pole with a hook on it; a **gaffe** is a social blunder or an indiscreet remark: *Bernard turned a bright red when he realised he'd made a gaffe.*

gale. See **cyclone, hurricane, tornado, typhoon**

Gallic, Gaelic

Gallic (from Gaul, the earlier name of France) relates to France and its people. **Gaelic** refers to Celtic descendants (Scots, Irish, Isle of Man) and their languages.

Gambia, The Gambia

The latter is the correct name for this tiny country on the West African coast.

gamble, gambol

Occasionally confused but their meanings are miles apart. To **gamble** is to play a game of chance for money; to **gambol** is to frolic about playfully: *He quickly gambled his fortune away; The lambs gambolled happily in the early spring sunshine.*

gaol, jail

Both are correct but the former is alive and well only in Britain.

Gay

In his book about Oxford, Christopher Hobhouse records that *The life is easy-going and tolerant; the company is intelligent and gay.* But that was in 1939; he certainly wouldn't write that today for fear of being grossly misunderstood. Nor would Franz Lehar who, in the famous song 'Girls are Made to Love and Kiss' from *Paganini* asks: Am I to blame if God has made me gay?

There are many who are deeply offended that this light-hearted and useful word has been hijacked to serve as a euphemistic term for homosexuality (since 1935, but effectively from the 1970s) and few would now attempt to use **gay** in its original sense.

While many British newspapers now use gay, (especially in headlines, for brevity's sake), *homosexual* is more prevalent where the sense contrasts with *heterosexual*. Gay is frequently used to describe male homosexuality, as in *The bar was packed with gay and lesbian couples.*

---

gelatin, gelatine
Generally the British prefer gelatin, and the Americans **gelatine**.

gender. See **sex, gender**

generous. See **prodigal, generous**

genial, congenial, congenital
To be **genial** is to be friendly, pleasant and good-tempered; to be **congenial** is to relate to and to share your friendliness with others of similar disposition:*The atmosphere during the whole trip was wonderfully congenial.* **Congenital** relates to any non-inherited abnormality acquired before or during birth.

gentleman, man
Usage of **gentleman** is mostly a social nicety. It can be used in a complimentary way: *That kind gentleman gave me his seat.* Or sarcastically: *That gentleman over there just rudely brushed past me.* The phrase *he's no gentleman* indicates clearly that the man has bad manners and probably a long list of other sins. Its most common usage is in the form of an address to a gathering: *Gentlemen, will you please take your seats?*

genuine. See **authentic**. Also see **replica, copy, facsimile**

genteel, gentle, Gentile
Two of these are generally well understood: **gentle** means 'tender and kindly', the opposite to 'rough, coarse and violent'; and a **Gentile** is a non-Jewish person. **Genteel** is trickier; it originally meant 'well-bred, respectable and refined', but is now often used in a mildly sarcastic way to send up ordinary people who affect or aspire to middle- or upper-class lifestyles.

geriatric, elderly
Geriatric is not a synonym for elderly. **Geriatric medicine** or **geriatrics** is the branch of medicine that studies and treats elderly people and their diseases.

Germany

The unified former West and East Germany is now the **Federal Republic of Germany**.

get, acquire, obtain, secure

Get is such a powerful, versatile but simple word that we often fall over ourselves trying to find a smarter substitute. Usually there isn't one. Sir Ernest Gower hated **acquire** but you can use it in a sort of shifty sense: *He acquired it from the back of a lorry.* There's not much call for **obtain**. **Secure** is like *get* plus a *favour*: *I've secured you two tickets for the big match tomorrow.* Many people object to the brutal **have got** as in: *I have got two tickets for the match tomorrow*, preferring the shorter, more mellifluous **have** by itself: *I have two tickets for the match tomorrow.*

geyser, geezer

A **geyser** is an active hot spring and used to be (in the UK) a domestic gas bathroom water-heater. A **geezer** is a slang term for a man, usually any older man, but the **geezer** is 'the boss'.

gibbet, giblets

The last recorded use of the giblet for capital punlishment ... (*Leicester Herald and Post*, 1995) proves that it is possible to confuse these two. A **gibbet** is a gallows from which (until the 19th century in Britain) executed criminals used to hang in public view. The **giblets** are various bits and pieces of a fowl which usually include the neck, liver and heart.

gibe. See **jibe, gibe, gybe**

gilt, guilt

Gilt is the result of gilding, that is: covering with gold or a preparation that imitates it. **Guilt** is the product of moral or criminal wrong doing. In most people, guilt can give rise to feelings of responsibility and remorse.

gipsy. See **gypsy, gipsy, Romany, traveller**

gist, grist

The gist (pron. jist) is the point or substance of an argument: *The gist was, as Mr Peters explained, that there would be no pay rises until after September.* **Grist** is grain intended for grinding. The phrase *it's grist to the mill* means it is something that can be turned to a profit: *To Fred, any old scrap metal, batteries, tyres and so on was all grist to the mill.*

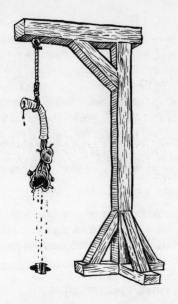

GIBBET, GIBLETS

give. See **donate, give**

god, God

The Greeks had **gods**; Christians have **God**, the supreme being, always with a capital 'G'. Similarly pronouns referring to *God* (*Him, He, Her, Thee, Thou,* etc.) should be capitalised. Sometimes a choice is difficult: *If you believe Goldsmith, the shares are a bargain. If you believe the market, disaster lies ahead. Personally, I believe Goldsmith. But god help him if he is wrong.* (*The Sunday Times*, 1993).

good, well

Using good as an adverb (*Elizabeth can cook quite good*) is incorrect; use **well**. On the other hand, Elizabeth's cooking can taste *good*. And you can **feel good** and also **feel well** – two different states. Tread carefully to retain clarity.

got, gotten, has got

Gotten travelled with the settlers from Britain to America where it is now

91

standard usage, but the word never returned to its native shores. Here, although we retain *forget/forgotten* and the biblical *beget/begotten*, the use of **gotten** produces furrowed brows and dismissal as American slang: *Fred's gotten to be a smartass these days.* In Britain, **got** is the past participle of **to get** as well as being the form used for the past tense: *She's got a great voice; They've got a nerve!* Used informally in speech there's little to complain about, but when written many people find 'has got' grating: *She has got a great voice; They have got a nerve.* With **has got** and **have got** the objection disappears when you drop **got**: *She has a great voice;* and *I have to go* instead of *I have got to go.* There are no firm rules for **got** but sentences often seem more elegant without it.

Gothic, Gothick

Gothic describes the Western European architectural style during the 12th–16th centuries, and the painting and sculpture associated with it. **Gothick** specifically denotes the 18th-century neo-medieval revival in architecture, art and literature.

gourmand, gourmet, epicure, glutton

Deepest in this trough is the **glutton**, who will eat anything and any amount of it. Then comes the **gourmand** who, while appreciating food, just loves to eat. Finally, the **gourmet** and the **epicure**, both of whom appreciate the finer points of eating and drinking except that, to the **epicure**, the joy of food is almost a religion.

gradation, graduation

A **gradation** is a gradual progression of stages, in size, tone, sound or degree, often imperceptible: *The sky was a striking gradation of purples and reds.* In this context, a **graduation** is a progression of measuring marks or calibrations.

graduate, undergraduate, postgraduate

An **undergraduate** is a student studying for a first degree who becomes a **graduate** when the degree is awardedwhen it is awarded. A **postgraduate** is, as a wag suggested, a dead graduate. The correct term is **postgraduate student**, who is studying for more advanced qualifications

grammar, syntax

Grammar is the system that binds all the elements that make up a language; **syntax** is the system (within grammar) that controls the order and relationships between words in constructions such as sentences.

gratuitous, gratuity

Sometimes confused with *gratitude*, **gratuitous** means 'something given free and unrequested'. Its use today is increasingly to define something that's unnecessary and uncalled-for: *The two men traded gratuitous insults for half an hour*. A **gratuity** is a gift, usually money, for services rendered.

green paper. See white paper, green paper

gregarious, egregious

These were once opposites: **gregarious**, meaning 'enjoying the company of others and tending to flock together'; and **egregious** (pron. *eh-GREE-jus*) meaning 'separate from the flock, or outstanding'. But while **gregarious** has retained its original meaning, **egregious** is now used almost exclusively to mean 'blatantly, deliberately bad, bald-faced': *I've never met such an egregious liar in all my life*.

grisly, grizzly

Grisly means 'gruesome'; **grizzly**, applied to hair and bears, means 'grey or streaked with grey'.

grist. See gist, grist

grow, growing

There is a trend, imported from North Africa, to a new use of **grow** and **growing** as a substitute for **increase**: *By encouraging communication we will grow the telecommunications market* (*The Times, Business Section,* 30.12.96). It is well-worn nowadays, but nevertheless it's worth pointing out that on all counts it's a cliché and incorrect. If you care about accuracy, remember that we *grow* Sweet Peas but *increase* markets.

guarantee, warranty

Although somewhat interchangeable, a **guarantee** is an assurance that a product or service will meet agreed standards or specifications; or an agreement to repair or replace. A **warranty** is usually more specifically a promise that what is being sold is the vendor's (for example a car), and is suitable and fit for the use claimed.

guess, suppose, think

To **guess** is to put forward an opinion or estimate based on little or no information. To **suppose** is to assume that something is true, again based on hazy information. To **think** is to arrive at a decision or point of view after conscious thought: *I guess stew will be on the menu again tonight; After his big sale last week, I suppose Jim will be first in line for promotion; We're all very tired so I think we should return home.*

Guides, Girl Guides

The former **Girl Guides** organisation in Britain is now known as the **Guides**. In the US, their equivalent is the *Girl Scouts*.

guilt. See gilt, guilt

gybe. See jibe, gibe, gybe

gynaecologist, obstetrician

A **gynaecologist** specialises in diseases of the urinary and genital organs of women; an **obstetrician** deals with all aspects of childbirth.

gypsy, gipsy, Romany, traveller

Gypsy (plural *gypsies*) is preferred to *gipsy but* **Romany** is the technically correct term for the true ethnic gypsy that is, a member of a race of wanderers, originating in India, who came to Britain in the early 16th century. The term **traveller** appears with increasing frequency, but is ambigious as it not only refers to Romany travellers, but also to more recently-formed groups of itinerants.

habit, habitual

A **habit** is an established or usual custom, so the term 'usual habit' is a redundancy – as is 'customary habit'. **Habitual** is the adjective, meaning 'by habit': *Unfortunately, for his job prospects, Tony was an habitual drinker.*

had had

There are times when we all get caught in a construction with the dual **had**: *If I had had the time I would have stayed to watch.* Although grammatical, it's not a pretty sight and best avoided by rewriting: *I would have stayed to watch but didn't have the time.*

hale, hail

These two soundalikes confuse because between them they have four common meanings: **hale** the adjective, meaning 'robust and healthy'; **hale** the verb, meaning to 'haul or drag'; **hail** the noun, meaning 'frozen raindrops or similar particles driven with great force'; and **hail** the verb, meaning 'to attract attention' or 'to greet enthusiastically'. Recognise these meanings and you'll know how to use them in such expressions as: *Even at eighty-six Ethel was still hale and hearty; Last week Gerry was haled before a judge; Even at eighty-six Ethel was still hale and hearty; Under a hail of gunfire they raced for the nearest cover; Outside the theatre, they hailed a taxi.*

hallo. See **hullo, hallo, hello**

hamlet. See **city, town, village, hamlet**

hanged, hung

A recently published book entitled *How To Get Hung* alarmed some people who thought it might be a do-it-yourself suicide manual; in fact it was by an art gallery owner advising artists how to get their work exhibited. To remove such ambiguity, a person is **hanged** (by the neck until dead); a picture (or your suit) is **hung**.

hanger, hangar

A **hanger** is a wire contraption on which you hang clothes; a **hangar** houses aircraft.

happen. See **transpire, happen, occur**

harangue, tirade

A **harangue** is a forceful, loud, long and eventually tedious speech: *Mr Oliver harangued the crowd for two interminable hours*. A **tirade** is much the same, but angrier.

harbinger. See **bell-wether, harbinger**

hare-brained, hair-brained

The first is correct, although the second is also now used, to describe something hastily and very badly thought out: *The proposal to give away free tickets was just another of Mildred's hare-brained schemes*.

HARE BRAINED, HAIR BRAINED

healthy, healthful

Healthy means 'having good health'; **healthful**, not much used now, means 'giving good health': *Barbara was always careful to eat healthful foods.*

heart attack. See stroke, coronary, heart failure

hello. See hullo, hello, hallo

harmful. See deleterious, harmful

Hebrew. See Jewish, Hebrew, Yiddish

helpmate, helpmeet

Both mean the same: 'a helpful and dependable friend, companion, husband or wife'. The less-used **helpmeet** derives from the archaic meaning of *meet*: 'proper, correct and fitting', that is, 'a suitable helper'.

hence, thence, whence

Think of **here, there** and **where**: they went **hence** (from here); they advanced thence (from there, or that place); **whence** (from where?) came the new arrivals? All are archaisms except **hence**, when meaning 'therefore, or for this reason': *The Smiths won £2,000 on the lottery, hence the new TV set.*

hereditary, heredity

Hereditary means 'transmitting or passing genetically or by inheritance'; **heredity** is the ability of living things to transmit genetic factors from one generation to another to determine individual characteristics. *Sir Gerald's hereditary title was bestowed upon him at the age of three; Whether his intellectual fastidiousness is a product of heredity or academic environment is anybody's guess.*

hiccup, hiccough

The simpler (and easier spelt) **hiccup** is now generally preferred.

Hindi, Hindu

A **Hindu** is a follows the Indian religion of Hinduism; **Hindi** is the language.

hire, rent, lease, let

Modern marketing has introduced a large degree of interchangeability here: you can now **hire, rent** or **lease** cars, vans, rave venues, vacuum cleaners, cement mixers, storage space, even people (*party clowns for hire; rent-a-crowd*). Strictly speaking, **rent** is the money you pay. To **let** an apartment or flat means that temporary possession of the property is granted on payment of an agreed **rent** or **rental**. The person who **lets** is the **lessor**; the person who pays the rent is the **lessee**.

histology, history

History we all know; **histology** is the study of plant and animal tissues.

historic, historical

Something significant that has a place in history is **historic**: *The long-delayed meeting will be one of the great historic events of our time.* **Historical** relates to events of the past: *Emma's novel about Nelson is based on historical evidence.*

hitherto, previously

Hitherto means 'up to this time, until now'; **previously** means 'until then, prior to': *Hitherto the company had succeeded in ignoring all their claims; Previously, the company rule had been simply to ignore their claims.*

HIV. See **Aids, HIV**

hoard, horde

The magazine *Cumbria Life* is discredited with confusing these: *Wordsworth in particular has brought hoards of visitors invading the very privacy so revered by the poets.* A **hoard** is a store or accumulation; a **horde** is an unruly and often unpredictable crowd of people. Obviously *Cumbria Life* meant **hordes**.

hoi polloi

Many believe this Greek expression refers to the rich elite. What it really means is 'the common people' and is usually applied in a derogatory sense *by* the rich elite: *Who knows or even cares what **hoi polloi** are doing tonight?* If you intend using the term, don't precede it with 'the'; it's already built in.

holiday. See **vacation, holiday**

holistic, holism, holy

Holistic has nothing to do with God or any sacred deity, and thus has no connection with **holy**. **Holism** and **holistic** refer to the doctrine that the whole of a system is greater than the sum of its parts. In treating human disorders, holistic medicine considers the whole person and not just individual organs.

Holland. See **the Netherlands, Holland**

holocaust, Holocaust

A **holocaust** is an act of truly terrible destruction; with its capital letter, it has come to mean and symbolise the Nazi genocide of the Jews during the Second World War. Use with caution.

home, house

Although increasingly regarded as synonyms, a **house**, as the saying goes, is not a **home**. To most people it seems reasonable that you can build, buy or sell a **house**, flat or apartment and live in a comfortable **home**. A **home** implies much more than a house: life, a family, roots, comforts; when we say that a home is 'wrecked', we mean something quite different than demolishing a house.

homicide, manslaughter, murder

Homicide is the killing of one person by another; the killer is also known as a **homicide**. **Murder** is the unlawful premeditated killing of another. **Manslaughter** is the unlawful killing of another but without 'malice aforethought' or premeditation, often under provocation, in the heat of passion, or through negligence.

honorary, honourable

An **honorary** position or title is one that is awarded as a recognition or honour (*an honorary degree*) or one that is unpaid (*honorary club treasurer*). To be **honourable** is to possess high principles or intentions: *Although many regarded him as being rather dim, Arthur was thought by all to be an honourable man.*

hoodoo. See **voodoo, hoodoo**

hope. See **anticipate, expect, hope**

Hopefully

If you are seeking advice on the use of the word **hopefully** you may read this **hopefully**, or **full of hope**, for that is its traditional meaning. But in the last few decades a second meaning has insinuated itself into the language: *Hopefully, the team will play much better next time.* Here, the meaning is 'let's hope', or 'it is hoped', and it has occasioned a lot of tut-tutting from the word police, despite the fact that we freely use, for example, similar adverbs, e.g. 'honestly', 'mercifully' 'naturally' in much the same way without criticism: *Honestly, we would have been there earlier but for the accident; Naturally, we'll be there tomorrow; Mercifully , we'll all be safe in our beds tonight once we manage to cross the river.*

The respectability of the 'new' meaning of **hopefully** can be readily defended, however. It originated from the German **hoffentlich**, meaning 'I hope so', which travelled with German migrants to the US last century, there to be translated as – *hopefully.* A hundred years later, it recrossed the Atlantic to Britain where it now firmly resides, although still a much misunderstood and mocked orphan.

host, hosted, present

Dictionaries sometimes label **hosted** as 'informal', but as a substitute verb for **present** (pronounced *pree-ZENT*), as in a television programme (*She hosted the show with amazing verve*); and on the Internet (*Website hosting is available*), it is being used more and more.

hotel: a hotel, an hotel

She once lived in Paris in **a hotel** *on the Boulevarde St Germain: an ideal life, on a scholarship, writing a book. She still goes to Paris, alone, stays in* **an hotel***, goes to bookshops and sits in cafes.* While *The Times* in this example has it both ways, the preference leans to the soft '*h*' sound of hotel: **an hotel**.

Horrible, Horrendous, Horrifying and Horripilation

How do you separate these? Most people use them indiscrimately as 'over the top' terms, with the result that they are usually used incorrectly: *It looks horrible* (my new hair-do); *It was horrendous* (the English exam); *It was absolutely horrific* (the fun-park's bare knuckle ride).

All three 'horror' words are used correctly in this comment by a child psychologist: *While horror films are designed to horrify, they do not make the children themselves into horrific people.* **Horrific**, meaning 'capable of provoking horror', should be used in this context only, but **horrid, horrendous, horrible** and **horrifying** are all fairly interchangeable by today's usage standards.

But now everyone has a new word to corrupt: **horripilation**: *One feels throughout a distinct horripilation, a quavering anticipation of something about to spring on us over the next page – Sunday Times Book Review*. **Horripilation** is the bristling of short bodily hairs; in other words, goose-flesh.

hotel, motel, inn, public house, pub, bar

Hotels and **motels** should include meals and accommodation as services but they are necessarily licensed to serve alcoholic liquor. **Public houses**, or **pubs**, are licensed (note *licensed*, not *licenced*), as are **inns** and **taverns**. These may or may not serve food or offer accommodation and the terms are to a great extent interchangeable. All have **bars**, from which drinks are dispensed, but a bar can also be an establishment, such as a **wine bar, club bar, doubles bar** (where double measures of spirits are served), **singles bar**, (where singles, or unattached or unmarried people, congregate) or **gay bar** (where gay men and lesbians meet).

hullo, hello, hallo

Originally the greeting was **hallo** or **halloo**; modern usage favours **hello** and **hullo**, take your choice.

human, humanity, humane, inhuman, inhumane

Human and **humanity** refer to the human race or humankind, and the words are usually used with favourable intent. To be **humane** is one of the civilising qualities of humankind and means to be considerate, kind and merciful. Conversely, an **inhuman** person lacks the qualities of humankind; to be **inhumane** is to be unfeeling, cruel and brutal.

humanist, humanitarian

A **humanist** believes in the superiority of human concepts and ideals – culture, philosophy, literature, history – over religious beliefs. **Humanitarians** are kind, philanthropic people with the interests of their fellow humans at heart: *The doctor denied he was an atheist but admitted to staunch humanist beliefs; The ship left on its humanitarian mission to Ethiopia.*

humus, hummus, houmous, hoummos

Humus is decayed organic matter in soil; **hummus** (or **houmous** or **hoummos**) is a chick-pea puree which originated in the Middle East.

hung. See **hanged, hung**

hurricane. See **cyclone, hurricane, tornado, typhoon**

hypocrisy. See **cant, hypocrisy**

hypocritical, hypercritical

To be **hypocritical** is to pretend to be what you are not, or to affect beliefs or views which are contrary to your actions. To be **hypercritical** is to be excessively critical and carping.

I

idea, opinion

An **idea** is a thought, a mental concept, a creation, an intention or a plan. An **opinion** is a view, judgment, assumption or estimation.

I, me

It is I – or, It is me? Between you and I, or *Between you and me?* With the first pair, just about everyone accepts that the *It is I* construction sounds affected; although *It is me* is regarded as colloquial, it also sounds right. Confusion surrounding the use of **I** and **me** has existed for centuries. Who would be bold enough to criticise Shakespeare for *All debts are cleared between you and I* (from *The Merchant of Venice*)? Modern idiomatic usage has virtually banished **I** even from constructions where it is grammatical, and the substitution of **me** is *almost* universal (you wouldn't say, for example, *You and me are going to be late*, or *Doreen and me sat next to each other*). Use your ears to avoid the grossest *I – me* solecisms. If still in doubt, rewrite: *Doreen sat next to me.*

identical to, identical with

Identical with is the originally correct usage, although today little fuss is made about **identical to**.

if, whether

Mostly interchangeable, although **whether** seems to be preferred where alternatives are indicated: *Did you notice whether David returned that book today?* Quite commonly you will hear *I don't know whether or not David returned the book;* here the 'or not' is regarded as redundant, but on the other hand it removes all ambiguity.

ilk, of that ilk

The traditional Scottish meaning of **of that ilk** is 'of the same place or name'. **Ilk** refers to a type or class of person: *I really don't like people of that ilk using the clubhouse.*

Idioms

The words and terms in *Word Check* are almost without exception from the orthodox English vocabulary. What are known as idiomatic expressions – *pay through the nose, don't rub it in, take it to heart, etc* – are mostly omitted. In any case, most people, perhaps instinctively, have little trouble with the use of idioms in their own language. But what does a foreigner, either learning English or even having quite a good command of it, make of this typical group of idiomatic add-ons to the word look?

look slippery	–	be quick
look up	–	refer to
look out	–	be wary
look down on	–	scorn
look up to	–	respect
look daggers	–	stare angrily
look yourself	–	act normally
look sharp	–	be alert
look alive	–	be awake
look see	–	make an inspection/investigate
look over	–	examine carefully
look to	–	pay attention to
look after	–	care for

ill. See **sick, sickly, ill**

illegible, unreadable

Illegible is usually taken to mean writing or printing that cannot be deciphered because of some fault, such as fading or other damage.
Unreadable means that the writing is impossible or very difficult to read because it is badly presented or simply very bad and boring: *They tried to read the markings on the gravestone but time had rendered them illegible; Bruce's essay was so full of errors the teacher pronounced it unreadable.* See also **legible, readable**.

illicit, illegal

Although for most purposes these terms are synonyms, **illicit** is more often used to denote something that is not allowed or approved of by custom or community standards, while **illegal** means unlawful, or forbidden by law: *They admitted they had conducted their illicit love affair over the past four years; Nobody realised that Maria was an illegal immigrant.*

illiterate, ignorant

An **illiterate** person is not necessarily **ignorant,** but does not know how to read or write. Many **illiterates** are in fact very knowledgeable, and surprisingly clever in surmounting their problem.

illegitimate, natural

An **illegitimate** child or person is born out of wedlock, that is, of parents who were not married at the time of birth. Social service workers now tend to favour **natural**, despite the danger of ambiguity: *The rumour was that he was the natural son of Sir William; He never realised that Martha and Carl were his natural parents.*

illusion, allusion, delusion

An **illusion** is a deception of the mind or eye; a **delusion** is a mistaken idea or false belief; an **allusion** is a passing reference to something: *The magician performed one brilliant illusion after the other; Margaret's dream of an easy life turned out to be a delusion; The speaker's allusion to Bill's enthusiastic attachment to the bottle was regarded as being in bad taste.*

imaginative, imaginary

Imaginary means 'existing in the imagination, unreal'; to be **imaginative** is to possess a heightened or creative imagination: *She loved drawing imaginary animals; Lucinda had always been an imaginative child.*

imbue. See **inculcate, imbue**

immigrant. See **emigrant, immigrant**

imminent. See **eminent, imminent**

immoral. See **amoral, immoral**

immunity, impunity

Immunity means 'the ability to resist something, usually harmful', or 'being free from some liability or obligation': *The injections gave him immunity from a range of tropical diseases; The diplomatic plates on the illegally parked car gave it* *immunity from the usual £50 fine.* **Impunity** means 'exemption from some unpleasant consequence' such as recrimination or punishment: *Carlo's political connections enabled him to rob and extort the native population with arrogant impunity.*

impassable, impassible, impasse

Something **impassable** means something that cannot be passed or travelled over': *During winter the old mountain track is quite impassable.* **Impassible**, an adjective deriving from *impassive*, is not a variant spelling but a different word meaning 'insensibility to injury and pain'. An **impasse** (pronounced *am-pass*) describes an extremely difficult situation in which any progress is blocked: *After three weeks of fruitless negotiation, both sides realised the talks had reached an impasse.*

IMPASSABLE, IMPASSIBLE, IMPASSE

impeach. See **convict, impeach**

impel. See **compel, impel**

imperial. See **empirical, imperial**

implicit. See **explicit, implicit**

imply, infer

To **imply** means 'to express indirectly, to hint or suggest'; to **infer** is to deduce or suppose by reasoning: *I inferred that they had a bad attitude to working, and strongly implied that I wasn't prepared to put up with their behaviour.*

105

impracticable, impractical. See **practicable, practical**

impromptu, extempore
Both mean 'spontaneous and unpremeditated', but **extempore** is customarily reserved to describe an off-the-cuff speech: *The children gave a wonderful impromptu performance on the makeshift stage; Lance was noted for the wittiness of his extempore speeches.*

improve, ameliorate
Ameliorate is frequently wrongly used to mean 'alleviate, mitigate, lessen, nullify or neutralise' when it really means 'to improve or to make better': *The new treatment ameliorated his condition immediately.* You can avoid ambiguity by using **improve**.

in, in to, into
In denotes a place, and is static: *Elizabeth is in the bathroom.* **Into** expresses motion and direction: *Elizabeth went into the bathroom.* **In to** implies a sense of purpose or 'in order to: *Elizabeth wandered towards the bathroom and then slipped in to powder her nose.* See also **on, on to, onto**.

inapt, inept
In the sense of 'inappropriate and ill-conceived', these are synonymous. But **inept** also means 'clumsy and incompetent': *The inclusion of the jingoistic song in the programme was considered to be decidedly inapt; It had to be admitted that Errol's carpentry skills were embarrassingly inept.*

incapable, unable
There is a difference between these two for those who wish to preserve it. **Incapable** means 'lacking the ability, capacity or power to accomplish something'; *incompetent* would be a near synonym: *Fred was utterly incapable of singing in tune.* But with a statement like *Fred was unable to climb the stairs* we are left in some doubt as to the reason; Fred might have a physical disability; or he might be able to climb them when he sobers up. **Unable** implies an inability to do something at a particular time or because of some special circumstance.

inchoate. See **chaotic, inchoate**

include. See **compose, comprise, constitute, include**

incredible, incredulous
Incredible means unbelievable or beyond belief, although it is now widely and wrongly used to mean 'wonderful, astonishing, remarkable, etc'.

Incredulous describes the inability to believe: *When John had told them the incredible full story they all remained incredulous.*

incubus, succubus

Gendered devilry here: an **incubus** is the demon who in the night lies upon sleeping women to have intercourse with them, whereas a **succubus**, a sister spirit if you like, descends in the night to lie upon sleeping men for the same purpose.

inculcate, imbue

His father had inculcated him in most of the rules of hunting; She was thoroughly inculcated with Theodora's legendary wisdom. Both these usages are common but incorrect. You cannot **inculcate** people, only ideas: *Mr Simmonds inculcated a new sense of purpose in the entire staff.* But you may **imbue** or inspire a person with ideas: *His father had imbued him with a sense of family pride; She was thoroughly imbued with Theodora's legendary wisdom.*

independence. See **interdependence, independence**

in-depth

As in *an in-depth analysis*, or *in-depth investigation* – a cliche to avoid.

index, indexes, indices

Both **indexes** and **indices** can be used as the plural of **index**. Interestingly *The Times* goes along with this but prefers **indexes** in the context of books.

indigenous, endogenous

Indigenous means originating in a given location, or 'native to': *The species of moss is indigenous to the Lakeland region.* **Endogenous**, formerly a rare word indeed, recently emerged as a term in economics, as in *Shadow Chancellor Gordon Brown seemed to be endorsing the post neo-classical endogenous growth theory.* The word means 'developing or originating from within an organism'.

indoor, indoors, outdoor, outdoors

Indoor and **outdoor**, the adjectives, describe physical situations: *The players still preferred the indoor courts to the recently built outdoor complex.* **Indoors** and **outdoors**, the adverbs, are used differently: *During the winter the players naturally preferred to play indoors rather than outdoors.*

induce. See **convince, persuade, induce**

inequity, iniquity, inequality

Inequity is injustice; an **inequitable** situation is unjust and unfair. An **iniquity**

is also an injustice, but one that is grievous and wicked: *James was appalled by the inequity of the judge's remarks; The new demands were little short of iniquitous.*
Inequality is the state of being unequal, out of balance, irregular: *The difference between the government's treatment of the two families was one of gross inequality.*

inestimable. See invaluable, inestimable

infect, infest

To **infect** is to cause an infection or to contaminate; to **infest** is to overrun in dangerous numbers: *The infestation of lice was undoubtedly the cause of the infection.*

infer. See imply, infer

infectious, contagious

Contagious diseases are transmitted by physical contact; **infectious** diseases are spread by micro-organisms in the air or in fluids, often disseminated by coughing and sneezing.

infinite, infinitesimal

Two easily confused opposites. Something **infinite** is so great that it has no limit; **infinitesimal** is so small as to be negligible: *It is a mystery why the scientists took such infinite pains to measure such an infinitesimal difference.*

inflammable, flammable

Inflammable means intensely **flammable**, but the ever-present danger is that, thinking the in prefix means 'not' in this case, some people might assume that **inflammable** means 'not flammable' or non-combustible. That's why we're seeing more and more **flammable** and **highly flammable** labels on products that are a fire risk.

informant, informer

An **informant** supplies information; an **informer** provides information with the intention of incriminating someone.

infringe, infringe on, infringe upon

The man infringed the law and paid the price is correct usage; **infringe** means 'to break or violate' and thus **infringe on** and **infringe upon** are redundancies. But many of us feel the need for the prepositions when **infringe** is used to mean 'to tresspass or encroach upon': *The farmer's animals constantly infringed upon the municipal park.* Keep your nerve and leave them out.

in heat, on heat, in season

All are acceptable terms (especially to the animals concerned).

ingenious, ingenuous, disingenuous

An **ingenious** person is clever, inventive and resourceful; an **ingenuous** person is someone who is naive and artless and thus more likely to be open, frank and candid. A **disingenuous** person is insincere and not as ingenuous as he or she might appear.

initiate. See begin, commence, initiate, start

injury. See accident, injury

in lieu of, instead of

In lieu means 'instead of, or in place of'. But if you accept the principle of using foreign words and expressions only in the absence of suitable English equivalents, use **instead of**.

inning, innings

In cricket it's an **innings**; in baseball an **inning**.

inoculate, vaccinate

Meaning 'to cause immunity from a disease by the use of a vaccine', these are now synonymous.

inquire. See enquire, inquire, enquiry, inquiry

insofar as, in so far as

In so far as the inflation rate is concerned, prices will inevitably respond is still general English usage, although the joined-up version is gaining in popularity. It joins similar combinations: *whomsoever, inasmuch, hereinafter, nonetheless and nevertheless*.

insolvency, bankruptcy

Insolvency happens when a person can't pay his or her debts when they are due. If sufficient assets can't be realised, the person may be declared **bankrupt**, the official, public state of insolvency, when assets are distributed to creditors. When a company goes bust, it goes into **liquidation**, either compulsorily or voluntarily.

instantly, instantaneous

Both mean the same: 'immediately, at once, without delay'.

institute, institution

In most cases, these are synonymous. The exceptions are when organisations choose either to call themselves **institutions** (*Royal Institution*) or **institutes** (*Massachusetts Institute of Technology*), and in the context of something well-known and well-established: *The artist was regarded as something of an institution in Dorset.*

instinct, intuition

Instinct is a natural impulse triggered by some stimulus; **intuition** is an unconscious, non-reasoning mental awareness: *Sensing a movement he instinctively stepped back; She intuitively realised she would never really feel comfortable with David.*

insurance. See assurance, insurance

insure. See assure, ensure, insure

intense, intensive

The two are different. **Intense** should be used to describe an extreme degree: **intense** heat, **intense** power, **intense** aroma. **Intensive** is about concentration: concentrated medical effort (**intensive** care); a thorough murder investigation (**intensive** enquiries).

interdependence, independence

These lookalikes are actually opposites. **Independence** is to be free from control, not dependent or reliant upon anything else; **interdependence** means to depend upon each other: *The couple had lived together so long that their interdependence was virtually total.*

internecine

From its original meaning of 'bloody carnage and slaughter' **internecine** is primarily used now to describe a conflict that is mutually destructive. Beware of a growing usage that implies that internecine merely means 'conflict within a group': *The struggling organisation was a viper's nest of internecine rivalries.*

internment, interment

Internment is detaining and confining someone, usually for security reasons during a conflict or war. An **interment** is a burial.

intrigue, intriguing

Although there still remains some resistance to the wider use of **intrigue**, meaning 'to arouse curiosity and interest', this has now substantially overtaken the original meaning of 'to plot secretly'. The same applies to **intriguing**.

intrinsic. See extraneous, extrinsic, intrinsic

Inuit. See Eskimo, Inuit

invaluable, inestimable

Invaluable means 'priceless' – something so valuable its worth is difficult or impossible to estimate. **Inestimable**, meaning 'beyond estimation' is a synonym but tends to be used to describe abstract rather than material qualities: *The chairman praised Jane for her inestimable contribution to the project.*

invariably, always

Invariably means 'fixed, unchanged, never varying'; **always** means 'uninterruptedly, at all times', but for all practical purposes they are synonymous. However many people tend to misuse **invariably** to mean *'almost always': Although he's missed the train on occasions, John is invariably on the platform five minutes early.*

inveigh, inveigle

To **inveigh** is to denounce or to speak bitterly about something: *The Opposition leader inveighed against the injustice of the Poll Tax.* Note that **inveigh** is followed by against. To **inveigle** is to convince or persuade by trickery.

invented. See discovered, invented

in vivo, in vitro

These terms, now common in the context of artificial insemination, define the two methods. *In vivo fertilisation* is when it occurs or is carried out in the living organism, while *in vitro fertilisation* is a laboratory process (*vitro* = glass) in which the fertilised ovum is reinserted into the womb. Hence the idiomatic 'test tube baby'.

invoke, evoke

Two well-worn confusables! To **invoke** is to appeal to or to call upon someone – often God or a god – for help or inspiration: *The camel driver fell to his knees and invoked the wrath of Allah upon his enemies.* To **evoke** is to summon or recall some feeling or memory: *The plaintive dirge evoked in her a rush of memories of her Highland childhood.* See also **evince, evoke**.

ion, iron, steel

The confusion probably arises in the UK because **ion** and **iron** are pronounced similarly in the UK (in the US they stress the 'r' in iron). An **ion** is an electrically charged atom or group of atoms; **iron** is, of course, the metal. Much of what we commonly call *iron* is actually **steel**, a much stronger iron-carbon alloy.

Ireland, Eire, Ulster, Irish Republic

Eire is the Irish word for **Ireland**, or, more correctly, the **Irish Republic** with its government in Dublin. **Ulster**, or **Northern Ireland**, consists of the six counties outside the Republic.

irony, sarcasm, satire

You are waiting for a bus, the rain is belting down and you are splashed by passing cars. The next person in the queue says, *Lovely day, isn't it*? That's **irony**: saying something the opposite of what you mean with the intention of mocking. **Sarcasm** is a bitter, derisory form of irony: *Well, thanks for telling everyone about our secret!* **Satire** is the witty demolition of stupidity, wickedness and folly, sometimes called **lampoon** or **spoof**.

irreparable, unrepairable

Irreparable means 'beyond remedy or repair': *His mother's criticism over many years had caused irreparable damage to his already fragile self-esteem.* **Unrepairable** is customarily used to describe objects rather than concepts: *The TV engineer said that the set was unrepairable.*

It, Its, It's

You can't go through a day without using **it** a few thousand times. Nor, it seems, can you go through a day without seeing **its** and **it's** used wrongly. The only time **its** has an apostrophe is when it is used as a contraction for **it is**: *It's raining; If it's not raining it's pouring!* The possessive form of **it** is **its** (no apostrophe): *The parrot fell off its perch.* If in doubt, read the sentence literally and aloud: *The parrot fell off it's perch would sound like The parrot fell off it is perch.* It's very simple.

---

iterate. See **reiterate, iterate**

It looks like, It looks as though

One of the longest-running sores in the whole of English grammar is – what's correct – *it looks like (it might) … it looks as though (it might, … it looks as if (it might) … it looks possible that (it might) …* etc. Editor, columnist and satirist Ian Hislop found himself in such a pile of poo (as he blithely put it) recently, and admitted quite candidly that he found it difficult, if not impossible, to extricate himself from the ordure. It's all a matter of taste, actually.

-ize, -ise

Only a handful of words require the *-ize* spelling (*size, prize, capsize*) while many have always taken *-ise* (*advise, arise, despise, devise, exercise, rise, surprise* are just a few). This has led to a tendency to favour *-ise* in British English while *-ize* is standard in the US. Most UK newspapers subscribe to *-ise* endings though many publishers use *-ize*.

J

jacket. See **coat, jacket**

jail. See **gaol, jail**

jealousy. See **envious, enviable, envy, jealous**

jejune

Latin scholars in particular insist that **jejune** should not be used to mean *naive, simple* and *unsophisticated* but its original meaning of 'insipid, dull, barren or insubstantial' – the word derives from the Latin for *hungry* and *empty*. Jejune does not mean 'juvenile': use 'childish', 'puerile', 'infantile' instead.

jetsam. See **flotsam, jetsam, ligan**

jersey. See **sweater, jersey, jumper, pullover, etc.**

jewellery, jewelry

Jewellery is the usual British English spelling; **jewelry** is standard in American English.

Jewish, Jew, Hebrew, Yiddish

While there remains a sensitivity about **Jew** being a pejorative term it is preferable to euphemisms as 'a Jewish person' and is generally preferred by the Jewish community anyway: *My fellow Jews approve it*, wrote one reader of the first edition of *Word Check*. **Jewess** is discouraged, however; **Jewish woman** is preferred. **Hebrew** and **Yiddish** are languages spoken by Jews; **Hebrew is** the official language of Israel, while **Yiddish** is a Hebrew-influenced vernacular version of German. Many Yiddish words have entered the English language via America: bagel and lox, chutzpah, schmooze.

jibe, gibe, gybe

To **gibe** means 'to taunt or jeer', and that is the favoured spelling in the UK. **Jibe** is an acceptable alternative and general in the US. **Gybe** (**jibe** in the US) is a nautical term.

join. See **enjoin, join**

The Joys of Jargon, Slang, Argot, Cant and Gobbledegook

Jargon is a collective word for micro-languages understood only by a small number of people. Pick up a computer magazine and you will find yourself face to face with jargon, which is typically occupational:

Science	chaology, cyborg, entropy, double helix, quark
Computing	wysiwyg, bus, dump, download, pixel, interface
Finance	call, bull, junk bond, OTC, white knight, spread
Medical	bronk, DNR, perrla, scoop, MFC

Slang is a separate vocabulary from the standard language, often used by specific social groups (Cockney) or during a period of time (Second World War II). Some slang words survive for a generation or two before disappearing; others make it to dictionary respectability. A **colloquialism** is an unconventional word or phrase you'd use casually in conversation. **Vernacular** is the native spoken language or dialect of a particular group or race. **Argot**, formerly 'the language of thieves', is now a synonym for *jargon*; **cant** is any hypocritically pious language. **Lingua franca** defines a language used by people of different mother tongues to communicate among themselves; pidgin, for example, is the *lingua franca* of the people of Papua New Guinea who are divided by hundreds of separate languages. **Gobbledegook** is pretentious, pompous, utterly confusing and obscure language, instantly recognisable when you fail to understand it. For example, in a bureaucratic response to a request for a bus shelter: 'it is axiomatic that residual requests in respect of prospective shelter sites identified as having priority, those named in earlier programmes of shelter erection will take precedence in any future shelter programme.

The Last Joyride

Can a word be deliberately banished, that is, sent to Coventry? Take the case of **joyride**. A typical dictionary definition is: *A ride taken for pleasure in a car, especially in a stolen car driven recklessly.* Unfortunately for many people, including the cars' owners, killed and injured joyriders and innocent victims, the result of such rides of often far from joyous. The toll of murder-by-joyride in the UK mounted to such an extent that in 1993 a national newspaper decided to ban the word: *This is the last time the word 'joyride' will appear in the Daily Mirror.* For a word that now means almost the opposite of what it originally meant, it is perhaps not a bad idea. But what might take its place? How about **car thief**?

---

jubilee. See **anniversary, birthday, jubilee**

judgment, judgement

In British English, **judgement** with an 'e' prevails, while **judgment** is reserved for legal decisions. However, this is changing, as many British publications adopt the American-English universal use of **judgment**.

judicial, judicious

Judicial refers exclusively to justice and the law courts; **judicious** means showing good judgement: *Dividing the property between the two brothers proved to be a judicious solution.*

jujitsu, judo, karate, kung fu

Jujitsu is the traditional Japanese samurai form of unarmed martial combat, from which **judo**, a more sports-oriented form, was developed. **Karate** is a similar art which uses sharper blows and chops to the body with hands and feet. **Kung fu** is the Chinese version, in which weapons are sometimes used. Exponents in these arts graduate from a 'white belt' through green, blue and brown to a final 'black belt'.

jumper. See **sweater, jersey, jumper, pullover, etc.**

junction, juncture

A junction is a location where several things meet: roads, railway tracks, electrical cables, etc. A **juncture** is a moment in time, such as a pause, a crisis or a turning point: *At this juncture it is essential that we review the situation.* The frequently used phrase *'At this juncture in time'* is redundant.

jury, juror, jurist

A **jury** is composed of members of the jury, or **jurors**. A **jurist** is a general term used to describe anyone well versed in law including legal graduates, scholars and writers.

just, about, just about

It's just about time to go and meet the train is a statement to which few would take exception. However it contains a very common contradiction: **just about**. The word *just* indicates accuracy and precision; *about* means 'near, or close to'. So what do we mean when we combine the two as in *just about*? Little or nothing, because one cancels out the other; either one or the other is redundant. Use **just** if you mean to be exact; **about** if you mean approximate: *There's just time for another drink; It's about time we left.*

K

karat. See **carat, caret, karat**

karate. See **jujitsu, judo, karate, kung fu**

karma

There are three vaguely accepted definitions of what **karma** is but no agreement on which one is right: **1.** For Hindus and Buddhists, it is the cosmic operation of retributive justice; a person's fate in life is determined by his or her own deeds in a previous incarnation. **2.** The doctrine of fate and destiny, or inevitable consequences. **3.** The mood or atmosphere of a person or a place. However, there is a fairly widespread negative reaction to anyone saying, for example, that a disabled person, or anyone with AIDS or terminal cancer, is in some way responsible for his or her predicament – due to bad or evil behaviour during a prior incarnation. It certainly sounds unfair to a Christian. The closest, for example, that an Anglican has to this belief, is that we all reap what we sow. Perhaps meaning (3) is, for Christians, the kindest definition of all.

kerosine. See **paraffin, kerosene, kerosine**

kerb. See **curb, kerb**

ketchup, catsup, sauce, chutney, pickle

Ketchup is vinegar-based condiment, usually tomato-flavoured, and often distributed directly on to food from a bottle; **catsup** is an alternative spelling usually found in American English. With our modern preoccupation with cooking and restaurant eating, a **sauce** (formerly **gravy**) is increasingly a piquant liquid accompaniment to a cooked dish. **Chutney** consists of coarsely-cut fruit and vegetables preserved by cooking with vinegar, salt, sugar and spices. **Pickle** consists of vegetables – onions, cauliflower, etc. – preserved in vinegar or brine.

kind, kind of, sort of, type of

It helps to know that **kind** is a singular noun and to be able to recognise when you need the plural form: *This kind of novel gives publishing a bad name; Many kinds of fruit are in the shops at this time of year.* The same applies to **sort of** and **type of**. Expressions such as H*e sort of has a funny effect on me* and *I felt kind of relieved it was all over* are cheerfully informal as is *I kinda like this town,* but not good written English.

kinky, quirky

Within a couple of decades, **kinky**, originally meaning eccentric or bizarre, has come to mean unusual or abnormal sexual behaviour. **Quirky** is safer if you wish to describe someone or something as peculiar, unconventional or unpredictable.

kipper, herring, bloater

Each of these starts life as a **herring**, the North Sea fish. When split, salted and smoked, it is called a **kipper**; a **bloater** is a herring cured whole without being split.

knave, nave

An area in St Mary's Church in Beverly in North Yorkshire, has been known for some time as 'The North Isle Knave'. Nobody is inclined to change it even though most parishioners are aware that it is really 'the north aisle nave.'

knell, knoll

KNELL, KNOLL

A **knell** is the tolling of a bell to announce a death or a funeral; a **knoll** is a small, usually rounded, hill.

knot

A **knot** is the unit of speed used by ships and aircraft and is one nautical mile (1.15 land miles or 1.85 km) per hour. Thus there is no need to say 'knots per hour'.

kudos

Remember, as Bob Hawke did when his popularity rose to 75%, that such kudos is transient. The '*is*' may sound strange but as **kudos** is singular it is quite correct.

kung fu. See **jujitsu, judo, karate, kung fu**

L

labour. See **belabour, labour**

lady, woman

The use of **lady** can convey courtesy and respect, or can evoke a sense of sophistication and elegance: *She's a real lady; It's usual to serve the ladies before the men; Mrs Griffiths is a wonderful old lady.* (See **gentleman, man.**) However, **lady** can also carry implications of condescension and should be used carefully: *Nancy Astor was the first lady parliamentarian* has less impact than *Nancy Astor was the first woman to be elected to parliament.*

lagged, lagged behind

The English purists will say, *For years the Oxford Street store has **lagged** its rivals,* but the overwhelming majority will say **'lagged behind'**, meaning to hang (back) or fall (behind). **Lag** or **lagged** 'behind', is far more knowing and elegant.

laid, lain, lay, lie

The veteran novelist Barbara Cartland describes her authorial technique: *My writing day starts at 1.30 when I lay on the sofa and dictate 6,500 words.* (interview in *The Times*). One hopes that Ms Cartland was **lying**, not **laying**, on the sofa. Remember the difference between **lay** and **lie** by reciting: *Lay down the law and lie on the floor.* In other words, to **lay** is to put or set down something, while to **lie** is to recline. The same goes for **laid** and **lain**: *After she'd laid the table for dinner she went to lie down; The corpse was lying on the floor; It had lain there for days.* Watch for **lay** when used as **lie** in the past tense: *She simply lay there and cried her eyes out.*

lama, llama

A **lama** is a Tibetan or Mongolian monk; a **llama** is the South American ruminant.

landslide, landslip

These are synonymous when referring to a mass of earth or rock giving way, but only **landslide** is used to dramatise an overwhelming election victory.

lapse, elapse

Lapse can mean 'a slight slip or failure' (*We all suffer from the occasional lapse of memory*), 'a gradual falling or decline' (*They watched as Sue lapsed into unconsciousness*), or 'to become ineffective or to expire' (*Unfortunately the family's insurance policy had lapsed*). **Lapse** can also indicate the passing of time, which is where it can overlap with the usage of **elapse**: *Time lapses slowly on that particular train journey; Elapsed time at the halfway mark of the race was three hours thirteen minutes and four seconds.*

last, latest

Have you read Salman Rushdie's last book? Sounds a bit ominous. What the speaker meant was, *Have you read Salman Rushdie's latest book?* Use **last** only when you mean to convey finality: *My grandfather travelled on the last horse-drawn tram in London.*

latitude, longitude

The imaginary navigational lines around the earth that meet at the Poles are called meridians of **longitude**; the similar horizontal lines that run around the earth parallel to the Equator are called parallels of **latitude**.

laudable, laudatory

Laudable means 'deserving praise'; **laudatory** means 'expressing praise'. But **laudable** is often used to express worthiness rather than unqualified approval: *The committee's efforts, though laudable, ultimately proved to be a waste of time.*

lavatory, toilet, loo, bathroom

Modern usage now frowns upon the traditional, basic **lavatory** as an upper-class affectation; **toilet** is now more or less standard in the UK, along with the more informal **loo**. In the UK, the **bathroom** is the functional room containing bath, basin and toilet; in the US, however, it is more often a euphemism for the toilet: *Look, Fido is whining – he wants to go to the bathroom.* Other euphemisms abound: *powder room, rest room, His'n'Hers, bucks & does,* etc.

laver bread

The menu of a prominent Cardiff hotel, before it was hastily corrected, offered diners *'breakfast complete with **larva bread**'* . This sounded suspiciously like fried bread and weevils. Not to be outdone the London store Selfridge's tried to sell customers the same delicacy packaged as *'**lava bread**'* – presumably very crunchy. The real Welsh breakfast dish is **laver bread**, made with a special seaweed.

lawful, legal, legitimate

Lawful means 'permitted by law'; **legal** means 'related to law'. **Legitimate** has a wider range of meanings – proper, natural, conforming to custom – but commonly refers to children born in wedlock.

lay. See laid, lain, lay, lie

Law AND Lawyers

A **lawyer** is a member of the legal profession and is usually a barrister or a solicitor. A **barrister** pleads on behalf of **defendents** (criminal defence) or **plaintiffs** (civil defence) in the courts; a **solicitor** is a legal advisor to his or her clients, and to barristers. An **attorney** is a practitioner in Common Law, while a **notary public** verifies contracts and deeds and administers oaths. A **silk** is a barrister who dons a silk gown on becoming a **Queen's Counsel**.

---

lead. See led, lead

leading question

A **leading question** is phrased in a way that tends to steer or lead the person being asked to give the desired answer. *And what did you see him do next?* is a fair question. *And then did he go to the draw an bring out the carving knife?* is a **leading question**. Such questions are regarded as unfair in a law court and usually disallowed.

leak, leakage

A **leak** is the accidental escape of something, often fluid or air but also information, secrets, etc. **Leakage** is the 'instance of leakage' but usually means 'the rate of loss caused by a leak': *Even though they thought they'd fixed the fault, the leakage continued.*

learn, learn of, learn about, understand

Consider this comment from *The Times*: *The sooner some union leaders learn his absolute determination to take Labour into government*… There's something wrong about this – perhaps because you can't **learn** 'his absolute determination' because this is a personal quality of Mr Blair's. **Learn** is a transitive verb which has these clear meanings: **1.** to gain specific knowledge. **2.** to acquire specific skills. **3.** to gain by a specific experience. **4.** to commit something specific to memory. In the context of the statement above it needs 'learn' in an intransitive mode: *The sooner some union leaders* (*learn about*) *his absolute determinatin…* or, *The sooner some union leaders* (*learn of*) *his absolute determination…* Or it could be attacked in another way altogether: *union leaders* **understand**… or *union leaders* **realise**.

learned, learnt

Although **learned** expresses the past tense of **learn**, usage favours **learnt**, leaving the way clear for the adjective **learned** (pron. *LER-ned*) meaning 'having great knowledge': *Halliday was easily the most learned of all the professors.*

leave alone, let alone

Usage tends to separate the senses these phrases are meant to convey. *Leave me alone* is a demand to the intruder to depart, to go. *Let me alone*, admittedly a similar command, is nevertheless intended to mean 'stop annoying me!' **Let alone** can also mean 'not to mention': *She could not read or write well, let alone spell.*

led, lead

The confusion arises no doubt from their similar pronunciation. **Lead**, the verb, meaning 'to guide, show the way or to take charge', is pronounced *leed*: *The committee asked Joan to lead the special enquiry.* But **lead** the metal is pronounced *led* as is **led**, the past tense of **lead**: *The man promptly led the detectives to the body.*

legation. See consulate, embassy, legation

legible, readable

Legible means 'writing or print that can be read or deciphered'. **Readable** is synonymous in this sense but has another common meaning: *I've always found Chandler's novels most readable*, meaning 'enjoyable'. See also **illegible**, **unreadable**.

legend. See allegory, fable, myth, parable, legend

less. See few, little, less

lessee, lessor

A **lessee** leases property from the owner, known as the **lessor**.

liable. See likely, liable, apt

Lend AND Loan

A reader's letter to *The Times* complains: *In my post today I received a letter from a local headteacher, offering the use of his school's facilities. Apart from various grammatical and spelling errors, his letter invited my firm to 'loan' his school's video. I do not know whether the concept of borrowing and lending is included in the national curriculum, but if headteachers are unable to master this simple idea, what hope is there for their pupils?*

What the headteacher should have known is that the verb **loan** is strictly a financial transaction; you **loan** money but **lend** a video. Perhaps he confused **loan** (the verb) with **loan** (the noun) which is used to describe any sort of lending, financial or otherwise: *Bert thanked him for the loan of the car.* What the headteacher presumably intended was to invite the reader's firm to *borrow* his school's video: *The headteacher kindly offered to lend his school's video to the local firm ...* or *... The headteacher kindly offered the loan of his school's video to the local firm.* Be warned, however; sloppy usage has effectively smudged the difference between these two words.

libel, slander

A **libel** is something written, published or broadcast that damages a person's character and reputation. **Slander** is a spoken defamatory statement.

liberal, Liberal, libertarian, libertine

If you are **liberal** you're generous, tolerant, progressive, open and receptive to ideas, and a champion of individual freedom. If you are a **Liberal**, you are or were a supporter (in Britain) of the former **Liberal Party**. A **libertarian** believes in freedom of thought and speech while – careful here – a **libertine** is a thoroughly immoral and dissolute philanderer.

licence, license

The confusion here lies in your ability or otherwise to remember that **licence** is a noun (*your driving licence, TV viewing licence*), and that **license** is a verb (*James Bond was licensed to kill; The vendor claimed he was licensed to sell hotdogs by the Council*). In other words, a **licence** is the piece of paper or evidence of permission granted; **license** or **licensing** is the act of authorising. In American English, the one word **license** is used both as the noun and verb.

licentious, licentiate

Licentious means 'sexually unrestrained'. A **licentiate** is someone who holds a licence or certificate of competence to practice a trade or profession.

lie. See **laid, lain, lay, lie**

lightening, lightning

Lightening means 'to become lighter or paler'; **lightning** is the dramatic flash seen in the sky during thunderstorms: *As the sky was lightening at dawn, distant flashes of lightning illuminated the horizon.*

light year

A **light year** is the distance light travels in a year, (about six trillion miles). The poet Seamus Heaney received some stick recently for appearing to use **light years** as a measure of time instead of distance: *Like starlight that is light years on the go/From far away and takes light years arriving.* A pun or two may have been the poet's defence, but they are so well buried that they do leave Heaney vulnerable to being – quite fairly – in ignorance and error. Light years do not take feet, yards or even miles to arrive!

like, as, as if, such as, just as

The so-called misuse of **like** is widespread and the word has the strange capacity to make even alert writers nervous. The problem is that **like** is so easy to use as an all-purpose conjunction: *My mother can't get through a busy day like* (as) *she used to; It sounded like* (as if, as though) *she was about to scream the house down; I prefer the early German composers, like* (such as) *Bach; Like* (just as) *in Pam's case, Liz received no compensation.* When using **like** in a sentence, read it over carefully; in many cases your 'ear' will warn you of possible misuse.

likely, liable, apt, prone

Likely is a useful word to express degrees of probability: *It is likely to be a fine day today.* **Liable** indicates a strong probability but, curiously, is almost always used in a negative sense (*It's liable to rain again today*), derived no doubt from *liability,* the primary meaning of which is 'being exposed to an (unpleasant) obligation'. **Apt** implies suitability, appropriateness or having a tendency to something: *At her age she's apt to tire easily.* **Prone** is a synonym for *apt,* but again is usually used negatively: *After a few drinks Betty was prone to talking rather too frankly about her friends; She said that all her children were prone to any germ that came along.*

limbo

Limbo is occasionally misused to indicate a gap or void : *He wondered what to do to fill the limbo between assignments.* A **limbo** is in fact an imaginary place for lost or forgotten things or persons: *The aftermath of the illness had left her in a sort of limbo, disoriented, floating and remote from the real world.*

line. See **queue, line**

liquidate, liquidise

In the financial sense to **liquidate** means to use assets 'to settle liabilities' or 'to pay off debts'. Most of us are also aware that it means 'to terminate, to kill'. To **liquidise** means 'to pulp food into a liquid': *It took the machine only seconds to liquidise the vegetables into a creamy soup.*

lira, lire

The Italian currency unit **lira** is singular; **lire** is plural.

litany, liturgy

A **litany** in the Christian religion is a repetitious prayer to which there is a fixed response by the congregation. The **Litany** (upper case '*L*') is the prayer contained in the *Book of Common Prayer*. If you use **litany** in a non-religious sense to mean 'a long, repetitious and tedious list or speech, use a lower case '*l*'. A **liturgy** is the prescribed ritual of public church worship.

literal, literary, literate, literally, littoral

If someone says, *He literally hammered the guy into the ground*, you should expect to see the flattened remains of the victim merging with the earth. But that is rarely what such speakers intend by using **literal**, which really means 'actual or actually'. Unfortunately many of us use it in the opposite sense; what we really mean is 'figuratively'. But how often would you expect to hear someone say, *He figuratively hammered the guy into the ground!* **Literate** means 'having the ability to read and write', and **literary** means 'pertaining to literature and books'. **Littoral** is the odd one out here: it is a shoreline.

Literally

The flagrant, even wilful, misuse and abuse of **literally** continues unabated. The main offenders are those who, when using **literally**, intend to mean (if they intend to mean anything) *not* **literally**: that is, **figuratively** or **metaphorically** – in fact the very *opposite* of **literally**. Here are just a few examples: *William Byrd, who literally had the ear of Elizabeth the First* … (Classic-FM Radio). *Everyone had their eyes glued to their radios – quite literally* (BBC) . *Blackburn Rovers are now taking Brian Clough's team literally to the cleaners* (Piccadilly Gold Radio). *Here under the roof at Earls Court is quite literally the world of boating* (Capital Radio).

---

livid, lurid

His angry, livid face blazed with the intensity of a furnace. The imagery is certainly

125

dramatic but **livid**, used here to indicate redness, is the wrong word. **Livid** means 'discoloured', as with a bruise, and if it indicates colour at all it is bluish-grey. **Lurid** is also sometimes misused to describe something red, glowing or fiery; in fact in colour terms it means 'yellowish, pale and wan', quite the opposite. **Lurid** is best used for its primary meaning which is 'vivid, shocking, sensational': *His lurid accounts of her infidelities alienated her previously adoring public.*

living room, sitting room, lounge, drawing room

Describing a room in a house in which to relax and entertain, the first three are now synonymous and their use is a matter of choice. However, a **drawing room** is understood to be a grander, more formal room for entertaining, of the kind you would expect to find only in a very large house.

loan, loaning

*'She is director of the Grosvenor House Art and Antiques Fair, to which the Duke of Westminster is **loaning** important items…'* (*The Times*, 2 June 1998). If this is a word we're still using today then it must be a real antique. If it exists at all today, it is a Scottish or Northern English dialect word meaning a country lane or a cow's milking area. As we have noted earlier under **lend** and **loan,** 'loan' is the noun (except when used as a verb in the case of financial transactions: *The bank loaned us the money with no objections*) and 'lend' is the verb (though **loan** as a verb is common in American English). Therefore in the quotation above the writer should have reported *'the Duke of Westminster is **lending** important items'.*

loath, loth, loathe

Commonly confused. **Loath** is an adjective and means 'reluctant and unwilling': *Although he needed the money Robert was loath to accept anything for helping to fix Brian's car.* **Loth** is an alternative spelling but rarely used. **Loathe** is a verb and means 'to detest, to feel hatred and disgust': *She loathed the very idea of going into hospital.*

locale, location, locality

A **locale** is a place which has a relationship with some event, a venue: *After some argument they allowed him to inspect the locale of the gunfight.* A **location** is a place where something is sited: *This is to be the location of the new factory.* A **locality** is a neighbourhood area or district.

loggia, logia

A **loggia** is a gallery or porch supported by columns; **logia** (plural) are the collected sayings of Christ.

look up, look up to

The idiomatic **look up** can mean 'refer to', 'to improve', 'to have respect for' and 'to make contact': *We'll promise to look up the Jones's when we're in Newcastle; Things began to look up for the boy.* Use judiciously to avoid misunderstandings; a sign in the window of a Sydney bookstore urged potential customers of Scottish descent to '*Look up your clan's tartan*'. To **look up to** means 'to have respect for': *John looks up to his intelligent cousin.*

longitude. See **latitude, longitude**

loose, lose

Use **loose** to describe anything free, unrestrained, unfastened: *She hated to wear anything but loose clothing; The vampire was on the loose again.* **Lose** describes loss: *Give him money and he's sure to lose it.*

lounge. See **living room, sitting room, lounge, drawing room**

low, lowly

Low has a great number of meanings: 'not high; a small supply; coarse and vulgar; quiet and soft; a sound made by cattle'. However **lowly** has but a single meaning which is 'humble, meek and low in rank': *Despite his wealth Frank always boasted about his lowly origins.*

lubricious, lugubrious

Lubricious means 'lewd and lecherous'; **lugubrious** means 'dismal and mournful'.

lumbago. See **arthritis, lumbago, rheumatism, arthritis**

lumbar, lumber

The **lumbar** region is at the lower end of the spine; **lumber** is sawn timber – or discarded household items sometimes stored in a *lumber room*. Less well known, a **lumber** can be a prison or a pawnshop, and a **lumberer** a pawnbroker.

lunch. See **dinner, supper, lunch, tea**

luxuriant, luxurious, luxuriate

Luxuriant means 'prolific, lush, rich and abundant': *Lisa had the most luxuriant hair.* Something **luxurious** is sumptuous and usually costly: *At the hotel they marvelled at the luxurious surroundings.* To **luxuriate** is to revel in pleasure: *She spent most of the evening luxuriating in the Jacuzzi.*

macrocosm, microcosm. See **microcosm, macrocosm**

madam, madame

Use **madame** when in France; otherwise **madam**. In France, **madame** is the equivalent of the English *Mrs*; in Britain it is used only formally: *Dear Madam* (in a letter); *If I were you, Madam, I'd complain to the management.*

mad, angry

Mad meaning **angry**: defenders of this usage quote the Bible and Shakespeare to support their cause but the original meaning is worth preserving: 'insane, senseless, foolish'.

mafia, Mafia

The **Mafia** (upper case '*M*') is the infamous international secret organisation founded in Sicily. The word is now used generally to denote a powerful clique or group: *Despite the mergers, the firm is still run by the Glasgow mafia.*

Magdalen, Magdalene

It's **Magdalen College**, Oxford, and **Magdalene College**, Cambridge.

maintain. See **claim, allege, assert, maintain**

majority, more, most

Maxwell pensioners are to be offered an outline settlement next Wednesday to fill the majority of the £440m hole left by Robert Maxwell's pension fund plundering. (Daily Telegraph). Some usages of **majority** can leave you scratching your head; here it is misused because **majority**, although it means 'most of', is used only of things that can be *counted*. As no part of a hole can be counted, *'majority'* in that sentence should be replaced by *'major part'*. **More** means greater: in quantity, number, extent or importance; so does **most**, except that it implies a greater proportion: *Although more people are now coming to church, most of the villagers still stay at home.*

mannish. See **masculine, mannish**

malevolent, malicious, malignant

Of this trio, **malevolent** means 'of evil intent'; **malicious** implies a desire to hurt and injure or to create mischief; **malignant**, in this context, means 'capable of causing serious harm to another person'.

More on Majority and Minority

One of the problems people have using **majority** and **minority** is whether these nouns take singular or plural verbs. Is it *The majority of the books in the library are never read*, or *The majority of the books in the library is never read*?

The answer lies in the sense indicated by the sentence. If the majority consists of a group (keeping in mind that both **majority** and **minority** apply only to entities that can be counted) or block, then singular would be appropriate: *The Prime Minister's view is that the government's majority **is** likely to be substantial.* If, on the other hand, the majority emphasises individuals, use plural verbs: *The majority of the adults in the tribe **are** meat eaters.* In the sentence about the library, the subject is about books – many individual books – so: *The majority of the books in the library **are** never read* is preferred. If in doubt, use *most* with a plural verb.

---

malfunction. See **dysfunction, malfunction**

mall

Three centuries or more ago a **mall** was a long tree-lined alley designed for playing the game of *'paille maille'* – a combination of croquet, basketball and aerial golf in which a ball was hit into a suspended iron ring. When the game palled the malls (pron. mal) survived (London's The Mall and Pall Mall are two) along with the name. But today, **mall** (pron. mawl) describes a creation quite architecturally different: an out-of-town complex all under cover with shops, supermarkets, cinemas, restaurants and vast parking lot.

man. See **gentleman, man**

mannequin, mannikin

A **mannequin** displaying clothes can be ravishingly alive at a fashion show or an inanimate dummy in a shop window. A **mannikin** (or **manakin,** or **manikin**) is a dwarf or very small man, and also a moveable model of the human figure used by artists and sculptors, reduced in scale and usually carved from wood.

manqué, marque

Manqué means 'unfulfilled, failed, would-be': *As with many members of the Groucho Club Tony was just another writer manqué*. The word, being French, is italicised. A **marque,** also from the French, is a brand or make, usually of a car, and not italicised: *The Stutz marque was noted for its looks, speed and insolence.*

manslaughter. See homicide, manslaughter, murder

mantel, mantle

Mantel is the shortened form of **mantelpiece,** which is the shelf over a fireplace. A **mantle** is a cloak or covering: *The pirates moved towards the ship under a mantle of utter darkness.*

marginal, minimal, slight

Something **marginal** is close to some lower or outer limit: *The farmers complained about the marginal profit yielded by the new season's potato crop.* Although many dictionaries now allow secondary meanings of 'small, insignificant, minimal, slight', the original meaning is worth keeping in mind.

marjoram, oregano

Although there's a lot of cross-fertilisation, *Origanum majorana* is **sweet marjoram**; the wild *Origanum vulgare* is **oregano**. Good cooks are rarely confused.

marriage with, marriage to

The invitation from Buckingham Palace read: *Wedding Breakfast following the Marriage of The Prince of Wales with Lady Diana Spencer.* A marriage is after all a union, which suggests **with** rather than **to** although many prefer the democratic **between**.

marten, martin

The **marten** is a furry, flesh-eating weasel-like animal; the **martin** is a bird of the swallow family.

masculine, mannish

Masculine refers to typical male characteristics; **feminine** is the opposite. **Mannish** is sometimes used to describe women with masculine looks, habits and qualities, often in a derogatory way: *They're strange, that pair; Judy is so feminine while Lucy is decidedly mannish.*

masterful, masterly

Masterful means 'imperious, domineering, self-willed'. **Masterly** describes someone endowed with extraordinary skill: *With a flurry of masterly strokes Anton finished the charcoal portrait.*

mawkish, maudlin

Mawkish means 'sickeningly sentimental, insipid'... yuk! **Maudlin** describes a state of tearful, sentimentality: *Jerome's biography of the bishop was damned by one critic as confused, tedious and mawkish; Harry lapsed into an inarticulate, maudlin account of his early life.*

maxim, axiom

A **maxim** is a concise saying expressing a recognised truth (*pride goeth before a fall; live by the quick and not the dead*); an **axiom** is a generally accepted principle used as a basis for reasoning and argument: *The debating society decided to test the axiom that 'every law has a loophole'.*

may. See can, may, might

may be, maybe

May be as two words indicates possibility and is used differently than **maybe** which means 'neither yes nor no, perhaps': *The conclusions may be correct after all; I may be at home tomorrow; Maybe the conclusions are correct after all; Maybe I'll stay at home tomorrow.* You will note that **maybe** expresses slightly more uncertainty and hesitation than **may be** in these examples.

mayday, May Day

Mayday, the international distress signal, is from the French *m'aidez*, meaning 'help me!' **May Day** is the holiday Monday closest to May 1 each year.

me. See I, me

mean, mien

Mean has many meanings but **mien** has only one: **mien** is a person's bearing, appearance or expression.

The Misuse of Mean

In his book *The Queen's English*, Harry Blamires identifies **mean** as 'the most abused verb in the language'. He particularly criticises its widespread use

131

to express relationships which have little or nothing to do with what **mean** properly connotes, and gives many examples from popular magazines and newspapers:

> *Having a European presence means a firm has to be flexible (Marketing Week).* Actually it doesn't mean that at all; what's required here is a verb that means what it says: *Having a European presence* **requires** *a firm to be flexible.*
> *The 2-metre flex should mean you can find a socket within easy reach of a mirror (Good Housekeeping).* A socket-seeking flex? *If there is a socket within easy reach of a mirror, the 2-metre flex will prove useful.*
> *Numbers of salmon are also reported to have increased. This probably means an improvement in water quality (See Angler).* Here **means** is vague and too sweeping; more precise verbs such as *indicates, suggests,* or *is evidence of* would be more appropriate.

---

meaningful

Although, according to the *Oxford English Dictionary*, **meaningful** has been around since the 1850s, it has appeared with increasing frequency since the 1960s when it became an 'in' word. Discriminating writers give it a miss, preferring more specific adjectives such as *important, significant, far-reaching, valid, critical, serious, etc.*

meantime, meanwhile

Meantime is primarily a noun (*In the meantime we'll simply wait*); **meanwhile** is primarily an adverb (*Meanwhile we'll wait as patiently as we can*); but both are fairly interchangeable as nouns and adverbs.

mecca, Mecca

Mecca, birthplace of Muhammed, is the holiest city of Islam; **mecca** (lower case) is used to describe a centre of aspiration or activity: *St Andrews is the mecca for all true golfing addicts.*

media, medium

The **media** are the agglomeration of newspapers, magazines, television and radio stations, cable and telephone networks whose business is communications. **Media** is the plural of **medium:** *The Times* is a print medium; the BBC is a broadcast medium. However **media** is increasingly used as a singular noun and attracting less and less criticism: *The mass media has a lot to answer for.*

meddlesome, mettlesome

Two different words although often thought to be merely different spellings of one. **Meddlesome** means 'interfering and intrusive'; **mettlesome** means 'spirited and adventurous': *The landlady was a meddlesome old woman; With a couple of my more mettlesome friends we explored the Turkish baths of the old city.*

mediate. See **arbitrate, mediate**

megaton, kiloton

A nuclear weapon of one **megaton** would be equal in destructive power to a million tons of TNT; a **kiloton** is equivalent to 1,000 tons of TNT.

melted, molten

The adjective **molten** means 'made liquid by extreme heating' (*Molten lava coursed over the volcano's rim*); a solid that turns liquid through heat **melts**, is **melting**, has **melted**.

Melodic Matters

Melody is a succession of musical notes forming a recognisable sequence: the **tune. Harmony** is the sounding together of combinations of musical notes as **chords. Rhythm** is the regular repetition of sound and stress: the **beat. Counterpoint** is the weaving together of two or more melodic strands. The **lyric** is the words of the song. The **book** (or libretto) is the text – the spoken words and the words of songs – for a musical or an opera.

---

ménage, manège

A **ménage** consists of the members of a household; **manège** is horsemanship: the art of training horses and riders. **Manège** is sometimes used as a fancy term for riding school.

mental illness

Political correctness has come down very heavily on terms describing the varieties and degrees of mental illness, and words such as *idiot, cretin* and *moron* have, by their popular, abusive meanings, overridden their original clinical definitions. However, **mental illness** and **mentally ill** are widely acceptable, as is **mentally handicapped**. Beyond those, write with care and sensitivity.

meretricious, meritorious

The first means 'superficial and flashy but empty and valueless'; the second means 'excellent and praiseworthy': *The prospective MP made a typically meretricious appeal to the party members; Although Jenny came only third in the race, her effort was considered to be the most meritorious.*

metal, mettle

Surprisingly, these are often confused. **Metal** is the mineral product (gold, copper, iron, etc.); **mettle** means 'spirit or courage': *They all realised that the challenge would test his mettle.*

metaphor. See simile, metaphor

meteor. See comet, meteor

meter, metre

In British English, a **meter** is a measuring guage (gas meter, speedometer); a **metre** is the metric unit of length (1.094 yards) and also the metre of rhythm in music and poetry. American English uses the single spelling **meter** to cover all meanings.

mettlesome. See meddlesome, mettlesome

microcosm, macrocosm

A **macrocosm** is a whole, an entire unified structure, such as the universe. A **microcosm** is a system on a small scale, a structure in miniature: *In Gilbert White's mind, his village of Selborne was a microcosm of the world as it then existed.*

middle. See centre, middle

midget. See dwarf, midget, pygmy

might. See can, may, might

milage, mileage

Both are acceptable spellings, with a preference for the traditional **mileage**.

militate, mitigate

Near opposites, yet often confused. To **militate** means 'to influence an action or event': *Surprisingly, most of the members were for militating against industrial action.* Note that **militate** is usually followed by *for* or *against*. To **mitigate** means 'to moderate, to soften, to make less severe': *Amy's failure to win the Championship Trophy was mitigated by her being awarded Best of Breed for poodles.*

millennium, millennia

The third **millennium** is now here, so watch the spelling – note two l's, two n's. It defines a period of 1,000 years. **Millennia** is the plural.

minimum. minimal, minimise minuscule

Minimum and **minimal** are used to mean 'the smallest, the least possible': *The minimum amount served from this pump is two litres; What problems we faced* *during the journey were minimal.* To **minimise** is to reduce to the smallest possible amount, degree, extent or size. **Minuscule** describes anything extremely small.

minority. See **majority, minority**

misconception. See **fallacy, misconception**

mistrust. See **distrust, mistrust**

mitigate. See **militate, mitigate**

moat, mote

A **moat** is a ditch filled with water to protect a fortification such as a castle; a **mote** is a tiny speck: *The sun made bright yellow shafts through the dust motes.*

Mogul, Mughal

The former spelling is now generally preferred when referring to the former Muslim empire.

mold, mould

For all its meanings ('a shape used to make castings'; 'to shape or form'; 'to influence', 'a fungus' or 'mildew', etc.) the spelling is **mould** in British English and **mold** in American English.

mollify. See **nullify, mollify**

molten. See **melted, molten**

moment in time, point in time

At this moment/point in time … are clichés and are redundant. Use **moment**.

momentary, momentarily, momentous

Momentary is the adjective and means 'lasting only a moment'; **momentarily** is the adverb meaning 'just for a moment, for an instant': *She was prone to suffer from momentary lapses of memory; As I went to meet him I was momentarily confused.* **Momentous** means 'of great significance or consequence': *The President's inauguration was a momentous occasion.*

money, monies, funds, cash

Money is a singular noun and it remains singular regardless of how much money is involved: a million pounds or dollars is still just **money**. The plural, **monies**, though archaic, is still in use: *Nearly half the monies set aside for the projects have been spent.* **Cash** is 'ready money'; **funds** are available financial resources including, of course, **money**.

mongolism

The medical condition formerly known as mongolism is now termed **Down's Syndrome.**

moot, moot point

Although **moot** is usually encountered in the phrase **moot point**, meaning 'a point worth arguing about', **moot** is perfectly capable of acting for itself: *The students agreed unanimously that the issue of alleged immorality at the University was moot.* In other words, the issue was arguable and ripe for debate.

moral, morale

Moral concerns right and wrong in human character and conduct; **morale** is a mental state of confidence and optimism: *The hypocritical moral standards of the officers had a bad effect on the morale of the troops.*

moribund

Moribund is frequently misused to indicate a state of dormancy, inactivity or sluggishness. Its true meaning is far more dramatic: something **moribund** is at the point of death or extinction.

mortgagee, mortgagor

The **mortgagee** provides the loan on a security, such as a house; the **mortgagor** borrows the money.

most, almost

Because the idiomatic use of **most** to mean **almost** is almost standard in American English (*Most everyone enjoys a good holiday*) it is now thought acceptable for British English to follow suit. It isn't.

motivate. See **activate, motivate**

motive, motif

A **motive** is the reason behind a course of action: *It was fairly obvious that Brenda's motive for the attack was pure jealousy.* A **motif** (pron. *mo-TEEF*) is a theme or idea typically repeated and expressed in graphic, musical or literary form: *The same motif of St Francis and a dove was repeated in all the stained-glass windows.*

mould. See **mold, mould**

mule. See **donkey, ass, burro, mule**

murder. See **homicide, manslaughter, murder**

Muslim, Moslem, Islam, Islamic

Muslim is preferred to **Moslem**. **Muslims** are followers of **Islam**, the
religion. **Islamic** is the appropriate adjective when referring to such things as
Islamic writing, Islamic art, etc.

must

The overuse of the word **must**, as in *A visit to the British Museum is an absolute
must,* can be discouraged by remembering that, in Anglo-Indian, a **must** is the
frenzied state of elephants in heat.

mutual, common

Charles Dickens is held responsible, in *Our Mutual Friend,* for the original
misuse of **mutual** to mean **common. Common** means 'something belonging
equally to two or more or all': *Although they came from widely different backgrounds
all the boys had a common interest: football; In the end the lawyers managed to find
some common ground.* **Mutual** means 'something reciprocated, something
shared, experienced or felt between two or more individuals or groups': *For
many years the two partners had enjoyed a mutual trust and respect.* Well-worn terms
such as *mutual agreement* (how can you have an agreement without it being
mutual?) are considered acceptable through established usage.

myth. See **allegory, fable, myth, parable, legend**

nadir, zenith

The **nadir** is the lowest point of anything; the **zenith** is the highest point.

naive, naive, naivety

All three can be written with or without the diaeresis (the two dots above the 'i') although if you use the alternative **naiveté** for **naivety**, it requires the French acute accent.

naturalist, naturist

A **naturalist** studies natural history; a **naturist** or **nudist** enjoys natural surroundings too, but without the hindrance of clothing.

naught. See nought, naught

nauseated, nauseous

A *Times* story described how initial irregularities in the motion of *Le Shuttle* trains rendered their drivers **nauseous** – a common error. What *The Times* meant was **nauseated**, the uncomfortable sensation of nausea or feeling sick. Someone or something **nauseous** is obnoxious and repulsive and capable of causing others to feel disgust and revulsion – or **nauseated.** It's worth mentioning here that the Latin term *ad nauseam* is more often than not misspelt *ad nauseum*.

naval, navel

Often confused. **Naval** refers to a navy, a country's seaborne armed force of warships and sailors. Your **navel** is the small depression left by the umblical cord in the skin of your stomach.

nautical, naval

Nautical refers to anything concerning ships, shipping, seamen and navigation; **naval** relates only to a country's navy, its ships, personnel and activities.

NAVAL, NAVEL

near by, nearby

Near by is used as an adverb only: *Margaret's mother lives near by.* **Nearby** can also be used adverbially as above, or as an adjective: *Margaret's mother lives in the nearby flats*.

near future, distant future, forseeable future

Although wonderfully imprecise terms, these are now idiomatic, and irremovable from the language. Careful writers might may prefer to use more explicit words such as *shortly, soon, eventually, ultimately,* etc.

necessities, necessaries, essentials

Few people preserve the differences here because they are extremely subtle. They have all come to mean the same, which is why we feel the need to add qualifiers to create *bare* **necessities,** *absolute* **essentials***, the* **necessaries** *of life*, etc.

needless to say

Logically, a meaningless phrase (if needless, why say it?) but nevertheless an established idiomatic expression. The same illogic applies to *it goes without saying*. Writers and speakers obviously find the phrases useful to call attention to a point about to be made.

negligent, negligible

To be **negligent** is to be careless and indifferent, to neglect something or someone, perhaps to a dangerous degree: *The court found the ship's engineer to have been grossly negligent in policing safety regulations*. **Negligible** means 'unimportant, trivial, insignificant': *Fortunately the effects of the tainted food on the men were negligible*.

neither nor, either or

Neither means 'not either of two', and thus, like **either**, is singular: *Neither of his two novels is read much nowadays*. And while **either** is followed by **or**, **neither** is followed by **nor**: *Neither Jane nor Thomas is to go to the cinema today*. However there can be plural constructions: *Neither Marcia's parents nor Harvey's friends **are** welcome here any more* (where both subjects are plural) and: *Either Marcia's parents or Harvey will **have** to decide who is to go to the airport* (one subject plural, one singular).

nemesis

Frequently misused to mean fate or destiny or even some adversary or rival, **nemesis**, derived from *Nemesis*, the Greek goddess of vengeance, means the prospect of a punishment: *At last the cruel leader became the people's prisoner, awaiting his nemesis alone in his cell*.

net, nett

The former is correct; **nett** is a pointless variant.

the Netherlands, Holland

Use **the Netherlands** in official and political contexts; otherwise **Holland**.

nevertheless, none the less

Nevertheless means 'however, in spite of, yet, notwithstanding': *I was quite ill; nevertheless I felt I should attend the meeting*. **None the less** (written as one word in American English) is a synonym but also covers the meaning 'not any the less': *Although I was none the less eager to attend the meeting, my illness prevented me*.

new

Watch for the unnecessary use of **new**: *'new discovery'*; *'new developments'*; *'new* *breakthrough'*. You would hardly expect to attract attention by announcing an *'old breakthrough'* would you? In these examples **new** is a superfluity.

New York, New York

New York is both a city and a state of the USA; hence, to avoid confusion, *New York City (NYC)* and *New York State*. Manhattan is not New York City but one of its five boroughs; the others are the Bronx, Brooklyn, Queens and Richmond.

nice

Of its two strands of meanings, only that of 'discriminating and precise' retains its original definition although few people are sure enough about this to ever use it: *John could always be relied upon to make nice distinctions in disputes over croquet rules*. The second strand of the meanings of **nice** has degenerated through over-use into 'agreeable, pleasant, attractive, kind' and so on, so that it is now a limp and lazy word for general approval: *a nice cup of tea, a nice chap, he made a nice job of it, nice one, Cecil!* Discriminating writers will replace **nice** with more specific adjectives to convey what they really mean.

nicety, niceness

While many writers avoid using *nice* because of its previous overuse, we shouldn't shun **nicety** and **niceness**, both of which have retained useful meanings. A **nicety** is a subtle point of detail, a delicacy of refinement: *Thomas was a master of the niceties of sarcasm.* **Niceness** is a safe and fresh way of conveying the combination of charm, sympathy, kindliness and modesty: *You couldn't help admiring Emily's niceness.*

Nissan, Nissen, Nisan

Nissan is the Japanese car manufacturer; a **Nissen hut** (called a **Quonset hut** in North America) is the semi-circular shelter structure, usually of corrugated steel. **Nisan** is the first month in the Jewish calendar.

noisome, noisy

Noisy needs no explanation, but **noisome** has nothing to do with noise or loudness; it means objectionable and offensive: *The visitors wrinkled their noses as they passed the noisome slurry tanks.*

nominal. See **token, nominal, notional**

none

The pronoun **none** can be singular or plural according to the sense in the context. If **none** expresses the singular idea of 'not one, not any' then it is singular: *All five books are well written but none* (i.e. **not one**) *has been a bestseller.* But where **none** suggests a multiplicity of 'not any', then it is plural: *We looked for suitable gifts but none were to be found.* In each of these examples your ear should tell you that *'none have been a bestseller'* and *'none was to be found'* sounds wrong. You'll also come across instances where despite following the 'rule' the sentences still sound awkward. Both *'None of the gang was caught'* and *'None of the patients was seriously ill'* are pedantically correct but in each case the plural *were* instead of the singular *was* would sound better. It's a matter of gingerly feeling your way and making sure that once you choose singular or plural, you stay with it.

none the less, nonetheless

Although traditionally written as three words and sometimes hyphenated, **nonetheless** as a single word is now generally acceptable.

no one, no-one

I was sure that no one was there means that nobody, no person, not anyone was there. **No one** is written as two words to avoid **noone**, although some prefer **no-one**.

normally, normalcy, normality

Normal once meant 'according to the rule or standard' but for a long while now we have been using **normal** and **normally** to mean 'usual, common, typical': *Today it's quite normal for a woman to sit unaccompanied in a bar.* Although **normalcy** is standard (or normal) in American English, **normality** is preferred in the UK: *At last the situation returned to some semblance of normality.*

notable, noted, noticeable, notorious

If you are **notable**, you are someone distinguished by some aspect of worthiness or character: *Both men came from notable military families.* If you are **noted**, it is usually because of some outstanding skill or achievement: *Henshaw was among other things a noted bassoon player.* If you are **notorious**, you are a celebrity for all the wrong reasons: *Dolores was notorious for running away with other women's husbands.* **Noticeable** means 'detectable, easily seen': *The effects of the accident on the patient were noticeable.*

notwithstanding. See pace, according to, notwithstanding

nought, naught

Nought is the correct British English spelling for zero (the numeral 0); **naught**, meaning 'nothing', is occasionally found in such statements as: *All* *their efforts came to naught.* In the US, **naught** is used in both senses and **noughts-and-crosses** is better known as **tic-tac-toe**.

noxious, obnoxious. See obnoxious, noxious

nubile

It would take a brave or foolish writer to use **nubile** in its original meaning to describe a woman: 'suitable or ready for marriage'. Its now well-established meaning is 'female, young and physically and sexually attractive' and is replete with suggestive overtones.

nugatory, nuggety

Something **nugatory** is worthless and trivial; someone **nuggety** is stocky and rugged.

nullify, mollify

To **nullify** means 'to make useless, to cancel out or to render null and void'. To **mollify** means 'to appease and soothe'.

numbers

For the sake of clarity and uniformity there are several preferences for denoting numbers. From one to ten, numbers are spelled out: *Seven players turned up but only five were without injuries.* Beyond ten, use numerals: *Of the class of 35, no less than 15 pupils were found to be suffering from colds.* Where numbers range from below to above ten, spell out: *The company's portfolio contained more than forty different stocks but only nine were performing well.* Don't begin sentences with numerals: *Fifteen pupils were sent home with colds.* Percentages are usually expressed in numerals: *The proportion rose rapidly from 5% to over 20% during the week.* The same usually applies to Manhattan streets: *42nd Street; 12th Street.* Fractions (1/3, 1/8) look better written out (one-third; one-eighth) in sentences, and while *a third* or *a half* imply approximately a third or a half, *one third* or *one half* seem more precise.

nutritious, nutritional

Certain foods may be **nutritious**, meaning 'nourishing'. **Nutritional** refers to the process of nourishing the body: *The nutritional needs of the patients require at least two nutritious meals a day.*

O, Oh, Ooh!

The single, capitalised **O** is now used only in religious, historic or poetic contexts: *O Thou, that in the heavens dost dwell; O my Luve's like a red, red rose.* **Oh** is the usual expression for mild surprise or pause: *Oh, that was close! Oh, I see.* **Ooh!** is reserved for bigger shocks.

objective, subjective

To be **objective** means 'to be uninfluenced by any prior beliefs, personal feelings or prejudices'. To be **subjective** is to be the opposite: to be over-influenced by personal considerations or relationships.

obligate, oblige

Of the two, **obligate** implies a moral or legal duty, whereas **oblige** means 'to render a favour or to accommodate': *The man had obliged him on several occasions, and now Peter felt obligated to repay his kindness.*

oblivious to, oblivious of

Although **oblivious to** is commonly seen, and also mistakenly used to mean 'ignorant or uncomprehending' (*Bob was completely oblivious to the importance of being polite*), **oblivious of**, meaning 'unaware or forgetful', is correct: *Bob was completely oblivious of the racket going on around him.*

obnoxious, noxious

Obnoxious means 'very unpleasant' and is often applied to aggressive behaviour: *Even though it was his fault, the other driver couldn't have been more obnoxious.* Something **noxious** is potentially injurious.

obscene, pornographic, erotic

Something **obscene** is 'disgusting and offensive to accepted standards of decency' – *Mrs Harris branded the exploitation of children to sell toys on television as obscene* – but more often 'sexually indecent, lewd and lascivious': *They were appalled by the obscene graffiti that adorned all the walls.* **Pornographic** means 'designed deliberately to arouse sexual excitement': *The centre spread of the magazine was dominated by a picture of Miss Behaving in a pornographic pose.* In the context of exciting sexual desire, **erotic** is a near synonym except that **erotica** is claimed to have the redeeming quality of being 'art'.

observance, observation

An **observance** is a ceremony or custom, and also the act of complying with a law or custom: *Almost the entire village supported the eleven o'clock observance; Observance of the new dog fouling laws was almost total.* **Observation** is the act of watching, or noting information: *He was awarded the science medal for his observations on the mating of the rare white seal.*

obsolete, obsolescent

If something is **obsolete**, it is out of use or out of date; if it is **obsolescent**, it is in the process of becoming obsolete: *It was fairly clear that the trusty old engine was facing obsolescence.*

obstetrician. See gynaecologist, obstetrician

obtain. See get, acquire, obtain, secure

obtuse. See abstruse, obtuse

obviate, obliterate

Obviate means 'to prevent in advance, or forestall': *The new car park should obviate the need for people to park in the street.* **Obliterate** means 'to remove or efface by destruction': *The remains of the old town were obliterated in a matter of days.*

Occam's razor

This strange term is being used and seen more and more. It's a maxim (*q.v.*) which encourages economy, first proposed by 14th-century philosopher William of Ockham. To apply the sharpness of Ockham's own razor, the principle states that suitably defined simple explanations of phenomena are more likely to be true. In short, the simplest explanation is most likely to be proved correct.

occupied, preoccupied

In the sense of using one's time, being **occupied** means being busy; being **preoccupied** means being absorbed, engrossed and oblivious of all around you.

oculist. See **Optical Options**

odd, queer

Most people today hesitate to use **queer** in its original meaning of 'strange and unusual' for fear of being misunderstood. Even an innocent remark such as *I'm feeling a bit queer* will provoke sniggers and guffaws. Now that the word's accepted meaning is 'homosexual', it's safer to use alternatives: *peculiar, curious, unreal, suspicious, dotty,* etc. Beward also of **odd** (*He estimated there were 30-odd people in the bus at the time*) in the sense of an unspecified number; in the above example, the hyphenated *'30-odd'is necessary to* remove ambiguity.

odious, odorous

Odious means 'unpleasant and detestable'; **odorous** applies only to smells, not necessarily unpleasant. To describe a bad smell, use **malodorous**.

offence

You can **give offence** (*He [Evelyn Waugh] crafted some exquisite novels, caused much merriment, and gave offence to nearly everyone he met*); **take offence** (*She took offence at the slightest criticism*); and **cause offence**: *Something in the man's psychological makeup prompted him to cause offence at every opportunity.* In American English, the spelling is **offense**.

offer. See **proffer, offer**

offered, offerred

Invariably a nail-biting decision. The correct spelling is **offered**.

official, officious

Official implies possessing a position of authority: *a government official, an official document.* **Officious** means 'self-important and unnecessarily intrusive, especially where advice is concerned': *The official in charge was officious in the extreme.*

off of

This double preposition is fairly common, especially in American English. But the *'of'* is redundant and incorrect. Thus *He told the boys to get off of the grass* should be *He told the boys to get off the grass.*

okay, OK

As an adjective, **okay** and **OK** are acceptable. As a verb, as in *The boss has just okayed William's idea*, the full spelling is preferred to *'OK'd'*.

old age pensioner, OAP

OAP, old age pensioner and just plain **pensioner** are used in British English, with pensioner the preferred usage. **Senior citizen** is usually found in American English.

older, oldest. See elder, eldest, older, oldest

ombudsman, ombudswoman

The style is to use both according to the sex of the office-holder.

one another. See each other, one another

one, one's, oneself

The use of **one** (*One isn't obliged to use the indefinite pronoun but it can be useful at times*) can often lead to pretentiousness. Use 'one' to start with and you must use **one's** and **oneself** throughout the sentence: *No matter how one tries to protect one's life, it is only too easy to hurt oneself in a war.* Grammarians shudder when a sentence begins with a reference to **one** which is then abandoned for specific pronouns: you, your, his, her, etc.: *One gets very angry when your tax bill arrives just after you've paid for your holiday.* This practice is acceptable in American English but not if you live within a thousand miles of the *CED*. Good writers will not use this form, preferring the more idiomatic: *No matter how much you try to protect your life, you can still get hurt in a war.*

ongoing, continuing

Ongoing is an 'in' word (*ongoing dialogue, ongoing situation, ongoing programme*), but there are better choices such as: *continuing, developing.*

only

The problem with the adverb **only** is that it is too often misplaced in a sentence: *Hawking only published his book after years of deep thought.* Does this mean that all Hawking ever did was to publish this one book? It seems so, but it is not true. What the sentence intended to convey was *Hawking published his book only after years of deep thought.* When using **only**, make sure it is placed next to the word it modifies.

on to, onto, on

Onto, once condemned by grammarians, is now well established, but that doesn't mean that it is always interchangeable with **on.** *Harry was fined when he drove onto the traffic island* and *Harry was fined when he drove on the traffic island* mean two different things. The first sentence suggests that, accidentally or deliberately, Harry's car mounted the traffic island, and then presumably stopped, whereas the second implies that Harry was having a merry time driving around and around on the traffic island. Nor is **onto** always interchangeable with **on to**: *When he'd repaired the puncture he drove on to his destination; Bill immediately passed the information on to the police; Although injured Zapotek kept right on to the finishing line*. In all three cases **on to** is used adverbially and using the preposition **onto** would be wrong.

onward, onwards

Onward is the adjective: *Despite the hail of gunfire the car maintained its onward course*. But **onwards** and also **onward** are adverbs, with the former more in general use in the UK: *The car kept coming, despite the fierce gunfire, onwards to the escapee's hideout*.

opponent. See adversary, opponent

opportunity, chance, possibility

Chance, as any gambler knows, is a force by which things happen without cause; **opportunity** is a favourable combination of circumstances; **possibility** is the chance for something to happen or exist.

opposed, opposite. See diametric, opposite, opposed

Optical Options

Ophthalmologists and **oculists** are medical practitioners who specialise in diseases of the eye; the former term is now preferred by the profession. An **optometrist** tests eyes and vision and prescribes optical aids such as spectacles, while an **optician** writes optical prescriptions and makes and sells spectacles. Artificial eyes are made by **ocularists.**

---

optimistic, confident

To be **optimistic** is to look on the bright side of things, to expect the best in everyone, to believe that good will triumph over evil, to be always cheerily hopeful. **Optimistic** generates a wide range of meanings. So if you wish to convey feelings of (for example) hope, confidence, expectation, light-heartedness, cheerfulness, idealism and so on, use specific adjectives.

optimum, optimal

Optimum is frequently mistakenly used to indicate 'the most, the greatest, the biggest or best'. In fact **optimum** (and its fancy synonym **optimal**) means 'the best result produced by a combination of factors'. The optimum selling price for a product isn't necessarily the highest or the lowest, but that which will do best for the vendor.

oral, aural, verbal

Oral refers to the mouth, thus spoken; **aural** refers to the ear, thus heard. **Verbal** refers to words but its use is invariably ambiguous because such terms as *verbal abuse* and *verbal agreement* are usually accepted as being of the **oral** kind, i.e. spoken. When you wish to convey that something is written do not use **verbal**; instead, use *written agreement, in writing,* etc.

orchestrate, organise

In its non-musical sense, **orchestrate** does not mean to **organise**, but to arrange something for a special or maximum effect: *Fresh from organising the Budapest Festival, Paul orchestrated a surprisingly well-received event by our rather motley collection of speakers.*

ordinance, ordnance

An **ordinance** is a regulation or decree; **ordnance** means 'military armament, munitions and supplies'.

ordinary. See **average, ordinary**

oregano. See **marjoram, oregano**

oriel, oriole

An **oriel** is a projecting window, usually from an upper storey; the **oriole** is a brightly plumaged songbird.

orient, orientate

Meaning 'to find your bearings', both are, as with their opposites **disorient** and **disorientate**, synonymous.

or, nor. See **neither, nor, either, or**

orotund, rotund

An **orotund** voice is rich and resonant; an **orotund** speech is loud and pompous. **Rotund** can also be applied to speech – meaning sonorous and grandiloquent – but is mostly used to describe the human figure: plump and round.

orthopaedic, paediatric

An **orthopaedist** was once the medical specialist who treated deformities in children, and this is why there remains some confusion with **paediatrician**. Nowadays an **orthopaedist** treats the bone, joint and muscle problems of children *and* adults; a **paediatrician** treats children only – and for any diseases. In American English the diphthongs are dropped: **orthopedic, pediatric.**

outdoor, outdoors

Outdoor is the adjective: *Jane loved all outdoor activities.* **Outdoors** is the noun: *Rupert loved to paint outdoors.* See *indoor and indoors.*

outing

Meaning 'a short trip or excursion', this word has been adopted by the homosexual community and is thus now subject to ambiguity and misunderstanding. In a homosexual context **outing** is related to *come out,* (which is to declare openly one's homosexuality), it means the exposure of or the declaration that a person is a homosexual, often against that person's will: *The sensational outing of the Bishop caused a national furore.* The parish church of Clare in Suffolk felt it was forced, in a porch notice (*The Times, 29.3.95*) to explain to parishioners: '*OUTING – no, not another in the succession of Peter Tatchell's exposures, but a coach trip to Framlingham next Thursday …*'

outward, outwards

Outward is the adjective: *Despite all the problems on the cruise ship, they enjoyed the outward journey.* **Outwards** (and also **outward**) is the adverb: *They couldn't help noticing that his rather large feet turned outwards.*

over, more than

Over is a very useful catch-all word, and there's the catch: over-use. Many object to its use in place of **more than**: *He weighed in at over fifteen stone; She collected over six hundred Barbie dolls.* The use of **over** in other contexts is also regarded as sloppy: *The complaint was over lack of redundancy payments ('caused by'); The strike was over increased employment guarantees ('for' or 'about'); She expressed her worries over the missing child ('about').* It's worth taking a little care over **over**.

overly

The use of this word is common enough and standard in American English (*Vera was not overly fond of cabbage*) but continues to be frowned upon. Use instead: *Vera was not over-enthusiastic about cabbage.*

overt. See **covert, overt**

P

PACE, ACCORDING TO, NOTWITHSTANDING

Fowler's says forthrightly that this Latinism 'is one we could well do without in English' because it is so widely misunderstood. Faced with a sentence containing *pace*: *But in the House of Lords there is no hilarity – pace Lord Salisbury's speech last night* ... many people are prone to think that *pace* means *notwithstanding*. Another guess is that it means 'according to'. In fact *pace* (pron. *pay-say* or *pah-chay*) is a nicety (q.v.) expressing polite disagreement but with due deference to, and is thus used to acknowledge the author of a quote: *The inscription in E. M. Forster's 'A Passage to India', "God si love" is not, pace Andrew Motion, a typographical mistake that was never corrected, but an observation noted at Moghul Sarai railway station and recorded in Forster's diary for January 1913.*

---

pacific, Pacific
A **pacific** person is against the use of force and thus war. **Pacific** refers to the Pacific Ocean, its islands and adjoining land masses (for example the Pacific Rim).

paediatric. See **orthopaedic, paediatric**

paid. See **earn, paid**

pair. See **couple, pair**

palate, palette, pallet
The **palate** is the roof of the mouth; a **palette** is an artist's board on which colours are mixed; a **pallet** is many things but most visibly the robust timber

tray on which are stacked heavy, bulky goods for easy lifting and transportation, or a small or makeshift bed: *Take up your pallet and walk.*

palpable, obvious

The word palpable is frequently misused for 'obvious': *The female buttocks in many of Man Ray's early photographs are so palpable nobody could miss them.* Palpable doesn't mean simply 'obvious': it means 'real, capable of being felt' and 'perceived by the sense of the mind or the sense of touch'. As an observer has noted, 'Buttocks in photographs may be breathtaking, obscene, delightful or even obvious, but they are not palpable.'

palpate, palpitate

When a doctor **palpates,** he or she examines by the sense of touch and pressure. **Palpitate** means 'to tremble' but is used most frequently to describe an abnormally fast and uneven heartbeat.

panacea

The team found that common aspirin and several days' rest was the panacea for the latest flu epidemic. Not untypically, **panacea** is used incorrectly here; a **panacea** is a universal remedy for *all* ills.

pandemic. See endemic, epidemic, pandemic

paraffin, kerosene, kerosine

In many countries – the US, Canada, Australia, etc. – what is called **paraffin** in the UK is called **kerosene** or **kerosine**.

parameter, perimeter

A **perimeter** is a boundary or limit: *The prisoners managed to get as far as the perimeter fence.* A **parameter**, a very much misused jargon word, is a mathematical term for a constant, with variable values, used to determine a problem – nothing to do with boundaries at all. Outside of higher mathematics you should have no occasion whatsoever to use **parameter**. Instead you may need such words as *limit, confines, frame, boundary, border*: *The new accountant was requested to work to the previous year's budget.*

paramount, tantamount

Surprisingly, these have been muddled. **Paramount** means 'of the greatest significance and importance': *Of all his ambitions, that of getting into university was paramount.* **Tantamount** means 'as good as, the same as, amounting to': *Wendy's jibe was tantamount to branding Barbara a liar.*

paranoid, paranoia

The loose use of **paranoid** and **paranoia** was one of Sir Kingsley Amis's pet bugbears. A throwaway aside such as *I get so paranoid about doing a good job when I'm speaking* (Australian cricket captain Allan Borders on the ABC, 1 May 1985) are just examples of countless trivialisations of paranoid and similar severe medical and psychological disorders which are dangerous and even fatal. **Paranoia** is a form of schizophrenia characterised by the progressive deterioration of the personality with hallucinations and delusions, or a disorder involving intense suspicions and fears that are unfounded; a **paranoid** person is one consistently exhibiting such behaviour.

parenthesis, brackets

Round brackets (like these) are used to parenthesise or set apart relevant matter within a sentence which could be dropped without altering the sense or grammatical construction of the sentence. The enclosed material might be extra information, an explanation or clarification, an afterthought, a comment. **Square brackets** [like these] are used to enclose an editor's or author's insertion: *It was a matter of opinion that if offered the position, he [Professor Brandmeyer] would most likely refuse it.* One common function of the square bracket is to enclose the adverb *sic* (from the Latin *sicut*, meaning 'just as') to indicate that incorrect or doubtful matter is quoted exactly from the original: *Pink and yellow concubines [sic] climbed in great profusion up the trellis.*

parlay, parley

In betting jargon, **parlay** means 'to stake all the winnings from one bet to the next'; to **parley** is to discuss informally with an opponent terms for ceasing hostilities.

parochial. See provincial, parochial

parsimony, penury

Parsimony means 'frugality and stinginess'; **penury** means 'extreme poverty': *The old man was parsimonious, which was why he was never penurious.*

part from, part with

To **part from** someone is to leave; to **part with** something is to give it away or give it up: *He parted from Beryl on the best of terms; The little girl absolutely refused to part with her favourite teddy bear.*

partial, partially, partly

Partial and **partly** both mean 'in part', with **partial** having the additional meaning of either prejudiced or incomplete, so use it only when the meaning

153

is clear: a *partial account* of some event could mean either that is an 'incomplete account' or a 'one-sided account'. **Partly** is more likely to be used to open an explanatory phrase: *Partly because she was ill, Mary cancelled her own birthday party.*

passed, past

Passed is the past tense of 'to pass': *We told the police that the car **passed** us at great speed.* **Past** can confuse writers because it can be a noun (*All that bitterness is now in the past);* an adverb (*They watched as the car accelerated past*), and a preposition: *They drove past us at great speed.*

pastiche, parody

Pastiche is sometimes used instead of **parody** but there is a difference. A **pastiche** is a play, painting or some other creation that imitates and borrows styles from other artists and periods. A **parody** is a humorous – intentional or unintentional – or satirical imitation of another individual's work.

pastille, pastil, pastel

'After the loss of that tidy sum he [Hattersley] may care to reflect on why he has been discarded like a green fruit pastel.' (*Daily Telegraph*, 10 August 1997). **Pastel** is a pigmented stick or crayon specifically manufactured for drawing or colouring. You are not encouraged to suck pastels, although **pastilles** (sometimes misguidedly called **pastils**) or flavoured lozenges can be chewed *or* sucked.

pathos. See bathos, pathos, bathetic, pathetic

peaceful, peaceable

Peaceful means 'tranquil, calm, undisturbed'; someone **peaceable** is attracted to peace and calm, and abhors aggression: *Jules was above all a peaceable man.*

peal, peel

A letter in *The Times* encouraging campanologists to travel: *Visiting other churches broadens the experience of ringers, as does the occasional peel.* A series of changes rung on bells is of course a **peal**; to **peel** is to remove or strip from a surface – peel from an orange, clothing from a body, etc.

pedlar, peddler, pedaller

Someone who **peddles** or hawks goods from house to house or person to person is a **pedlar** in the UK and a **peddler** or **pedler** in the US. A **pedaller** is usually found riding a bicycle.

peel. See peal, peel

peeping, peeking

To **peep** or **peek** is to take a quick or furtive glance – while both are synonyms, **peep** is preferred in the UK, **peek** in the US. **Peep** is also a more suggestive word in that it can imply 'looking secretly from a hidden place'; hence *peephole* and *Peeping Tom*.

peninsula, peninsular

A **peninsula** is a piece of land almost surrounded by water, while **peninsular** is the adjective, as in *Peninsular War* and the full name of P&O: The Peninsular & Oriental Company.

penny, pee, pence, p

What a quandary! When the British currency was decimalised in 1972, the 240 pennies that made up the old pound became 100 pence to the new (decimalised) pound. To differentiate between the two values, the new penny coins were called **new pence,** which was quickly abbreviated to **'np'** and, subsequently, to **'p'**. While this looked fine when written (85p) it was a less than mellifluous sound when pronounced – *pee* – with its long usage to mean 'passing urine'. The French don't say *twenty-four eff* for 24 francs, nor are Americans bound to say *ten see* for 10 cents, but the British now fluctuate between **pee** and **pence**.

penury. See **parsimony, penury**

people, persons

Where the sense of a group needs to be conveyed, or there is an uncountable or indeterminate number of individuals, use **people**: *Hundreds of people hurled themselves at the turnstiles.* Where a sense of individuality needs to be preserved, or the number of individuals is small or countable, **persons** is appropriate: *The number of persons injured in the blast is likely to reach double figures.* However, **persons**, which has had more usage in the US, is gradually giving way to **people**, as **persons** retreats to semi-legal language: *In person or persons unknown.*

per, a

We worked ten hours per day is considered inferior to the plainer *We worked ten hours a day.* Restrict the use of **per** to commercial or legal contexts (*per annum, per diem*).

per cent, percent, percentage, proportion, part

Percentage and **proportion** are habitually used when neither a percentage nor a proportion is remotely involved in the statement: *A large percentage of the* *shareholders voted for the changes* (probably meaning 'many'); *The biggest proportion of the profits will be ploughed back into research* (probably meaning 'most'). When a percentage figure or a known proportion is involved, fair enough; otherwise use *part, most, many, few, little,* etc. **Per cent**, as two words, is still maintained in Britain while **percent** is more or less standard in the US.

perceptible, perceptive, percipient

Perceptible means 'observable or able to be recognised or measured': *The lights on the far shore were barely perceptible.* **Perceptive** and **percipient** mean 'quick to see and understand': *The captain proved to be quite perceptive when he chose Gary for the chess team.*

peremptory, perfunctory

Peremptory means 'final, decisive, allowing no questions and objections'. **Perfunctory** means 'careless, half-hearted, without enthusiasm': *After drilling in such a perfunctory manner, the squad was peremptorily ordered to the cookhouse.*

period of time, period in time

These common phrases or cliches are, strictly speaking, redundancies; after all, *time* is a *period,* albeit a continuous one. Use **period** or **time** separately, not together.

permanent, perennial

Perennial does not, as many people believe, mean 'year after year'; its correct meaning is **permanent**, unfailing, unceasing, long-lived.

permeate, pervade, penetrate

These, together with **saturate** and **impregnate**, are near synonyms, but there are subtle differences. **Permeate** is the action of passing through by diffusion: a gas or smell can permeate a room. **Pervade** means to 'spread through, gradually and subtly': a sense of fear can pervade a roomful of people. **Penetrate** implies physical or psychological breakthrough: an explorer can penetrate a jungle; a counter-espionage agent can penetrate a spy ring, etc.

perpetrate, perpetuate

Perpetrate means to cause, commit or carry out some act that (usually) is underhand, deceptive or even criminal; **perpetuate** means 'to continue indefinitely, to preserve by making eternal': *Guy Fawkes perpetrated an assassination plot, the meaning of which is perpetuated by the annual Bonfire Night festivities.*

perquisite, prerequisite

These are easily and often confused. A **perquisite** ('perk') is a benefit or privilege, often regarded as a right: *The company pointed out that high on the list of perquisites were a luxury car, an executive dining room and membership of the Key Club.* A **prerequisite** is a precondition: *One of the prerequisites of membership of the society was total abstinence.*

persecute, prosecute

To **persecute** is to ill-treat, harass or oppress someone; to **prosecute** is to bring a criminal action against a person. **Prosecute** is also sometimes used to mean 'carrying out a task or undertaking': *The parking inspector prosecuted his duties with the utmost vigour.*

Persecuted Unjustly... and Other Pleonasms

A **pleonasm** is a simple idea expressed with more words than is necessary. How many times have you heard *'past history'* when everyone knows that all history is in the past? A gift is something given, so what on earth is a *'free gift'*? Here are a few pleonasms that lurk in everyday speech and writing:

future prospects	actual facts	small detail
general consensus	universal panacea	moment in time
close proximity	interspersed among	general public
new innovations	downward plunge	consensus of opinion
advance warning	completely full	relic of the past
join together	usual habits	violent explosion
original source	revert back	repeat again
audible click	final outcome	serried rows

---

personal, personnel

Personal is an adjective relating to a person's private life (*personal hygiene, personal expenses, a personal question*), while **personnel** is a noun describing the staff of a company or organisation: *Jack was the senior personnel officer of quite a large company in the Midlands.*

personally

To act **personally** implies without the help or involvement of others: *I take a great interest in the club's activities but, personally, I hate going to the meetings.*

personify, impersonate

To **personify** is to attribute human characteristics to an object or abstraction: *Old Mr Wilkins was greed personified.* To **impersonate** is to pretend to be another person, usually by copying that person's appearance and mannerisms.

persons. See **people, persons**

perspicacity, perspicuity

Perspicacity is the ability to clearly understand; **perspicuity** is the ability to express lucidly, to state clearly. As Eric Partridge put it, *'Perspicacity is needed to grasp the distinction, and perspicuity to explain it'*.

persuade. See **convince, persuade**

pertinent, pertinacious

Pertinent means 'relevant'; to be **pertinacious** is to be resolute in purpose, stubborn and unyielding: *The lawyer insisted that the witness's past was entirely pertinent to the case; The case would have been lost but for the pertinacious attitude of the defence team.*

peruse, read

Peruse is often mistakenly believed to mean 'to read casually, at a glance'. In fact it means the opposite, which is to read and examine carefully and critically: *He seemed to take forever as he perused the document.*

pervade. See **permeate, pervade, penetrate**

perverse, perverted

To be **perverse** is wilfully to deviate from normal expectations; to be persistently obstinate: *You could always count on Agnes to cause trouble but tonight, perversely enough, she was all sweetness and light.* To be **perverted** is to deviate from the norm to abnormal, immoral or corrupt behaviour and standards; *The police charged him with perverting the course of justice.*

petition, partition

A **petition** is a request or plea to some authority, usually in the form of a written document signed by a very large number of people supporting the demand: *They all signed the petition to urge the government to abandon daylight saving.*

Petrol and Other Hydrocarbons

Petroleum is what comes out of the oil well, and **petrol (gasoline** or **gas** in the US) is refined from it. **Paraffin** (called **kerosine** or **kerosene** in North America, Australia and other countries) is also distilled from petroleum. What comes out of the pumps marked **DERV** (abbreviation for Diesel Engined Road Vehicle) is **diesel** oil, one of the heavier fractions broken down from the crude petroleum.

pharmacist. See **chemist, druggist, pharmacist**

phase, faze

A **phase** is a state or period in a sequence of events: *Both her children went through the dreaded 'Terrible Two's' phase.* Surprisingly it is sometimes muddled with **faze**, meaning 'to disconcert, confuse or worry': *The fact that his trousers had split didn't seem to faze him one bit!*

phlegm, phlegmatic

Apart from being infernally difficult to spell and pronounce (*flem, fleg-MAT-ik*) these two are also hard to relate to each other; but there *is* a relationship. Rarely, you may come across a remark that a person has **phlegm**. In this case, it is not respiratory mucus of the throat-clearing kind (also called **phlegm**) but meaning that the person is 'self-possessed, imperturbable, cool'. Hence **phlegmatic**: unemotional, indifferent, stolid, not easily excited.

pick. See **choose, pick**

picturesque, picaresque

Picturesque means 'visually pleasing and charming'; **picaresque** describes an episodic form of fiction featuring the adventures of a rogue hero.

pidgin, pigeon

Because these are pronounced alike they are occasionally confused. **Pidgin** is a bastardised language, made up of elements of one or more languages, which is understood by people whose own languages render communication with each other difficult or impossible. In Papua New Guinea, pidgin linguistically helps to unite over six hundred different tribes and groups, each with its own language.

piebald, skewbald

A **piebald** horse has black and white markings; a **skewbald** horse is brown or fawn and white.

Pilgrim Fathers. See **Founding Fathers, Pilgrim Fathers**

pirate, buccaneer, corsair, privateer

Although more reminiscent of the 17th century, these terms are occasionally used in modern contexts. A **pirate** was someone who had committed a robbery, hijacking or other felony not only on the high seas, but in any place, port or river under the jurisdiction of the British Lord High Admiral. **Buccaneers** were Caribbean pirates of the 17th century; **corsairs** were pirates or privateers operating in the Mediterranean; **privateers** were captains or ship-owners licensed by the British Admiralty to commit piracy – a proportion of their loot being delivered to the Crown.

pitiful, piteous, pitiable

Pitiful means 'arousing pity' but can also be used to mean 'deserving contempt': *The amount they finally raised for the family was truly pitiful.* **Piteous** and **pitiable** are synonyms though less used: *They found the old man in a piteous/pitiable state.*

plaid. See **tartan, plaid**

plaintiff, plaintive

A **plaintiff** is someone who brings a civil action in a court of law: *Through her barrister, the plaintiff listed a dozen grievances against her neighbours.* **Plaintive** means 'mournful and melancholy': *At night the aid team couldn't escape the plaintive cries of the grieving mothers.*

platonic, Platonic, plutonic

Platonic (capital 'P') relates to the philosophical teachings of Plato; **platonic** (small 'p') is almost always associated with the term **platonic love**, meaning a love or affection that is free from sexual desire: *Despite everyone's suspicions, David and Ruth insisted that their friendship was purely platonic.* **Plutonic** is a geological term pertaining to rocks that have originated from the earth's molten mass.

plebiscite, referendum, poll, ballot, election

A **plebiscite** is a direct vote by citizens on an issue of supreme national importance such as a change of sovereignty or frontier. A **referendum** is usually accepted to mean a direct vote by citizens to confirm a proposed change in the law or constitution or to vote on an issue of great public importance. A **poll** is the casting and recording of votes in an **election**, a democratic process in which candidates are approved by the **electorate** for government or local government office. A **ballot** is the practice of electing candidates or deciding a course of action by marking the choice on a paper which is deposited in a sealed **ballot box** and afterwards counted.

plurals. See **Singulars and Plurals**

podium. See **dais, lectern, podium, rostrum**

point of view. See **standpoint, point of view, viewpoint**

policy. See **ambition *vs* policy**

politic, politics, political

Politic (pron. *POL-ih-tik*) means 'prudent, sensible, shrewd': *The management decided it was politic to refrain from commenting on the issue.* **Politics**, the noun, describes the practice of government; **political** is the adjective. **Politics** can be singular or plural: *Politics is not a science, but an art* (Bismarck); *The Prime Minister is one reason why politics are so deeply unfashionable these days.*

Poo, Pooh

At least one British newspaper 'stepped in it' when reporting on an auction at Bonham's in London at which a lump of fossilised dinosaur dung was to be offered for sale. In its report, the paper jocularly referred to the item as 'a piece of polished **pooh**'. This brought on an avalanche of complaint mail – this letter is typical: *Bonham's is not auctioning 'polished pooh' but polished* ***poo***. *By failing to maintain this important distinction, well-loved phrases such as "Wherever I go there's always Pooh", come to take an unfortunate meaning which Pooh-lovers like myself find odious.* The writer was, of course, referring to the famous children's storybook character Pooh, from *Winnie-the-Pooh* and *The House at Pooh Corner.*

populist, popularist, populariser

Populist derives from the 19th-century US People's Party and is still sometimes used to describe a politician on the side of the 'little man'. A **populariser** is someone who makes causes attractive and acceptable to the public. A **spin doctor** is someone (usually in politics) paid to put a favourable 'spin' on potentially damaging news or policy. **Popularist** is occasionally incorrectly used for **populariser** but as a word it was pensioned off a century ago.

pool. See snooker, billiards, pool

portable. See potable, portable

poring, pouring

*'Here is John Major **pouring** over his newspaper'* (*Observer,* 17 July 1998) reports columnist Richard Ingrams. This particular gaffe often occurs, even in *The Times*: *'There was the lone figure of Sir Charles… pouring over plans…'* What is obviously intended is **poring**, meaning 'to make a close study or examination'.

pornographic. See obscene, pornographic, erotic

portentous. See pretentious, portentous

position. See **situation, position**

positive, positively
Some authorities object to using the adjective **positive** to replace the adverb **positively**, as in *think positive* instead of the grammatically correct *think positively.*

possible, plausible, feasible
Possible means that something could exist, happen or be done; **feasible** means that something really can be done. If an argument or statement appears to be true or reasonable, it is **plausible**: *The plan was plausible, for although the river was subject to flooding, it was still feasible to construct the bridge.*

potable, portable
Potable means 'drinkable'; **portable** describes anything that can be carried easily.

POTABLE, PORTABLE

pouring. See **poring, pouring**

practical, practicable
Practical has a wide range of meanings, including 'useful, usable, sensible, realistic, efficient': *Although it was practicable to scale the wall with a rope, they agreed that a more practical plan would be to find a ladder.* **Practicable** means 'feasible, capable of being done and put into practice'. Both words have opposites: **impractical**, meaning 'although possible, ineffective, inconvenient or useless', and **impracticable**, meaning 'impossible, unfeasible, unattainable': *The idea of combining the two wedding receptions was finally written off*

as impractical; Everything that science had taught him screamed that a perpetual motion machine was impracticable.

practically, virtually

The difference in meaning between these two words is now practically/virtually non-existent. **Practically** used to define 'in practical terms, for practical purposes, in practice', whereas now it is used as a synonym for 'almost, very nearly, as good as, to all intents and purposes'. **Virtually** today means 'nearly, practically, having the same effect' – so that modern meanings of both words have collided as in this example, where either word can be switched: *Living on anything they could find, the people were practically starving, and clean water was virtually non-existent.*

practice, practise

*The doctor had **practised** medicine for over forty years, thirty of them from his **practice** in Harley Street.* **Practice** is the noun: *piano practice, it is not the usual practice to tip, let's put theory into practice*; while **practise** is the verb: *the tribe practises ritual murder, he's a non-practising Anglican.* In American English, **practice** serves as both noun and verb.

pragmatic, practical

A **pragmatic** individual approaches a problem with practical considerations and results in mind rather than with theories. Even so, the pragmatic approach is not necessarily practical. A **practical** person is also not too impressed by theories but knows how to do things and actually gets them done.

prawn. See scampi, shrimp, prawn

precede, proceed, supersede

To **precede** is to go before or come before; to **proceed** is to continue or to go forward: *The Archbishop preceded the Queen as they proceeded up the aisle to the altar.* **Supersede** means to displace or replace someone or something: *Many people regretted that the Authorised Version had been superseded by the Revised English Bible.*

precipitate, precipitant, precipitous

All three derive from the Latin *praecipitare* (to throw down headlong), and the first two are concerned with unexpected and hasty action. *She precipitated her dismissal by swearing at the supervisor; You could say that Dawn's swearing at the supervisor was a rather precipitant action.* Here **precipitated** is used to mean 'caused to happen sooner than expected' and **precipitant** to mean 'impulsive and hasty'. The primary meaning of **precipitous** is 'extremely steep'; *She lost her nerve on the mountain's precipitous ascent.*

précis, résumé

A *precis* (in English, appears in italics and the accent is optional) is a brief written summary of the essential points of a text or speech. A *résumé* (retain the accents) is a descriptive summary, usually of some event. In American English, **resume** (no accents) is also a *curriculum vitae* or CV.

predicate, predict

Predicate seems to be catching on as a synonym for **predict** – it is not. **Predict** means 'to foretell', whereas the traditional meaning of **predicate** is 'to imply, affirm or assert': *The spokesman predicated that the election result would turn on the issue of inflation but declined to predict the result.* In American English, **predicate** invariably means 'based' and it is increasingly (and unfortunately) being used in this sense in the UK : *His views on economic policy are predicated on the need to lower inflation; In Mr Ashby's mind there was no question of losing, so everything was predicated on winning.*

prediction, predilection

Predilection has nothing to do with predicting. To have a **predilection** means 'to have a preference or predisposition for something': *Kathleen confessed to a predilection for old-fashioned sticky puddings.*

Precooked and Other Prefixes

On offer at most supermarkets are **precooked** meals. But can anything be **precooked**? It is either cooked or it isn't; and how can you cook something before you cook it? Perhaps such meals should be **pre-tested** – but just how do you accomplish that? Is a **pre-test** a test before a test? Then there is the **pre-planned** wedding, no doubt for a couple who are *pre-engaged*. These are redundancies or nonsenses, take your pick.

Yet **pre-empt** and **pre-emptive** are perfectly respectable dictionary words (from the Latin *praeemere*, to buy beforehand), the desirable status also awarded to **precondition.** But when does a *condition* become a *precondition* – or do we really mean **prerequisite**?

---

pre-empt, prevent

To **pre-empt** is to do something or obtain something beforehand, or to appropriate something in advance of other claims: *John's generous offer pre-empted any further bickering among the family.* To **prevent** is to hinder or stop an action.

premier, premiere

Premier means 'first or foremost' and is often used as a title for a country's leading statesman. **Premiere** is used exclusively to describe the first performances of plays and films, and can be a noun or a verb: *Shortly after its premiere in London next week the musical will premiere on Broadway.*

premise, premises

Premises describes land and buildings: *The firm has just moved to new premises in the High Street.* **Premises** is always plural, whereas **premise** is singular, meaning an 'assumption, theory or hypothesis': *The general's strategy was, in the opinion of many of his officers, rather too heavily based on the premise that the enemy was too weak to attack.*

preoccupied. See occupied, preoccupied

prerequisite. See perquisite, prerequisite

prescribe, proscribe, ascribe

The first two are almost opposites. **Prescribe** means 'to recommend a course of action or to lay down rules'; **proscribe** means 'to banish or forbid': *Bill's doctor had prescribed a course of antibiotics and three days in bed; Smoking is proscribed on the Underground.* **Ascribe** means 'to attribute, to credit with': *The scientists ascribed the unsettled weather to volcanic activity in the Pacific region.*

presently. See soon, presently

pressured, pressurised

The witness told the court that he had been constantly pressurised not to give evidence. This is an example of very loose usage of a scientific term concerned with the compression of gas or liquid. **Pressured** is to be preferred.

prestigious

This is an interesting example of how persistent misuse of a word can change its meaning. Until the late 19th century, the sole meaning of **prestigious** was 'cunning, tricky, fraudulent', springing from **prestidigitation**, or sleight of hand. Somehow, it became linked with **prestige** – when its meaning took a leap, too: 'to have status, influence and fame': *Of all London clubs the Reform is regarded as one of the most prestigious.* Nowadays, only etymologists would be aware of the word's original meaning.

presume. See assume, presume

presumptuous, presumptive

These are often confused. **Presumptuous** behaviour is arrogant, insolent, impertinent, and unwarranted: *It was presumptuous of the chairman to start the meeting with only half the members present.* Something **presumptive** is based on a presumption – the belief that something is or will be true: *The case was considerably weakened by the presumptive evidence that a body existed even though it had not been found.*

pretence, pretense, pretext

Pretence (**pretense** in American English) is the act of pretending; its near synonym, a **pretext**, is a fictitious reason or false excuse: *He abandoned the pretence of having MI5 connections; He lured her into confessing, on the pretext that he was her friend.*

pretentious, portentous

A **pretentious** person is showy, self-important and pompous and inclined to make exaggerated claims. Although one meaning of **portentous** is also 'self-important and pompous', its primary meaning is 'ominously foreshadowing some momentous or awe-inspiring event': *James was convinced that his dream was a portentous warning of what marriage to Annabel would be like.*

pretext. See pretence, pretense, pretext

prevaricate, procrastinate

These are commonly confused. To **prevaricate** is to act falsely or evasively with the intention of deceiving; to 'be economical with the truth' by deliberately being misleading: *When asked if the problem would be dealt with immediately the Minister prevaricated with a barrage of waffle and dubious statistics.* To **procrastinate** is to waste time – 'never to do something today that you can do tomorrow'; *It was clear that the Minister was indulging in the gentle art of procrastination on the question of getting the Beef Ban lifted.*

preventative, preventive

Both mean 'to prevent something from happening or recurring'. In the medical sense, **preventative** is increasingly being used as a noun: *The view of the preventive medicine lobby is that, against the common cold, vitamin C is an effective preventative.*

previously. See hitherto, previously

prima facie. See *a priori, prima facie*

Primates and Primates

An ape is a **primate**, which is defined as a placental animal with flexible hands and feet, good eyesight and a highly developed brain. A **primate** is also an Archbishop. Confusion reigned recently at the Wisconsin Regional Primate Center which, when compiling an *International Directory of Primatology*, wrote to the Anglican Archbishop of Canada, the Most Revd. Michael Peers, requesting details of his reproductive status, sex ratio and age structure. The Archbishop complained mildly that the Centre seemed to be trying to make an ape out of him but eventually the confusion was sorted out with apologies all round.

principal, principle

A pair of classic confusables! In a recent article in *The Guardian* the writer managed a confusable 'hat-trick': *There isn't even a principal at stake here... Sir Bryan said he still accepted the compensation principal but, as far as BT is concerned, accepting the principal is unlikely ever to translate into actual contributions.* In all three cases the correct word is *principle*. The meanings of **principle** are fairly straightforward: it can be a fundamental truth, a belief or doctrine, an agreed rule of action or conduct. **Principal** can be an adjective (meaning 'of primary importance') or a noun (meaning 'a person who is the leader, the head, first in importance'): *The school principal said that his principal aim was to insist on students observing a code of strict moral principles.* In the financial sense, **principle** is money, capital or property on which interest accrues: *His father had taught him to spend the interest if you must, but never touch the principle.*

prior, prior to, before

In *I have a prior engagement*, **prior** is used in its proper adjectival sense, meaning 'previous'. Some writers, however, are prone to use the quasi-legal **prior to**: *Prior to the meeting we had a few drinks.* Replace with the more direct **before**.

prise, pry, prize

To **prise** is to force something open, usually by levering: *After considerable effort she managed to prise the lid from the jar; They finally prised the information from the prisoner.* Although an alternative spelling is **prize**, its use only causes confusion with the long-established meaning of **prize**: the reward or honour given for success or for winning something. The use of **pry open** for **prise** in American English is creeping into the UK and, again, is being confused with the traditional meaning of **pry**, which is to snoop and meddle or poke your nose into someone else's affairs.

pristine

Often misused to mean 'spotlessly clean', **pristine** in fact means 'pure and uncorrupted, original and unspoiled': *The experts hoped to restore the ancient lamp to its pristine state.* See also *Catachrestically Speaking…*

privateer. See **pirate, buccaneer, corsair, privateer**

privy, privvy

'My fear was that some larger game was going on to which I was not privvy.' Readers of the *Sunday Telegraph* on 22 November 1998 were probably relieved to learn that not all privys were secrets or exclusive. But if they had tried to find **privvy** in the dictionary they would have been disappointed, because there is no such word. The word **privy** does all human jobs; It can mean 'participating in something secret, as well as a lavatory, especially an outside model'. There are also privy purses, councils, seals, chambers and, privy to no one except when occupied, common garden privies.

probity, property

The royal family nowadays is a model of property compared with those days (Letter to *The Sunday Times*, 1995). What the writer meant was **probity**, a quality combining honesty, integrity, fairness and open-mindedness.

procrastinate. See **prevaricate, procrastinate**

Prepositional Problems

Are you **angry with** Simon, or **angry at** Simon? Do you **cater for** Julie's whims, or **cater to** them? Have you ever been **compared to** a famous person, or **compared with** one? Using prepositions is a bit of a mating game, often idiomatic, sometimes illogical, and a constant curse for virtually every writer.

Problematical prepositions fall into groups. In some cases a certain preposition is prescribed: *Thomas was **oblivious of** the din* – not *oblivious to the din*. Then you discover that half the population is using that forbidden preposition 'to' anyway. In other cases different prepositions will supply different meanings: *June **agreed with** Jim about buying the house* is not the same as *June **agreed to** Jim buying the house.* Then there are instances where there is a choice; for example, **affinity with** and **affinity between**. And finally there are prepositions that aren't needed at all: **visited with** and **infringe upon** are two common redundancies.

Here are some of the prepositional matings that can cause confusion:

acquiesce in

affinity with/between (not **to** or **for**)

agree to (accept); *agree with* (concur)

alternative to

apropos of, or *apropo*
ask of / for
averse to
brood on / over (but not **about**)

capacity to / for
cater for (US = *cater to*)
compare to (liken to); *compare with* (to look for differences, similarities)
concur in (an opinion); *concur with* (someone)
conform to / with

connive at (illegal action); *connive with* (someone)
consequent on / upon
die of (not *die from*)

differ from (be unlike); *differ with* (disagree)
different from (preferred to *different to*, and also to *different than*)
disgusted at (something); *disgusted with* (someone)
encroach (without a preposition, but usually followed *by on/upon*)
identical to (not **with**)
inferior/superior to (not **than**)
knack of
meet with (problems, delays); *meet* people (preposition is redundant)
oblivious of (preferred to *oblivious to*)
opposite to (not *opposite from*)
partake of
participate in
substitute for (not *substitute with*)

sympathy for (having compassion for another); *sympathy with* (sharing feelings with another)

odigal, generous

To be **prodigal** is to be recklessly wasteful and extravagant, to be **generous** is to be unselfish and ready to give freely.

product

Product – not **a product** or **the product** or **products** – is used increasingly as jargon, in a catch-all fashion. A film industry spokesman remarked on Britain's failure to make more commercially successful movies: *Today there's very little worthwhile product coming out of our studios.*

proffer, offer

What little distinction there was or is between the two is exceedingly fine, but **proffer** is more formal and implies offering or tendering in expectation of acceptance: *The amount proffered by the management was calculated to make the men think twice about calling another strike.*

169

prognosis. See **diagnosis, prognosis**

program, programme

Programme is the traditional British spelling; **program** in the US. However **program** has enjoyed wide use in Britain (mainly due to the computer industry) to the extent that two spellings and two meanings are emerging: **programme** for TV, radio, theatre performances, etc. (*Where are tonight's television programmes?*), and **program** for schedule, project, plan, proposition, etc: *The owners finally released details of their building program.*

promise. See **assure, ensure, insure, promise**

prone, prostrate, recumbent, supine

All four refer to the action of lying down – but all have different meanings. To lie **prone** is to lie face downwards; **prostrate** assumes the same position but suggests exhaustion and helplessness. **Recumbent** is lying in any comfortable position, while **supine** is lying listlessly (spinelessly?) on the back, looking upwards.

propensity, proclivity

Both mean 'having a natural tendency or inclination' although **proclivity** is sometimes given a twist to imply 'naughty or unnatural', as in: *We all knew about Heather's sexual proclivities.*

prophecy, prophesy

Prophecy is the noun; **prophesy** is the verb: *The old farmer prophesied a hard winter, but his last prophecy about the weather had been totally wrong.*

propitious, auspicious

These synonyms mean 'favourably inclined' although a few writers like to preserve a fine difference of meaning: **auspicious**, meaning 'the circumstances are a good omen pointing to success', and **propitious**, meaning 'the conditions are directly conducive to success': *Everyone felt that the inauguration was an auspicious occasion; The chairman judged by the happy tone of the meeting that it would be a propitious time to introduce the subject of increased membership fees.*

proportion. See **percentage, proportion, part**

proposal, proposition

While both mean 'something suggested', **proposal** is more of an offer, as in *a proposal of marriage*; a **proposition** is a stronger suggestion, even an assertion, that might invite discussion before agreement: *The team looked carefully at the detailed proposition that had been put to them.* That said, they are both fairly interchangeable.

prosecute. See **persecute, prosecute**

prosthesis, prothesis

A **prosthesis** is an artificial or mechanical replacement of a damaged or missing part of the (usually human) body: *After her mastectomy, Anne resumed normal life thanks to an expertly-fitted prosthesis.* **Prothesis** is an extra sound placed at the beginning of a word, as in the Spanish *escriber* (to write) from the Latin *scribere*.

Prostates and Proctors

A not uncommon malapropism is: *He's seeing the doctor because of his prostrate trouble.* **Prostrate** means to lie face down, while the **prostate** is the male reproductive gland that tends to peter out with increasing age. And a **proctor**, perhaps because it rhymes with *doctor*, is sometimes thought to specialise in diseases of the anus. In fact, a **proctologist** does that; a **proctor** is a university official, one of two elected annually.

---

protagonist, antagonist

Mr Castle-Reeves is fortunate to have two stalwart protagonists to help him in the forthcoming by-election. The use of **protagonist** to mean 'ally or supporter' is a common error; a **protagonist** is the leading character or key player in an event, and thus there can never be more than one: *He was grateful to have the millionaire shipowner as his protagonist for the difficult election ahead.* An **antagonist** is an adversary or opponent.

protest, protest against

Many grammarians object to the use of **protest at, protest against** and **protest about**: *The angry students protested against the closing of the cafeteria.* It is customary to use **protest** alone as a verb, as in *She protested her innocence*, but in parallel examples such as *The nurses protested the government's rejection of their pay claim*, it cries out, as Fowler puts it, for the insertion of **against**.

proverbial

Although as a nurse she travelled extensively through Africa she never fell victim to the proverbial tropical tummy. Unless there is a proverb about 'tropical tummy', which is doubtful, one shouldn't refer to the ailment as *proverbial*. Here is

proverbial used correctly: *Always arriving and departing, George was like the proverbial rolling stone.*

provided that, providing that

Provided and **providing** are conjunctions that traditionally are followed by *that: Provided/providing that Jill and Sue arrive on time we'll just make it to the train.* However usage is beginning to favour the abandonment of *that* and little harm seems to have been done: *Provided the company instals the smoke-removing equipment, they should get the licence.*

provincial, parochial

In the UK, **provincial** tends to be applied to anything and anywhere outside London, but strictly speaking it means 'relating to the provinces'. The term is often used (by city dwellers) in a derogatory way: *Her taste in theatre, my dear, is rather provincial.* The compass of **parochial** shrinks to parish boundaries; it also implies a viewpoint that is narrow and limited in outlook and interest.

prudent. See discreet, circumspect, prudent

prudery, prurience

These are opposites. **Prudery** is the affectation of excessive modesty and primness, especially with regard to sex. **Prurience** is having an excessively morbid interest in sex and eroticism.

pry. See prise, prize, pry

Psycho Matters

This can be an area of potentially embarrassing confusion. **Psychosis** is the generic term for disorders of the mind; **psychotics** suffer from **psychoses** (plural of **psychosis**), and **psychiatry** is the branch of medical science which deals with mental disorders and their diagnosis, treatment and prevention. **Psychotics** may be **psychopaths**, persons with anti-social personality disorders; **schizophrenics**, whose minds and feelings have parted, causing withdrawal from reality; or **neurotics**, persons with unbalanced minds suffering from obsessive behaviour, unreasonable fears and hysteria. **Psychology** is the study of the mind and its behaviour; **psychoanalysis** is a treatment method based on the patient's conscious and subconscious memories of his or her past life, and **psychotherapy** is the treatment of nervous disorders generally.

---

punctilious. See **meticulous, punctilious, conscientious, thorough**

pupil, student

Although somewhat interchangeable, a **pupil** is a child at school who is taught in disciplined classes, while a **student** studies at a centre of higher education and is expected to be self-disciplined. However, secondary-school pupils are often referred to as students.

purport, purported

Purport means 'supposed to be, or claims to be': *With its official stamps and seals, the document purports to be genuine.* **Purported** is now often used to mean 'rumoured': *They were intrigued by the purported £15m government subsidy.*

purposely, purposefully

Purposely means 'intentionally, on purpose': *That man tripped me and did it purposely!* **Purposefully** means 'determined and resolute': *Miriam took a deep breath and purposefully rose to address the meeting.*

pursuant to, pursuivant

Pursuant to means 'in accordance with, in agreement with': *Pursuant to regulations, passengers must now disembark from the port exits.* The word is nowadays regarded as legalistic and a bit old-fashioned. **Pursuivant** is a term used in heraldry.

Q

qua

The occasional appearance of this Latin word understandably rattles many people. It acts as a sort of abbreviation and means 'in the role of, in the capacity of': *Emma sought his opinion, not qua her legal adviser but as a friend, on the question of her claim against the Smiths.*

quantitative, qualitative

Quantitative refers to measurable quantities and proportions; **qualitative** refers to quality, of characteristics, properties, attributes and singularities: *The agency agreed to commission a qualitative study of the effects of a price rise, while the client would look after the quantitative issues.*

quantity, number

Use **number** only when the items are countable: *To make the juice, you need a large number of oranges and a generous quantity of water.*

quantum leap

This term is used somewhat loosely: *The lecturer's opinion of his class took a quantum leap when it achieved the second highest pass rate in the county.* Strictly speaking, a **quantum leap** is a sudden highly significant change, or breakthrough, from its use in physics meaning the sudden jump of an electron, atom, etc., from one energy level to another (*CED*).

quasi, quasi-

Although it can be used independently as an adverb, meaning 'as if, or as it were', **quasi** is usually used and encountered in its combining, hyphenated form: *quasi-official, quasi-religious,* etc. This too means 'as if, as it were, almost but not really': *The tribunal had the necessary quasi-judicial powers to hand down a binding decision.*

queer. See odd, queer

question, begging the

To **beg the question** is to assume the truth of a proposition that remains to be proved. A secondary meaning, not unknown in politics, is avoiding giving an answer by posing another question.

queue, line

A **queue** in British English is a **line** in American English. The use of the latter term in the UK usually attracts objections, as in this letter to *The Times*: *I am disappointed to see that even The Times's leader columns are succumbing to the relentless invasion of American English. In your leader on the National Lottery you state that 'stores which sell tickets have lottery-only lines on a Saturday'. Don't you mean 'Shops... have lottery-only queues'?*

quietness, quietude, quiescent

Quietness and **quietude** are synonyms describing a state of little or no sound or movement. **Quietude**, however, is commonly used to describe a state of peace and tranquility: *During her convalescence, Sarah enjoyed the quietude of their Cornwall retreat.* **Quiescent**, the adjective, can also mean **quiet** but its primary use is to indicate a state of inactivity or dormancy: *The villagers were relieved to find that the volcano was quiescent.*

quite, rather

Quite is commonly used in two different ways and this inevitably leads to ambiguity. First, **quite** can mean 'completely, totally, entirely, absolutely': *The runner flung himself to the ground, quite exhausted.* Then, **quite** can mean 'somewhat, sort of, rather': *The horse was going quite well until the fifth hurdle.* The latter usage is not nearly so common in American English as it is in Britain. If you were to say to an American, *I think the movie is quite good,* he or she would take it that you meant it was really very good, whereas in fact what you meant was that the movie was 'okay, so-so, acceptable'. In most cases any ambiguity can be removed by substituting *rather*.

quixotic

Often misused to mean 'foolishly pointless', **quixotic** actually means 'hopelessly idealistic and ridiculously chivalrous', and is derived from the adventures of Don Quixote.

quorum, quota

A **quorum** is an agreed number of people required to be present before a meeting can be held; a **quota** is 'a proportion, a limit, an agreed number or amount'.

quote, cite

Both overlap in their meaning of 'referring to or repeating something said or written': *To support his argument the MP quoted/cited several authoritative opinions on the subject.* **Cite** also means 'to summon', especially to be summoned to appear in court: *The new neighbour was cited in Mary and Ralph's divorce case;* and 'to mention or commend', usually for bravery: *During the Vietnam War he was cited on three occasions.*

R

racism, racialism

The two have in the past been allotted separate meanings by some dictionaries (the *Routledge Dictionary of Race and Ethnic Relations* has **racism** = discriminatory attitudes and beliefs; **racialism** = abuse directed at another race); nowadays, both are viewed as synonyms, with the shorter **racism** being preferred.

rack. See **wrack, rack**

racket, racquet

The Times sensibly prescribes **racket** for tennis, for noise and commotion, and for fraudulent enterprise. **Racquet** remains an acceptable alternative spelling for the tennis racket.

rain, reign, rein

RAIN, REIGN, REIN

Rain we all know about; to **reign** is to rule or exercise supreme authority, and a **reign** (the noun) is a period during which a particular monarch rules: *The reign of George III was a turbulent one*. To **rein in** is to check or control, and a **rein** (the noun) is the strap which controls and guides a horse or other animal. **Rein** is also used in two opposite senses: *to keep a tight rein* (restrain) and *to give free rein* (allow freedom): *The constant rain of criticism did nothing to stop Henry VIII giving full rein to his appetites throughout his entire reign*.

raise, raze, rise

To **raise** is to elevate; to **raze** is the reverse: 'to destroy completely, to level with the earth', so the well-known phrase *The house was razed to the ground* is tautological. **Raise** is also creeping in to mean 'rear children', but most British parents still seem to prefer to raise sheep and bring up a family. You also **raise** your head but **rise** in the morning and **rise** from your bed. In British English, a **pay rise** is the equivalent of the American **raise**.

rang, rung

The team rung the bells for half an hour is incorrect: the team *rang* the bells. **Rung** is the past participle of the verb *to ring*, so it would be correct to say *The team had rung the bells for half an hour*.

range. See spectrum, range

rapt, wrapped, rapped

Rapt means 'engrossed and absorbed' (*The children listened with rapt attention to the storyteller*); **wrapped** means 'enveloped, enfolded, blanketed': *The trappers were well wrapped against the bitter cold*. **Rapped** describes the act of striking something sharply (*The caller rapped several times on the door*) and also the fast, rhythmic monologue delivered over a music track: *Public Enemy rapped non-stop until well after midnight*.

rather. See quite

ravaged, ravenous, ravished, ravishing

Ravaged means 'extensively damaged, ruined or destroyed', although the word is sometimes used in a romantic sense: *Sheila was swept away by his sunburned, ravaged face*. To be **ravenous** is to be famished, starving. **Ravish** requires some care in usage; its primary meaning is 'to enrapture, to be carried away with great delight', but it is also associated with violence and rape and therefore the possibility of ambiguity is likely. **Ravishing** is safe; it means 'enchanting, delightful, lovely'.

react, respond

A **reaction** is a spontaneous and immediate **response** to some stimulus, so **react** should not be used as a substitute for feeling, answer, reply, opinion or response – all of which require considered thought. *The mayor's reaction to the crisis was to sleep on it* is the sort of usage that has become acceptable today, but careful writers would use **response**.

readable. See legible, readable

real, really

There should be no problem with the adjective **real**; it means 'existing in the physical world; true, actual, genuine'. But the adverb **really,** which we use constantly, can cause headaches. The *Daily Mirror Style Book* describes **really** as '0.1 per cent colouring matter' but acknowledges its usefulness in providing an artificial boost to otherwise dull statements: *The career of hairdresser Karen, 20, from Middlesex, is really taking off…* If you drop the *really,* the announcement does go rather flat.

really. See actually, virtually, really

rebut, refute, repudiate, deny

There are several shades of meaning among this lot. To **rebut** is to contradict by argument with the support of evidence; to **deny** is to merely insist that an allegation or statement is false; to **repudiate** is to disown, reject or refuse to admit a charge or claim; to **refute** – the strongest and most convincing denial of all – is to *prove* that an accusation is false. Neither **rebut** nor **refute** is a synonym for **deny** or **dispute.**

receipt, recipe

A **receipt** (pron. *rih-SEET*) is a written acknowledgement that something (money, goods, a letter or document) has been received; a **recipe** (pron. *RES-ih-pee*) is a formula of ingredients and instructions to make something, usually in cookery.

recollect. See remember, recollect

recount, re-count

To **recount** is to relate or recite the details of a story or event: *Jim recounted his amazing adventures to a fascinated audience.* To **re-count** is to count again: *Because the ballot result was so close, a re-count was demanded.*

recoup, recover

Recoup means to 'regain or replace a loss', usually financial: *The company*

managed to recoup the previous year's losses with a series of shrewd investments.
Recover is synonymous but is used in a broader way: *When she recovered from the fainting spell she also recovered her composure.*

recover, re-cover

To **recover** is to regain or retrieve something after losing it; to **re-cover** something is to cover again: *They decided to have the old suite re-covered in dark red velvet.*

recrudescent. See resurgent, recrudescent

reduce. See exhaust, deplete, reduce

reduce, lessen

These are mostly interchangeable, except that **lessen** tends to be used where numbers are involved in the quantity: *By reducing his petrol consumption, he lessened the number of weekly trips to the garage.*

redundancy. See tautology, pleonasm

referee. See umpire, referee

referendum. See plebiscite, referendum, poll, ballot, election

reflection, reflexion

In the senses of an optical image, and careful consideration, the first spelling is preferred; **reflexion** should be reserved when it is used in the anatomical sense.

refute. See rebut, refute, repudiate, deny

regard for, regard to

To have **regard for** someone is to respect and admire that person: *He told us he had the highest regard for her.* The phrases **in regard to**, **with regard to** and **as regards** mean 'concerning, in relation to or with reference to': *With regard to the matter you raised yesterday, it is being dealt with.* The expressions are rather stiff and formal, and wordy.

regardless, irregardless

Although it is occasionally heard (and sometimes written) **irregardless** is not a word. **Regardless** is used in two senses: as an adjective to mean 'unthinking and reckless' (*The two men fought on the balcony, regardless of the danger of the six-storey drop*), and as an adverb meaning 'in spite of everything': *Its rudder damaged, spinnaker gone and sails in shreds, the yacht sailed on regardless.*

register, registry

A **register** can be a record of names, transactions, events, correspondence, data, etc.; a **registry** is a place where registers are kept: But watch out: a Register's Office (not Registry) where births, deaths and marriages are recorded, and civil marriages celebrated.

registrar, bursar, bursary

A **registrar** keeps registers and official records; a **bursar** manages the financial affairs of a school, college or university. A **bursary** is a scholarship awarded by a school or college.

regret, remorse

To **regret** (verb) or to express **regret** (noun) is to feel sorry, sympathetic, upset or repentant about something unfortunate that has occurred. **Remorse** is synonymous except that it implies that the person feeling remorse is the one guiltily responsible.

regretful, regretfully, regrettable, regrettably

The first two mean 'to feel sorry or to express regret', while the second pair is used when sorrow or regret is *caused*: *Regretfully, I am forced to cancel our plans for the visit; The problems caused by the cancellation are regrettable, but I had no other choice.*

regulate, relegate

To **regulate** means 'to adjust, control or restrict'; to **relegate**, as most football fans know, means 'to consign to an inferior position'.

reign. See rain, reign, rein

reiterate, repeat, iterate

To **repeat** means: 'to do, make or say something again'. **Reiterate** is a near synonym but tends to be used to express the repetition of a word, statement, account or request: *He carefully reiterated the terms of the agreement to make sure they were fully understood.* **Iterate** is a little-known and even lesser-used synonym for **reiterate.**

relapse, remission

A **relapse** is a return to a previous condition or former state; a **remission** is a respite from or abatement of a detrimental condition or the symptoms of a disease: *About 15% of multiple sclerosis patients have a fairly benign form of the disease, but 80% have remissions alternating with relapses that become successively worse.*

relation, relative

In the context of kinship, the two nouns are synonyms.

relatively, comparatively

Use only when there is something to be relative to, or something to compare with: *Although it appeared to be a most ambitious project, he said it would occupy* ***relatively/comparatively*** *little of his time.*

remember, recollect

To **remember** means 'to become consciously aware of something forgotten' or 'to retain something in the conscious mind'. To **recollect** is not instantaneous but requires some, often considerable, conscious mental effort: *Little by little she recalled the terrors she'd experienced on the journey.*

reminiscence, reminiscent

Some writers have difficulty using these. A **reminiscence** (noun) is a memory of some event or past experience: *The old sea captain was full of fascinating reminiscences.* **Reminiscent** (adjective) means 'stimulating memories' or 'stimulating comparisons with someone or something': *The paintings were reminiscent of the murals she'd seen in Venice many years before.*

remission. See **relapse, remission**

remorse. See **regret, remorse**

remuneration, renumeration

Possibly because of its presumed association with *numerate*, the misspelling of **remuneration** as **renumeration** is not uncommon. The former is correct, and is a reward or payment for work done or services rendered.

renascence, renascent, renaissance, Renaissance

Renascence is an alternative spelling of **renaissance**, meaning revival or rebirth, usually in the context of culture or learning: *The professor claimed that the world was witnessing the renaissance of the art of hieroglyphic communication.* **Renascent** is more often seen than **renascence**, and means 'growing and becoming active again'. The **Renaissance** (capital 'R') is the period, from the 14th to the 16th century, marking the European revival of art and classical scholarship, the end of the Middle Ages, and the rise of the modern world.

repel, repulse, repellent, repellant

Although both **repel** and **repulse** mean 'to force or drive back', they have other meanings, the usage of which can cause confusion. The related word

repulsive, for example, means 'causing distaste or disgust', but we do not say *His filthy, drunken state repulsed the other passengers* – instead we use **repelled**. Nor is **repel** appropriate when the meaning is 'to drive away or reject'; here usage demands **repulse**: *She repulsed his proposal by flinging the flowers to the floor.* **Repellant** can appear as a noun or adjective: *She found his behaviour repellent; The insect repellent seemed to be effective.* **Repellant** is incorrect.

replace. See **substitute, replace**

replica, copy, facsimile

It is generally accepted that a **replica** is a duplicate made by the original artist or maker, or made under his or her supervision. A **facsimile** is a copy of something exact in every respect and detail. A **copy** is the most general term and can be a mechanically produced duplicate (a photocopy, for example, or a printed reproduction), a written word-for-word transcription, or a hand-made imitation.

replicate, repeat

Although increasingly used as a synonym for **repeat, replicate** means rather more than that. Technically, a **replication** is a repetition of a study or of research, using the same data and methods, to confirm whether the results will be the same.

repository. See **depository, repository**

repudiate. See **rebut, refute, repudiate, deny**

request, behest

A **request** is a demand or expression of desire: *The hostess had requested that all the men wear black tie.* **Behest** is a near-synonym meaning 'authoritative request' and is used mostly in a formal context: *The children had attended the service at their late father's behest.*

requisite, requirement

These are near synonyms, broadly meaning 'something required'. But **requirement**, a noun, suggests an obligation or something demanded: *One of the requirements for the job was absolute punctuality,* while **requisite**, an adjective, implies 'something essential or indispensable': *Emily knew she had the requisite qualifications for the job.*

resin, rosin

These should not be regarded as alternative spellings or synonyms. **Resin** is a gummy exudation from certain trees and plants (for example, amber, copal), but the word is now also applied to a wide range of synthetic plastics. **Rosin** is the residue from the distillation of turpentine used in varnishes, paints and for treating the bows of stringed instruments.

resister, resistor

A **resister** is a person who resists, or who fights against something; a **resistor** is a component that introduces resistance into an electrical circuit.

resolve, solve

Resolve is often mistakenly used to mean **solve.** Sherlock Holmes did not resolve the case of the 'Crooked Man', he solved it. You **solve** a problem or mystery when you find an explanation for it: *Jim took less than two hours to solve the Rubik Cube puzzle.* To **resolve** means 'to firmly decide something, or to determine a course of action': *The meeting resolved to petition the Home Secretary.*

respectably, respectfully, respectively

Respectably means 'in a way that is honest, decent and deserving respect': *Although desperately poor the family was always dressed respectably.* **Respectfully** means 'with respect': *The men doffed their hats respectfully as the cortege went past.* **Respectively** means 'in the order given': *John, Amy and Sarah are aged twelve, nine and five respectively.*

respect of, in respect to, with respect to

In respect of and **with respect to** are pseudo-formal phrases commonly used to mean 'with reference or relation to'. **In respect to** is sometimes seen but is meaningless, and should not be used.

responsible. See accountable, responsible

restful, restive, restless

Restive and **restless** are the opposite of **restful,** which means 'peaceful, calm, inviting rest': *Aunt Elizabeth looked forward to the restful atmosphere of the lakeside hotel.* A **restless** person is one who cannot be still and quiet, while someone **restive** frets under restraint. The latter is mostly applied to animals: *The horses grew restive as the storm drew closer.*

restaurant, restaurateur

The latter owns or manages the former; note the spelling.

result. See upshot, result

résumé. See *précis, résumé*

resurgence, recrudesence

Resurgence means 'revival, reinvigoration, new life': *The huge numbers at the rally were a strong indication of the resurgence of nationalist feeling.* **Recrudescence** is sometimes wrongly used as a synonym which it most emphatically isn't; although it means 'to reappear or break out', it means this only in the sense of *worsening: The doctor was dismayed by the recrudescence of the wound, which they thought had healed weeks ago.*

retribution, restitution, reparation

Reparation is the act of making amends, or redressing a wrong, or repairing or restoring some damage or injury. **Restitution** can have an identical meaning but it also has recognition in law as the act of compensating for loss or injury, especially by returning something to its original state, for example, the removal of graffiti by the perpetrator. The meaning of **retribution** (from the Latin *retribuere* which means 'to repay') carries with it overtones of punishment and revenge, as well as and Divine judgement and should be used only to mean the act of punishing or taking revenge for some sin or injury.

revenge, avenge, vengeance

Revenge is personal retaliation: *I eventually got my revenge by having him arrested for harassment.* To **avenge** a wrong, the punishment is meted out by a third party as a form of rough justice: *They avenged my father's murder.* **Vengeance** is interchangeable with **revenge.**

reverse. See **converse, inverse, obverse, reverse**

review, revue

In a theatrical context, a **revue** is a performance of sketches, comedy routines, songs and dancing; a **review** is a critical assessment of any public performance: *Although the revue was enthusiastically received by the audience, the cast was shattered by the theatre critic's savage review.*

Rh negative, Rh positive

Short for 'rhesus factor', an antigen that produces antibodies that destroy the red blood cells in foetuses and new-born infants. Human blood containing the antigen is Rh positive; blood that does not contain the Rh factor is Rh negative.

rheumatism. See **arthritis, rheumatism, lumbago, sciatica**

rigour, rigorous, rigor

Rigour is a state of strictness, inflexibility, severity and hardship; **rigorous** is the adjective: *The monks were subjected to three years of rigorous discipline.* **Rigor** is the medical term for a violent attack of shivering, and also for the stiffness and rigidity of body tissues, as in *rigor mortis.* Both are spelt **rigor** in American English.

rime, rhyme
Rime is a rather archaic word for frost, used almost exclusively in a poetic context perhaps because it **rhymes** with *clime, climb, lime, mime, time,* etc.

riposte, retort
A **riposte** is a quick, sharp, sometimes witty reply. A **retort** is much the same, but is usually reserved to indicate a degree of anger and sarcasm.

robbery. See **burglary, robbery, stealing, theft**

rocks, stones
Boys throw **stones** in Britain; in the US they throw **rocks.** The separate words and their meanings (a **stone** is a small lump of **rock;** a **pebble** is even smaller, and rounder) are worth preserving.

Roman Catholic. See **catholic, Catholic**

roost, roast
The battle between **rule the roost** and **rule the roast** is a long and noble one, dating from 13th-century France. In the 1920s Fowler's, *Modern English Usage* and Chambers Dictionary, two of a number of authorities, still opted for 'roast' although, by the 1950s, Fowlers for one had switched its allegiance to 'roost'. Today, 'roost' is the most accepted.

Romany. See **gypsy, gipsy, Romany, traveller**

rostrum. See **dais, lectern, podium, rostrum**

rotund. See **orotund, rotund**

round, around, about
She looked round, or, *She looked around?* In the unintentionally comic first example, there is a temptation to substitute **around**, but this would be a departure from British usage; in British English, **round** is a linguistic fixture, while **around** is its standard equivalent in American English. In the UK and in the context of proximity, the differences are preserved; for example, to 'walk around the park' and 'to walk round the park' mean two different things; the first means to walk through and in the park, while the second means to

actually walk round the perimeter of the park. Nevertheless some flexibility in usage is obviously desirable, and we're already stuck with some usages. *We waited around; The smell lingered around for days; All year round; fenced all round; The wheels turned round; The boxer gradually came round...* are just a few. **Around** is also increasingly used to mean 'approximately': *We've had around three hundred replies.* **About** is to be preferred.

round robin

Many believe this term means a document that's distributed to or signed by a number of people who are agreed about a certain cause. Specifically, however, a **round robin** is a document signed in such a way (with the signatures arrayed in a circle, for example) to disguise the order in which they signed. In sporting terminology, a **round robin** is a tournament in which each player plays against every other player.

rouse, arouse

Both mean 'to awaken, to stir out of inactivity', but **rouse** tends to imply a physical response (*The sergeant roused the men from their bunks*) while **arouse** suggests a more emotional reaction: *Sally's frequent disappearances began to arouse his suspicions.*

rout, route

A **rout** (pronounced rowt) is a disorderly retreat; an overwhelming defeat; **to rout** (verb) is to cause a defeat or retreat: *The rabble was promptly routed by the well-trained guards.* **Rout** also has the less-used meaning of 'to dig, to turn over'; today's usage prefers **root**: *The pigs rooted among the leaves for acorns.* A **route** (pronounced root; rowt in the US) is the course planned or taken from one place to another during a journey. And watch the spelling of **routeing**: *Fred was in charge of routeing the buses.*

run, runs, manages, operates, directs

Grace runs a women's fashion shop in the High Street. The use of **run** and **runs** in this sort of context is sloppy, especially when there is no shortage of more specific substitutes: **manages, operates, directs, conducts**, etc.

rung. See rang, rung

rustic, rusticate

Something **rustic** is associated with the country or rural life, supposedly simple, peaceful and unsophisticated. To **rusticate** can mean 'to banish to the country', but its common meaning is to be sent down from a university as a punishment. In the architectural sense, **to rusticate** means 'to carve or cast deeply textured designs in masonry'.

S

saccharin, saccharine

Saccharin is the sugar substitute; **saccharine** means excessively sweet: *After a while the singer's saccharine voice began to get on my nerves.*

sacred, sacrosanct

Sacred means 'dedicated to religious use: holy, and not to be profaned'. **Sacrosanct** is more intensive, meaning 'pure and incorruptible, incapable of being violated'.

sadism, masochism

Sadism is the abnormal desire to inflict physical pain on others for (usually) sexual pleasure; **masochism** is the abnormal desire to be physically abused or humilated by another, again usually for sexual gratification.

salary, wages, remuneration

A **salary** is usually fixed as an annual rate, and paid by the month or week; **wages** are rates usually paid by the hour, day or week. **Remuneration** is payment for work or for services provided, not necessarily on a regular basis.

salon, saloon

Salon survives almost exclusively as a *hairdressing salon* or a *beauty salon*. A **saloon** in Britain is one of two or three drinking bars in a pub; in North America it is commonly a sleazy establishment serving alcohol. In the context of automobiles, a **saloon** in Britain is a **sedan** in the US.

same, similar

Harry sold six cars last week, and a similar number this week. What is meant here is *the **same** number this week;* **similar** means 'resembling something or someone'.

SALON, SALOON

sanatorium, sanitarium, sanatarium

A **sanatorium**. is a hospital or establishment for the treatment of invalids and convalescents; **sanitarium** is the American English spelling. **Sanatarium** is incorrect.

sanguine, sanguinary

Writers find this pair confusing to use. **Sanguinary** has one bloody meaning: 'attended with much bloodshed, bloodthirsty, flowing or stained with blood'. **Sanguine** also has its bloody aspect; it means 'blood-red and ruddy'. But it is also frequently used to mean 'optimistic, cheerful and confident': *Charles was quite sanguine about the team's prospects.* Use both with care.

sank, sunk, sunken

Sank is the past tense of **sink**, as is **sunk**: *With great relish Wilbur sank/sunk his teeth into the hamburger.* **Sank** is correct as an active verb: *She sank with all hands.* **Sunk** is correct as a passive verb: *The ship had been sunk by a torpedo.* **Sunken** is mostly encountered as an adjective: *sunken spirits, sunken cheeks, sunken treasure.*

sarcasm, satire. See **irony, sarcasm, satire**

sauce. See **ketchup, catsup, sauce, chutney, pickle**

scampi, shrimp, prawn, langoustine

Scampi are prawns fried in breadcrumbs or batter. **Prawns** are the crustaceans that grace prawn cocktails and range from the 1–4 in. Atlantic deepwater or Greenland prawns to the giant (up to 12 in.) Tiger prawns from

South-east Asia. **Shrimp** are a large family of marine decapods fished around Britain, of which the *Crangon vulgaris* is the main edible member. **Langoustine** to the French are **Dublin Bay prawns** to the British and look like miniature lobsters.

scan, glance, scrutinize

Scan can have opposite meanings. It can mean 'to look over in a casual manner': *Mr Hewitt picked up the newspaper and scanned the headlines.* However, **scan** can also mean 'to examine closely and thoroughly' and electronic scanners have been designed to minutely and systematically **scrutinize** objects. Make sure that your usage of **scan** is unambiguous. In this context, a **glance** is a quick look: *She had only time to glance at the table before the train left the station.*

scare, scarify

To **scare** is to frighten; to **scarify** is to scratch, abrade, break up or wound: *The general launched into a scarifying denouncement of the behaviour of his troops.*

sceptic, septic

A **sceptic** (in American English, *skeptic*) is a doubter who is unwilling to believe anything without superabundant proof. Something **septic** causes infection and putrefaction; in a **septic tank**, sewage is broken down by bacteria.

sceptical. See **cynical, sceptical**

sciatica. See **arthritis, rheumatism, lumbago, sciatica**

Scotland, Scotsman, Scot, Scotch, Scottish

Natives and institutions of Scotland are **Scottish** or **Scots**: *Scotsman, Scotswoman, Scottish smoked trout, Scots language, Scottish writers*, etc. The use of **Scotch** is mostly confined to *Scotch broth, Scotch mist* and, of course, *Scotch whisky*.

scotch

To **scotch** a rumour is to suppress it. Plans can be **scotched**, too, when the word means 'to put an end to, to prevent, to block': *The overnight rain scotched plans to resume play this morning.* **Scotch** in these contexts is not a slang expression but a word deriving from the Old French *escocher*, 'to cut'.

Scouts, Boy Scouts

The former Boy Scouts are now known in Britain simply as **Scouts**; Wolf Cubs are just **Cubs**; Girl Guides are **Guides**.

scrimp, skimp, skimpy

Both **scrimp** and **skimp** mean 'to be sparing, frugal, stingy': *Their mother* *scrimps/skimps on food for the family but smokes like a chimney.* **Skimp** has a second meaning which is to do something carelessly, hastily and in a slapdash manner: *The builder skimped on the job so we're suing him.* **Skimpy** means 'brief and scanty' and is usually applied to clothing: *Wearing only a skimpy dress, she nearly froze while wating for the bus.*

Scripture, scriptural

When used as a shortened form of **Holy Scripture, Scripture** and **the Scriptures** are capitalised. The adjective **scriptural** is lower case.

scull, skull

Scull can be a single oar, a long, narrow racing boat, or the action of pulling on one or a pair of oars: *To the cheers of the crowd, Watson sculled his way to victory.* The **skull** is the bony skeleton of the head.

SCULL, SKULL

scuttle, scupper

These are not interchangeable. A **scupper** is an opening on the deck or side of a ship for draining off water. A **scuttle** is also an opening, but it is a covered hatchway for access. If such openings are made below the waterline, the ship can be **scuttled**, or sunk. Away from seafaring, **scuttle**, but more usually **scupper**, are both used to mean 'to wreck or ruin': *The arrival of half a dozen other ice-cream vans scuppered Bert's plans to make a killing.*

seasonal, seasonable

Seasonal means 'occurring at a certain season' as in *seasonal storms* and *seasonal labour.* **Seasonable** means 'suitable to' or 'in keeping with the season': *The weather was seasonable for April.*

191

secure. See **get, acquire, obtain, secure**

seldom, seldom ever

Julie seldom ever arrives on time contains a redundancy: **seldom ever**. **Seldom** by itself, meaning 'not often or rarely', is sufficient.

sensitive, sensual, sensuous

Sensitive means 'acutely susceptible to influences, highly responsive to stimuli, or easily offended'. Except that it shares the meaning of 'the ability to perceive and feel', **sensibility** is not a synonym but means 'having the capacity to respond to emotion, moral feelings and intellectual and aesthetic stimuli'. **Sensual** pleasure derives from physical indulgences such as eating, drinking and sex. Something or someone **sensuous** is capable of arousing or pleasing the senses: *She closed her eyes as she listened to the sensuous progression of Ravel's 'Bolero'.*

sentence, sentience

It is not unknown for **sentience** to be corrected by some busybody to **sentence**. Many people are unaware the word exists and few writers have occasion to use it, but it means 'having a sense of awareness, as distinct from mental perception and intelligence': *The case for animal rights rests on the recognition of animal sentience.*

sew. See **sow, sew**

sewage, sewerage

Sewerage is the sewer system, and **sewage** is what passes through it.

Sex and Gender

It is first of all essential to grasp the fact that there are only two sexes (male and female) and three genders that apply to words (masculine, feminine and neuter). Despite this, **sex**, once exclusively used to denote the difference between male and female, has now through usage gained new meanings. This one – *The couple claimed they had sex five times a day* – to mean 'sexual intercourse' – has virtually levered the word away from its primary meaning. Because of the biological connotations of **sex** (the word), many writers and feminists in particular have nominated **gender** as its substitute to mean the difference between being male and masculine, and female and feminine. **Gender** now covers the social functions, status and expectations of males and females: **gender roles** instead of **sex roles** and **gender gap** instead of **sex gap** are now standard terms. There exists also a quest for **gender-free**

language (lawyer, dentist, doctor, student are okay; chambermaid, barmaid, businessman, chairman and clergyman aren't). There is, however, still plenty of sex about: **sex appeal, sex shop, sex-starved, sexploitation, sex change**, but not **sexpot** which, argue feminists, narrows the woman's entire identity to her sexuality and presents her as a 'woman-as-temptress' stereotype.

shall, should, will, would

There is a simple way through the usage tangle this quartet presents to many writers: **shall** and **should** are used with the first person, singular and plural, **will** and **would** with all the other persons: *I shall, we shall, he will, she will, they will, you will, it will; I should, we should, he would, she would, they would, you would, it would*. We do, however, often make exceptions for emphasis: *I will! You shall!* However, the distinctions above are rarely observed in ordinary speech and increasingly ignored in writing (in American English *shall* is hardly ever heard or seen; *will* is standard) to the extent that there is the danger of their disappearing altogether, helped on their way by the use of contractions (**I'll, she'll, he'll, they'll**) which conveniently can mean either.

shambles

The Government's BSE slaughter policy was today described in the Commons as a 'shambles'. An apt description, perhaps; a **shambles** (singular) is an animal slaughtering area. It is used nowadays to describe a scene of chaos and carnage: *After the drunken fracas, the saloon bar was a shambles.*

shear, sheer

Shear means 'to cut off' (hair), 'break off' (metal, etc.), or 'strip off' (privileges, powers, authority). **Sheer** can mean 'fine and transparent' (silk, stockings, underwear), 'steep' (road, cliff) or 'absolute' (*The woman laughed for sheer joy*). **Sheer** also means 'to deviate or swerve', but in this sense **veer** is a less ambiguous choice.

shewn. See shown, shewn

Shia, Shi'ite

The two main groups of Muslims are the **Shia** (preferred to **Shi'ite**) Muslims and the **Sunni** Muslims.

shibboleth

Shibboleth is misused variously to mean 'an entrenched custom', 'an old saying', or 'a sacred belief'. In fact it was the old Hebrew word for an ear of corn and was used as a password by the Gileadite tribe in order to identify their enemies, the Ephraimites. *'Say shibboleth'* they would demand. If the reply was *'sibboleth'*, another Ephraimite bit the dust – 42,000 in all. Today, a **shibboleth** is a catchphrase, test or custom that reliably distinguishes the members of a particular group from another.

shop, store

A **shop** in Britain is a **store** in the US. In the UK, however, **department store** describes a large shop with many departments.

shortage, shortfall

A **shortage** is an insufficient amount or a deficiency; a **shortfall** is the failure to meet some requirement or target, and the extent of it: *The fundraising goal suffered a shortfall of some £15,000.*

should, would. See shall, will, should, would

shown, shewn

Shewn is an archaic spelling of **shown**, but some people still persist in using it.

shrimp. See scampi, shrimp, prawn, langoustine

sick, sickly, ill

To **be sick** is a euphemism for **to vomit**, so **ill** is usually substituted for **sick** to mean a state of sickness or being unwell. The usage is about evenly divided because we still say *sick pay, sick leave, sickness benefit, sick child,* etc. A **sick/ill** Australian resolves the dilemma by saying *I'm crook.* A **sickly** person is unhealthy, weak and disposed to frequent ailments.

silicon, silicone

Silicon is the chemical element which as silicon oxide is all about us in the form of quartz and sand; **silicone** is a synthetic silicon compound used to make lubricants, water repellants and a range of other products.

silly. See crass, silly, stupid, gross

Similar To, Similar From, Different To, Different From...

Mr Ivor Kenny, a *Word Check* user from Plymouth, Devon, offers this thought:

If (as you frequently do)
You accept as correct *different to,*

Why not, with equal aplomb
Give endorsement to *similar from*?

While many famous writers have written **different to**, and even *The Times* has used the Americanism **different than,** the preferred usage is **different from** as is, of course, **similar to.**

simile, metaphor

Both are figures of speech. A **simile** makes a comparison or indicates a similarity, usually preceded by *as, as if,* or *like: He is as thick as two planks; The party went like a house on fire.* A **metaphor** makes a more direct analogy: *You're a doll; She's a pain in the neck.* A **mixed metaphor** combines two incompatible comparisons: *We've got a real headache on our hands; This decision is a very hard blow to swallow.*

simple, simplistic

The two are not synonyms. **Simplistic** means 'excessively simplified to the point of naivety'. The difference is made clear here: *Dalton's deductions were brilliantly simple, but the solution put forward by Keene was just too simplistic.*

sitting room. See **living room, sitting room, lounge**

It's A Problem Situation

A **situation** is, simply, a position, a location, or a state of affairs. But more often than not **situation** is used to inflate the importance of a statement: *It was a typical confrontational situation* for *It was a typical confrontation* is a fair example. A *crisis situation* is simply a crisis; an *emergency situation* is just an emergency. But with overuse threatening to topple **situation** from fashion, its cousin **position** seems to be taking over: *The position in regard to the need to increase railway fares is that it is being kept under review.* This again is gobbledegook which, when translated, could mean *The possibility of increasing railway fares is being considered.* Use **situation** and **position** with care and discrimination.

size, sized

A *large-size pumpkin* or a *large-sized pumpkin*? Both usages are acceptable although the adjective **sized** is usually preferred.

skewbald. See **piebald, skewbald**

skull. See **scull, skull**

slander. See **libel, slander**

sleight, slight

Sleight means dexterity, as in the *sleight of hand* displayed by a magician, but as a word it is rarely used by itself. **Slight** means 'small, slim, insignificant' and also a 'snub or insult'.

slow, slowly

Remorseless usage has converted the adjective **slow** into a substitute for the adverb **slowly:** *Drive slow past the school; Doesn't Thomas walk slow?; Is the train running slow again?* The adverbial use of **slow** is now wide spread, but you will be recognised as a writer of discernment if you use **slowly** where it *should* be used: *Drive slowly past the school.*

slow up, slow down

These idiomatic twins mean the same.

smelled, smelt

Smelled, not **smelt**, is preferred as the past tense and past participle of **smell**.

snook, snoot

Because **snoot** is slang for the nose, the rude gesture made by placing a thumb on the nose with the fingers outstretched is not uncommonly called **cocking a snoot**. It seems a shame therefore to point out that this is completely wrong. The name for this particular gesture is in fact a **snook**, and the correct phrase is **cocking a snook**.

snooker, pool, billiards

Snooker is played on a billiard table with a white cue ball, fifteen red balls and six other coloured balls which are all potted in a certain order. **Pool** is essentially an American game and is played with coloured and numbered balls plus a cue ball. In **Eight-ball pool** players must sink their own balls before those of an opponent, plus the black eight-ball, to win the game. **Billiards** is played with two white balls and a red ball with players scoring by potting the red ball, the opponent's ball, or another ball off either of these two.

so-called

This is regarded as a put-down or sneer term, such as **self-styled** or *soi-disant*, **would-be** and **self-proclaimed**. It indicates that what follows is to be held up to doubt, question or ridicule: *The so-called animal lovers claimed they had collected a petition of ten thousand names.*

solecism, solipsism, sophism, sophistry

In linguistic terms, a **solecism** is a violation of conventional usage, such as breaking a grammatical rule, misusing a word, mixing metaphors or mispronouncing a word. **Solipsism** is the belief that only the self is real and knowable, and the denial of the existence of any knowledge beyond one's own existence. **Sophism** is clever and persuasive but nevertheless specious argument. **Sophistry** is an example of this type of argument, or the art of specious reasoning.

solidarity, solidity, sodality

Solidarity expresses a unity of interests, opinions, feelings and responsibilities that binds members of a class or community: *The size of the contributions gave an indication of the solidarity of the strikers.* **Solidity** is the state of being solid. **Sodality**, a fairly uncommon word, means 'friendship and fraternity'.

solve. See resolve, solve

somebody, someone. See anybody, anyone, somebody, someone

sometime, some time, sometimes

Some time and to a lesser extent **sometime** are used to indicate 'at some unspecified time or another': *The Smith family moved away some time ago; We promised we would meet sometime.* Fowler makes a point that **sometime** should be reserved for its adjectival sense, meaning 'former': *The sometime president of the Board of Trade was at the meeting* – but usage will undoubtedly ignore this advice. **Sometimes** means 'occasionally, now and then'.

somewhere, someplace

The traditional and perfectly adequate **somewhere** appears to be standing up rather well to the American English import **someplace**.

soon, presently

Although the original meaning of **presently** (immediately) was supposed to have been obsolete for couple of centuries, it is still in evidence, which causes confusion with its contemporary meaning of 'soon, in a while'. Curiously the old meaning never died out in Scotland, so the Scots should win some points for consistency. In American English, too, **presently** is accepted as meaning 'now, at the moment': *James Mahoney is presently one of the key advisers to the President.* If you wish to avoid ambiguity, use **soon, now, currently, shortly**, etc. See also **directly**.

sophomore, freshman

In the US, a **freshman** is a student of either sex in the first year of secondary school or is a first-year undergraduate at a university. A **sophomore** is the second-year equivalent.

sort of. See **kind of, sort of**

sorted out, sorted

It's time to get that personal pension sorted! exhorted a recent financial services advertisement (*Daily Telegraph, 1996*). Only a year or two before the headline would have exclaimed, more traditionally, *It's time to get that personal pension sorted out!* Dropping the *out* (the blame is placed on East End London speech: *Okay, let's ge' i' saw-hid*) is a recent fashion but the abbreviated phrase is sticking like glue to current usage. You have been warned.

soul, sole

Kielder Ferries is a profitable family-run cruise business that enjoys the soul ferrying rights on Kielder Water, now one of Northumberland's largest tourist attractions (advertisement in the *Newcastle Journal*, 1994). Not only a profitable business but a classical one, ferrying souls across the water! What the ad intended to say was **'sole** ferrying rights' – meaning exclusive or unshared.

source, cause

The difference between the two is illustrated here: *The source of his headache was that blow to his head.* In fact, the blow was the **cause** of the headache; the **source** may have been a punch by a boxer, a brick thrown at him, or a wall he ran into. A **cause** is something that produces an effect; a **source** is a point or place from which something originates.

sow, sew

You **sew** with a needle and thread (*sewed, sewn*) and **sow** seeds (*sowed, sown*). A **sow** (pronounced to rhyme with *how*) is a female pig.

spasmodic, sporadic

Spasmodic means 'happening in short, irregular and unexpected bursts or spasms' (*His displays of academic excellence tended to occur spasmodically*), while something **sporadic** occurs intermittently, at scattered intervals: *The thunder continued sporadically throughout the afternoon.*

specially. See **especially, specially**

specialty, speciality

These are interchangeable, although **specialty** is standard in American English and **speciality** is preferred in the UK.

specie, species

Specie defines coins and coinage, as distinct from paper money. A **species** is 'a kind, or variety' or, most commonly in biology, 'a group within a genus which can interbreed and which may contain subspecies and varieties'.

specious, spurious

Both words share the basic meaning of 'being false and not genuine', but they are not synonymous. Something **specious** may appear to be superficially genuine, true or correct but in fact turns out to be false, untrue or wrong: *It took them a while to see through Brett's specious claims about his medical qualifications.* Something **spurious** makes little effort to mask its falseness.

spectrum, range

Spectrum is often used as a synonym for **range**: *He enthused over the spectrum of possibilities.* Use **range** in such contexts; it's plainer and clearer.

spelt, spelled

Spelt is generally found in British English, and **spelled** in American English: *The judge spelt out the alternative to prison.*

spilt, spilled

Spilt is generally found in British English, and **spilled** in American English: *The overturned tanker spilt an estimated three thousand litres of milk over the road.*

Spin doctor. See populist

spoilt, spoiled

Spoilt is generally found in British English, and **spoiled** in American English, but remember that there is no such word as *despoilt* – it's **despoiled.**

spokesman, spokeswoman, spokesperson

In the view of *The Times*, all of these are 'ugly' words; while **spokesperson** would be the most politically correct, it is also the most awkward sounding. Avoid them and the blight of political correctness by substituting more specific terms: *official, representative, aide,* etc.

staid, stayed

Staid means 'sedate, sober, serious, stuffy', so it's difficult to see how it could ever be confused with **stayed,** meaning 'remained in the same place'. But it has been, even by the poet T. S. Eliot who, in the first edition of a 1939 verse play, *The Family Reunion,* let slip the following:

> You have staid in England, yet you seem
> Like someone who comes from a very long distance.

staggering

For some unaccountable reason, **staggering** is quite often used as a substitute for adjectives such as *astonishing, amazing, surprising,* etc.: *The gala concert raised the staggering sum of £65,000.* Sums of money do not stagger, and as **staggering** means 'proceeding unsteadily and about to fall', it seems to be a most inappropriate substitute. Avoid this particular usage.

stalactite, stalagmite

A **stalactite** (*c* for ceiling) hangs down; a **stalagmite** (*g* for ground) projects up from the ground. Remember that 'tites' come down.

stammer, stutter

Although through usage and abusage, these are now regarded as synonyms, the technical difference is still worth preserving. A **stammer** is a speech disorder characterised by involuntary repetitions, hesitation and silences as the speaker attempts to utter the next word. A **stutter** is a similar disorder in which the speaker repeats the beginnings of words, particularly consonants, before being able to complete them.

stanch, staunch

Both are correct, but as a verb meaning 'to stem the flow of blood', **stanch** is more widely used, leaving **staunch** as an adjective meaning 'firmly loyal and steadfast'.

standpoint, point of view, viewpoint

Some object to **standpoint** but it is a respectable word deriving from the German *standpunkt*, meaning 'a position from which something is viewed', either in a physical or abstract sense: *From the client's standpoint the construction so far was a mess.* **Point of view and viewpoint have the same meaning.**

stationary, stationery

Stationary means 'fixed, not moving, standing still'; **stationers** sell writing material, which is called **stationery**. A useful mnemonic is '*stationary = stand; stationery = letter*'.

statistic, statistics

Statistics can be singular or plural, depending on the sense: *Statistics is an inexact science; The statistics are indicating a Conservative victory.* But **statistic** is always singular: *The one statistic that impressed the voters was the low inflation index.*

stimulant, stimulus, stimuli

Both nouns mean 'something that produces an arousal or increase in activity' and are near synonyms. However a **stimulant** is almost always used in a physiological context (*Jane could never get going in the morning without strong coffee or some other stimulant*) while **stimulus** is used to indicate something that arouses action or acts as an incentive: *There was little doubt that the overtime payment served as an effective stimulus to increasing production.* **Stimuli** is the pural of **Stimulus**.

stile. See style, stile

stolid, solid

Stolid means 'impassive, dull, showing little feeling or perception'. **Solid**, used in a similar context, means dependable: *When it comes to supporting the school, John's as solid as a rock.*

stone. See rock, stone, pebble

store. See shop, store

storey, story, storeys, stories

A **storey** (**story** in American English) is a floor or level in a building: *Jim lost his wallet in the multi-storey car park.* The plural is **storeys**. A **story** (plural **stories**) is a tale, a narrative. The plurals of both words share the same spelling: **stories**.

straight, strait, straightened, straitened

Phrases and combinations that include these words require care: *straight and narrow* (although it's *strait and narrow* in the Bible!), *straight-edge, straight-faced, straightforward, straight bat; dire straits, strait-laced, straitjacket, straitened circumstances.* You **straighten** something by making or bending it **straight; straitened** means 'restricted'. A useful mnemonic is *The Hunchback of Notre Dame didn't live in straightened circumstances.*

strategy, stratagem, tactics

Strategy is the planning of an operation; **tactics** involve putting the strategy into effect. A **stratagem** is a scheme designed to deceive.

stricken. See struck, stricken

Stroke, Coronary, Heart Failure

A **stroke** is a cerebral haemorrhage, a burst blood vessel in the brain, or a cerebral thrombosis, a blood clot in the brain, that often results in paralysis. A **coronary**, or more correctly a **coronary thrombosis**, is caused by a clot in the coronary artery, stopping the supply of blood to the heart. **Heart failure** or **heart attack** covers a variety of disorders in which the heart is suddenly unable to cope with pumping blood to the body. Most heart failures are treatable. A **cardiac arrest** occurs when the heart stops pumping.

struck, stricken

Stricken is sometimes mistakenly used as the past tense and past participle of **strike**: *Adverse comments on behaviour should be stricken from the records of a dyslexic student*. The intended word is **struck. Stricken** means to be 'affected or laid low by an illness'.

student. See **pupil, student**

stupid. See **crass, sully, stupid, gross**

style, stile

A **stile** is the arrangement of wooden steps to help you climb over a fence; **style** embraces a wide range of meanings: 'the manner in which something is done; a form of appearance or design; a refinement of dress and manners', etc.

subconscious, unconscious

Subconscious has two meanings: that of being only partly aware, and, more commonly, the thoughts that occupy the hidden level of the mind and influence our actions: *The analyst concluded that subconsciously Helen had a deep hatred for her sister*. To be **unconscious** is to be unaware: *She was unconscious of the danger she was in*. It can also mean total loss of consciousness: *After the accident the young man was unconscious for three days*.

subjective. See **objective, subjective**

subsequently. See **consequently, subsequently**

substitute, replace

These are subtly different. **Substitute** means 'to put in the place of', while **replace** means 'to put back again in place': *He carefully replaced the candlesticks but substituted a cheap imitation for the priceless bowl.*

succeed, follow

These are often regarded as synonyms but they are not. To **follow** means 'to go or come after and in the same direction': *Almost every child in the neighborhood followed the marching band.* To **succeed**, in this context, means 'to come next in order or sequence': *It was expected that Charles would succeed his father as senior partner in the business.*

successive. See **consecutive, successive**

succubus. See **incubus, succubus**

such as. See **like, such as**

Suit, suite

Although pronounced differently (*sut, sweet*), confusion between the two is not unknown: a **suit** of clothes but a **suite** of furniture; strong **suit**, follow **suit**; a **suit** of cards; a **lawsuit**; but a presidential **suite** (of rooms in a hotel), a musical **suite**, a **suite** of attendants.

summoned, summonsed

You can be **summoned** to appear at a public enquiry, or to a court hearing. If, however, you are presented with a **summons**, you are therefore **summonsed**.

sunk. See **sank, sunk, sunken**

superficial, cosmetic

We've made a few changes but they're only cosmetic is a usage now very much in vogue. **Superficial** is more to the point and preferred.

supersede, surpass

Supersede means 'to supplant or replace with something or someone superior to the original'. Note: **supersede** is often misspelled *supercede*. To **surpass** is to be better or greater than or superior in excellence or achievement: *Her results at the last Olympics surpassed even her own previous records.*

suppose. See **guess, suppose, think; also assume, presume**

surge. See **upsurge, surge**

surplice, surplus

A newspaper in south-west England recently reported that *students at Salisbury Cathedral School who, after becoming full choristers, were presented with **surpluses** to wear over their cassocks.* These, presumably, were not surplus stock, but the real thing – **surplices**.

surrounded

Surrounded means 'encircled or enclosed' – so phrases such as *completely surrounded* and *surrounded on three sides* are redundant or incorrect.

swam, swum

Harry and Peter swum out to the buoy is wrong. The past tense of **swim** is **swam**: *Harry and Peter **swam** out to the buoy.* **Swum** is the past participle of **swim**: *The water was so warm and inviting they could have swum all day.*

swap. See swop, swap

Sweater, Jersey, Jumper, Pullover, etc.

In matters of clothing, usage departs from often vague or out-dated dictionary definitions, so it's difficult to describe precisely what a jumper is, or a sweater, or any similar upper garment. Here's a cross-section of opinion: A **sweater** is knitted, neither tight nor loose, either with or without sleeves, and is a synonym for **jumper**; the latter term being used more to describe a child's garment. A **jersey** or **guernsey** was originally a heavy woollen sweater made for warmth; the same garment, in lighter material, is now fashionably called a *maillot*. A **pullover** can be with or without sleeves and is loose enough to slip easily over the head; it tends to be a male garment. The **cardigan** is distinguished by having buttons up the front and is longsleeved; in a **twinset** it is worn over a matching short-sleeved sweater. A **T-shirt** (or tee-shirt) is usually short-sleeved, usually made of cotton, and with no collar or buttons. A **tank-top**, extremely fashionable in the 1970s, is a lightweight vest-like garment with wide shoulder straps. The trade or generic term for all of the above is simply **tops**.

---

swingeing, swinging

Swingeing (pron. *swin-jing*) means 'severe in degree': *People tend to forget that the so-called Swinging Sixties also saw swingeing tax increases.*

swop, swap

Meaning 'to exchange', **swap** is universal and preferred; **swop** is a purely British variant.

swot, swat

These are two different words. To **swot** is to study or cram for an examination; to **swat** is to smack or hit sharply: *We did little all day but swat flies and mosquitoes.*

swum. See **swam, swum**

sympathy. See **empathy, sympathy**

syndrome, synergy, symbiosis

Each of these is about relationships. A **syndrome** is a combination of symptoms or signs that suggests some disease, disorder or problem. **Synergy** is now popularly used to mean 'productive relationship' or 'mutually beneficial relationship', but what it really means is the action of two groups or entities that when combined produce an effect of which each is incapable alone. **Symbiosis** is a biological term defining the interdependency of two animal or plant species.

Syndromitis

It has been suggested that the 1990s was the decade of the syndrome. While many syndromes have been established for some time (*Down's syndrome* (formerly mongolism); *Munchausen's syndrome* (and the more recent *Munchausen's syndrome by proxy* where the sufferer deliberately inflicts illnesses on others in order to draw attention to him or herself); *Cushing's syndrome, Guillain-Barre syndrome, etc.*) they are easily outnumbered by the more recent coinages. Some of these are serious medical conditions such as *Acquired Immune Deficiency Syndrome (Aids)* and *Gulf War syndrome* but others are trivialisations such as *empty nest syndrome*, describing families in which the children have grown up, leaving mum and dad with a house far too big for them. One that emerged with increasing frequency at the end of the second millennium was *Jerusalem syndrome*: 'a delusive condition affecting some visitors to Jerusalem, in which the sufferer identifies with a major figure from his or her religious background'.

---

syntax. See **grammar, syntax**

synthesis. See **analysis, synthesis**

T

tactics. See **strategy, tactics, stratagem**

Don't Get Out of Line When Using Tandem

Tandem, Philip Howard observed in *The Times*, is a word whose meaning is being eroded 'by slipshod extension, which Fowler defined, in his elitist way, as occurring when some accident gives currency among the uneducated to words of learned origin'. Howard quoted some lapses from his own newspaper: *Polaris and Trident will run in tandem for a short time; A Germany working in tandem with its partners could play a lead in this rewarding democratic reform'*; and a caption to a photo of two daring hang-gliders, hanging on to their frail craft side-by-side, asserting that they were in tandem when, visibly, they were not.

Tandem, from a pun on the Latin *tandem* meaning 'at last, at length, in the end', is intended to mean 'one behind the other' as with a tandem bicycle. The meaning is worth preserving because, as Howard points out, there are plenty of words to mean side-by-side, but only one to mean 'in line ahead and behind'.

---

tantamount. See **paramount, tantamount**

tantalise, tease

To **tease** means 'to lightheartedly annoy someone', or 'to arouse desire with no intention of satisfying it' or 'to offer something with no intention of supplying it'. To torment or irritate means substantially the same, so how different is **tantalise**? There is a subtle difference, and it derives from the

frustrating experience of the ancient Greek king Tantalus. He was condemned
to stand in a pool of water which receded every time he stooped to drink, and
under trees which drew back every time he reached to pick the delicious fruit
that hung from them. To be tantalised is to be tormented and frustrated by the
sight of something dearly desired but inaccessible.

tartan, plaid

Tartan is the distinctive patterned cloth used for certain Scottish garments,
including the kilt and the **plaid** – the shawl worn over the shoulder.

tasteful, tasty

Tasteful is something that embodies or employs aesthetic discrimination and
good taste: *The reception rooms were tastefully furnished.* **Tasty** means 'flavourful
to the palate', although colloquially it has also come to mean 'sexually
attractive'.

tautology

Tautology, *pleonasm*, *redundancy* and *prolixity* all means the use of unecessary
words. A **tautology** is the same point repeated: *I'll be leaving at 7 a.m. in the
morning; It's a rather puzzling mystery; What a disastrous tragedy!; What a lovely pair
of twins!* … and so on. See ***Persecuted unjustly and other Pleonasms.***

temporal, temporary

Temporal relates to real life, to the secular as opposed to the spiritual, to
earthly time rather than to eternity. **Temporary** means 'impermant, lasting
for a limited time only'.

tendency, trend

A **tendency** is an inclination, a leaning, a disposition towards something:
When he'd had a few too many, George had a tendency to fall asleep. A **trend** is a
general movement: *The current trend is for people to book their holidays early.*

tenterhooks

There are no such things as 'tender hooks' or 'tenderhooks', yet these
mysterious objects keep surfacing in ill-informed sentences. The word is
tenterhooks, traditionally the nails or hooks on a frame for stretching canvas
or cloth: *She's on tenterhooks waiting for her exam results* means she's in an agony
of suspense waiting for the outcome.

testament, testimony, testimonial

A **testament** is a will, the document by which a person disposes of his or her
estate after death, as in *last will and testament.* **Testimony** is evidence, proof or

confirmation, sometimes given under oath: *Fred's rapid climb up the company hierarchy was testimony to his 24-hour-a-day charm offensive*. A **testimonial** is a personal endorsement of a person's character, ability and experience: *Sam said he'd be delighted to provide a testimonial for David's youngest son*.

that, which, who

That and **which** are relative pronouns that are becoming more and more interchangeable despite long standing rules about their usage. However, at least some of these rules should be observed. **That** is used to refer to persons, animals and things; **which** to animals and things; **who** and **whom** exclusively to persons. Use **that** to define the meaning or intention of the preceding word or phrase: *The hotel that Helen stayed at has burnt down*. **That** defines or identifies the hotel for us. Use **which** when the identifying information is already supplied in the sentence: *The Imperial Hotel at Bath, which Helen stayed at last year, has burnt down*. Whether to use **who** or **that** for persons can be a problem but, generally, **that** is used to refer to *any* persons, and **who** to a particular person: *The mechanics that fixed this car ought to be shot; My mate Jim, who was supposed to fix this car, ought to be shot*. But using **that** for persons can sometimes look and sound odd. Here for example is *The Times'* columnist Simon Jenkins, a consummate stylist: *To all that protest that this is primarily an exhibition of handicraft design…* Most writers would in this instance use **who** and indeed are largely solving the problem with the indiscriminate substitution of **who** for **that**. In other contexts, **that** is a word we're abandoning. That very sentence is a good example; grammatically and pedantically it should have been written: *That is a word that we're abandoning*. Whether used as a conjunction or as a relative pronoun, we're dumping **that** wholesale. The current view on this is that when the meaning is clear, **that** can be safely dropped: *Are you pleased [that] I bought it? I know [that] she'll arrive tomorrow. Don't you think [that] it's a great car?* All three statements are unambiguous with **that** omitted. But don't get too carried away! *Mr Benton said yesterday some shares dropped as much as 20%* could mean two things: that Mr Benton made the statement yesterday (*Mr Benton said yesterday [that] some shares dropped as much as 20%*); or that Mr Benton said that some shares dropped 20% yesterday: *Mr Benton said [that] yesterday some shares dropped as much as 20%*. If you were the owner of those shares you'd be pretty interested to find out exactly what Mr Benton meant. The appropriate insertion of **that** makes either sentence crystal clear. So when in doubt, retain **that**.

theft. See **burglary, robbery, theft**

their, there, they're

A confusing trio – they look different but sound the same. **Their** is a possessive pronoun, the possessive of **they**: *This is their car.* **There** means 'in or at that place': *She left the car there but now it's gone.* **They're** is a contraction of 'they are': *They're trying to break into our car.*

their, they

The use of plural pronouns such as **their** and **they** in a singular sense is one of grammar's most slippery slopes. Faced with a 'his or her' couple, or uncertain of the gender of the antecedent, we're more or less forced to use constructions like *Nobody will stop us, will they?; Anyone can do as they please; Has anybody not yet completed their projects?* All three sentences combine a singular antecedent (*nobody, anyone, anybody*) with a plural pronoun (*they, their*) and all are considered acceptable except perhaps by pedants. Grammatical alternatives are clumsy (*Anyone can do as he or she pleases*) or outrageously ungrammatical: *Nobody will stop us, will he or she?* Usage here is a matter of commonsense and using your 'ear'.

think. See **guess, suppose, think.** Also **believe, feel, think**

thorough. See **meticulous, punctilious, conscientious, thorough**

though. See **although, though**

thrilled, enthralled

To be **thrilled** is to experience tingling excitement, an intense wave of emotion. To be **enthralled** (held in **thrall**) is to be captivated, spellbound, in a state of fascinated attention: *Julie almost stopped breathing, enthralled by the sheer poetry of the ballet.*

through, thru

Thru is a gross barbarism – there's nothing shameful in writing *Open from Monday through Saturday*, meaning 'from Monday to and including Saturday'.

tight, tightly

The adjective (**tight**) and adverb (**tightly**) are regarded as often interchangeable: *He held her tight/tightly.* But whereas **tight** suggests a condition (*The cork was jammed tight*), **tightly** implies action: *James held him tightly around the neck.*

till, until

Till is the informal and short form of **until**, meaning 'up to the time when': *I'll love you till the end of time.* Both are interchangeable but **until** is preferred especially at the beginning of a sentence: *Until Jim arrives we'll just have to twiddle our thumbs*.

timidity, temerity

Timidity is the tendency to be easily frightened, shy and fearful – or **timorous**. **Temerity** means almost the opposite: 'foolish, reckless boldness': *Only Felicity would have had the temerity to question the consultant's judgement*.

tirade. See harangue, tirade

titillate, titivate

Titillate means 'to tickle or excite'; **titivate** means 'to smarten up'.

toilet. See bathroom, toilet

token, nominal, notional

All three are frequently misused to mean 'minimal'. In the sense of 'symbolic gesture', **token** and **nominal** are closely related: a nominal payment and a token payment, meaning 'partial payment', are the same thing. **Token** also means 'slight, or of no real account': *The Party regarded his contribution of £20 as merely token support*. **Nominal** means 'not in fact, in name only'; a nominal charge is one removed from reality in that it is small compared to its real value: *Brian was allowed to buy his company car for the nominal payment of £100*. Something **notional** relates to concepts and hypotheses rather than to reality: *The engineers' notional cost for a single unit was thought to be in the region of £150*.

TNT, dynamite, gelignite

Dynamite, a compound of liquid nitroglycerin and absorbent material, was the invention of Alfred Nobel in 1866; he followed this with blasting gelatin or **gelignite** in 1875. **TNT** or tri-nitro-toluene is the most recently developed of the trio and safest from friction and shock.

ton, tonne

A British **ton** is 2,240 lbs; a short or American **ton** is 2,000 lbs; a metric **tonne** is 1,000 kilograms or about 2,200 lbs.

Toothy and Toothsome

In the *New York Times* recently the American wordsmith William Safire railed against the misuse of the word **toothsome**. His target was the magazine *Newsweek* which had described a model as 'blond and toothsome', clearly intending this to mean that the young lady possessed an outstanding set of gleaming choppers. Even Norman Mailer, writing in *Time* magazine, fell into the **toothsome** trap, using it to mean **toothy**. 'Let's fight cavities', quipped Safire, 'but stop the decay of a good word'. **Toothsome** means 'attractive, alluring, delicious or appetising' depending upon what is being described; it does not mean *toothy* any more than *fulsome* means 'full'.

Tortuous, torturous

Tortuous means 'twisting, winding, devious'; **torturous** means 'inflicting torture and pain': *Following the dark tortuous underground passages became a torturous nightmare.*

total

Total has become an immensely popular word, tending to be used in preference to the often more appropriate *complete, whole, entire,* etc. It is also used when not needed: *The gate receipts reached a total of £14,657,* when obviously £14,657 *is* the total amount; and *This game is going to end in total annihilation for Manchester United* when annihilation means to 'completely defeat or destroy'. In both examples **total** is redundant. However it is difficult to carp at one new and imaginative use of the word: *The police told him that the thieves had **totalled** his car,* meaning they had completely wrecked the car.

toward, towards

Both, meaning 'in the direction of' or 'in respect of', are interchangeable. Use according to taste, sound and appearance: *He steered the yacht toward/towards the harbour; The storm broke towards dawn.*

town. See city, town, village, hamlet

toxin, tocsin

Toxin is poison caused by bacteria; a **tocsin** is a bell rung to raise an alarm.

trace, chart

The architect's design for the atrium can be charted back to ancient Rome. Here the writer has used **chart** as a synonym for **trace**, which it isn't. To chart something is to plot it in advance; to trace something is to track back: *The navigator charted a course that would take them directly over Boston; Judith managed to trace her ancestors back to the late 18th century.*

trait, character

Character – of a person, object or group – is the combination of qualities that distinguishes them: *Fred was rather a weak character; it was not in Trudy's character* *to be aggressive.* A **trait** is some aspect or feature of a person or that person's behaviour: *One of Auntie's most endearing traits was her boundless optimism.*

transpire, happen, occur

Transpire does not mean **happen** or **occur** but to 'become known gradually, or come to light': *It transpired that, because she had accidentally overheard some gossip, Jean at last grasped the probability that John and Julie were having an affair.*

trauma

This word has become debilitated by misuse and over-use. Originally restricted to mean 'extreme pathological or psychological shock severe enough to have long-lasting effects', **trauma** has for some time been trivialised: *I simply couldn't stand the trauma of going for another job interview.* Return **trauma** and **traumatise** to the medical cabinet.

traveller. See gypsy, gipsy, Romany, traveller

trend. See tendency, trend

triple, treble

Meaning threefold, both are interchangeable except in the terms **treble clef** (in music) and **treble chance** (football pools); and **triple jump** (the hop, step and jump event in athletics).

triumphal, triumphant

Triumphal means 'celebrating a triumph or victory'; **triumphant** means 'victorious or successful, and rejoicing in the glory': *The team returned home, tired, drunk and triumphant.*

troop, troupe

Riverdance – the dance troop that took the Eurovision Song Contest by storm – is now beset with ego clashes and petty squabbles. (The Sunday Times). A **troop** is a large assembly or a flock but more usually a military formation, hence **troops**. What the writer intended was **troupe**: a group or company of performers.

true facts. See facts, true facts, factitious

truism, truth

A **truism** is not something that is merely true but a glaring self-evident truth, often expressed as a platitude: *Every man was once a boy.* See also: **veracity, truth**

try and, try to

Try to is logically correct and in most cases sounds better to the ear, except perhaps in such established phrases as *try and get me* and *try and make me*.

T-shirt. See **sweater, jersey, jumper, cardigan, pullover, etc.**

turbid, turgid

Turbid means 'clouded, muddy, opaque', **turgid** means 'swollen, bloated, inflated'. A river in flood can be both turbid and turgid.

twice, thrice

Twice means two times; **thrice** means three times. **Thrice** is rarely encountered these days but here are both words in use in *The Times*: *He was shot twice in the chest as he stepped outside his home to pull a tarpaulin over his car, a nightly routine after it had been paint-bombed thrice in recent months.* Modern usage would tend to favor *'three times'*.

U and non-U

In Britain, **U** means 'upper class' or associated with it, while **non-U** means not upper-class. The terms are not creations of Nancy Mitford as is popularly supposed, but of the linguist Professor Alan Rose who first used them in *Neuphilologische Mitteilungen*, a Finnish language journal.

ultimate limit

Heather was driven to the ultimate limit of her patience. **Ultimate limit** is tautological; **limit** by itself would suffice.

umpire, referee

Both undertake the same duties (conducting a game according to the rules) but attend different games: **umpire** for tennis, hockey, cricket and baseball; **referee** for football, ice hockey, rugby and boxing.

unable. See **incapable, unable**

unaware, unawares

Lookalikes but actually two different words and meanings. If you are **unaware** (adjective), you are not aware or you are ignorant of something (*Betty was unaware of the danger*); if you are caught **unawares** (adverb), something has happened without warning and you are surprised: *Betty was caught unawares in her nightgown.*

unconscious. See **subconscious, unconscious**

under. See **beneath, under**

underlay, underlie

To **underlay** is to place something beneath or to support something from beneath – think of carpet underlay. To **underlie** means 'to lie under something or to act as a foundation': *Deep and complex analysis underlies the champion's every move.*

understand, appreciate, comprehend

I appreciate the reasons for your refusal demonstrates the questionable use of **appreciate** as a substitute for **understand; appreciate** really means 'to feel grateful or thankful'. **Comprehend** is a synonym for **understand** but with the inference of 'complete understanding': *Joe eventually comprehended my warning.*

unexceptional, unexceptionable

Something **unexceptional** is normal, ordinary or commonplace; something **unexceptionable** is beyond criticism or objection: *He remarked that the jury's verdict might seem severe in some respects but was generally unexceptionable.*

uninterested. See disinterested, uninterested

unique

Unique means 'without like or equal, the only one of its kind'. Yet we persist in using pointless modifiers such as *so unique, absolutely unique, most unique* and so forth. If you think something may be unique, don't say *nearly unique*, but *It is so rare, so exceptional, that I think it may be unique.*

unique facsimile

'These party masks are faithfully reproduced from bygone days and are unique facsimiles of the Edwardian and Victorian originals' No, they are not; they are mass-produced **copies** of the original. An **original**, if there is only one, is unique, and it is possible to have a **unique facsimile**; sculptors sometimes have a single exact copy cast from their original sculpture.

universal

An obituary in the *Arundel and Brighton News* began: ' "*Father Gerry*", as he was *universally known in the Reigate and Red Hill area…* ' . Unfortunately, Fr Gerry's fame was rather more suburban than universal, the meaning of **universal** being 'typical of the whole of humankind… existing or prevailing everywhere' or 'unlimited'. Better choices for the obituarist would have been *always, generally, invariably,* etc.

Unless

There is a tendency among journalists and columnists to use **unless** as an extended pregnant pause: *Some will demand that China's door to the West must be closed if not slammed, because, despite Deng's promise, international contempt has not been replaced by respect. Unless. Unless a great question is finally faced and answered…* Where this usage achieves the stylistic effect without affectation, well and good; otherwise it is pretentious and best avoided. The same applies to a similar conceit – *'And yet. And yet.'* – which is also cropping up with irritating frequency. See also **What ever and whatever revisited; and except, unless.**

---

unlike. See **like, unlike**

unprecedented

The careless use of this word, which means 'first, original, unparalleled, unheard-of' can land you into trouble. Announce something or some event as **unprecedented** and the chances are that it is not, and that someone, somewhere, is likely to pop up and smugly point out your error. Make sure of your fact before labelling it **unprecedented.**

unreadable. See **illegible, unreadable**

unsatisfied. See **dissatisfied, unsatisfied**

until. See **till, until**

untimely death, instant death

Death is never timely and as far as we know, no matter how agonisingly drawn out the process preceding it, it is always instant. Don't fall for these fatal cliches.

unwanted, unwonted

Unwanted means 'not wanted': *The last thing she intended was to make the child feel unwanted.* **Unwonted** means' unusual, out of the ordinary': *She was fascinated by him and followed his every move with unwonted curiosity.*

upon, on

With a couple of exceptions, **upon** and **on** are interchangeable: *She sat on/upon the chair.* However you would hardly begin a fairy story by intoning, *Once on [upon] a time*; nor does the ear respond favourably to *The suburbs stretched for mile on [upon] mile…*

upshot, result

The two are synonymous except that **upshot** can suggest a 'surprise, final result': *After all the arguments and appeals the upshot was that they awarded Abbot the gold medal.*

upsurge, surge

To **surge** is to swell, bulge, well up, gush, rush, heave or flow (or in any combination of these): *The increasingly uncontrollable crowd surged towards the exits.* **Upsurge** suggests a rising or increasing surge: *The police attributed the upsurge of violence to the growing presence of drug dealers on the estate.*

upward, upwards

Upward is an adjective (*upward mobility, an upward slope*), and while it is also an adverb the alternative **upwards** is preferred in this role: *They climbed upwards for what seemed like an eternity.*

urban, urbane

Urban refers to the city, as in *urban living, urban architecture*; **urbane** means 'poised and sophisticated: *Ten years or urban life had transformed the country boy into a witty, urbane gentleman.*

use to, used to

It is not uncommon to hear a sentence like this: *They always use to take a holiday in January*, to which nobody would take exception. But write the sentence down and you have the dilemma: is it **use to** or **used to**? The latter is strictly correct although **use to** is more or less standard in American English and normal in interrogative sentences such as *Didn't you use to live in Manchester?* The same applies when **used to** is used adjectivally: *After ten years I'm now used to the cold winters.*

use, utilise, usage

Use is synonymous with the other two words in most cases and should be preferred. **Utilise** (or **utilize**) also has the narrower meaning of 'making useful or turning to profitable account': *The company utilised the old factory to manufacture office furniture.* **Usage** – especially in the context of the English language – is the recognised practice of something: *The Professor was an expert in English usage.* It is also applied where quantities are involved: *Domestic water usage in Kent rose 30% last month.*

usable, useable

Both spellings are acceptable, although the shorter **usable** is now generally preferred.

vacant, vacuous

Vacant means 'empty or unoccupied'; **vacuous** means not only empty but 'blank, bereft and mindless': *The stranger unsettled everyone with his vacuous stare.*

vacation, holiday

In British English a **vacation** is a **holiday**; in American English a long holiday break is known as a **vacation** and one-day breaks (Thanksgiving, Christmas, Easter, etc.) are called **holidays**.

vaccinate. See inoculate, vaccinate

valuable, invaluable, valued

Valuable means 'having great value, or being worth a lot of money'. **Invaluable** means 'priceless, precious beyond valuation': *Her friendship at this difficult time was invaluable to him.* Apart from its use in contexts such as *I'm going to have my watch valued*, **valued** means 'esteemed and highly regarded': *Of all the things David valued, her friendship was paramount.*

Van Gogh, Vincent van Gogh

Dutch names observe the convention that **van** is in lower case when it is part of the full name (*Vincent van Gogh; Anthony van Dyke*) but capitalised as **Van** when used only with the surname: *The museum owned no fewer than nine superb Van Goghs.*

venal, venial

To be **venal** is to act dishonestly and to be readily and easily corrupted and bribed. **Venial** also comes from the Latin and means 'pardonable' – as of a wrongdoing that is of a minor nature and is of little or no consequence.

vendetta, feud

A **feud** is a dispute or quarrel between two people, families or groups. It can be bitter and prolonged and even involve killing, when it is called a **blood feud**. Or it can merely amount to competitive rivalry: *The two newspapers were always feuding over their distribution areas.* A **vendetta** (from the Italian, meaning 'to avenge') is a rather more serious conflict, usually involving one family (typically Sicilian or Corsican) against another, and revenge killings.

vengeance. See revenge, avenge, vengeance

veracious, voracious

Veracious means 'habitually truthful and careful with facts'; **voracious** means 'greedy, rapacious, insatiable'.

veracity, truth

Truth is something that is true, that is fact. **Veracity** is the capacity for being truthful, accurate and honest: *We can depend upon his admirable veracity for the truth to come out.*

verbal. See oral, aural, verbal

verger, virger

'*A woman virger at St Paul's Cathedral claimed yesterday that she had, in effect, been demoted to the role of a checkout girl*' began a story in *The Times* in April, 1995. A good many readers would have sprung for their dictionaries, wondering if they'd been spelling **verger** wrongly all their lives! But **verger** is correct; the **virger** spelling has been obsolete for 150 years.

via

It is fairly common to see **via** used like this: *They travelled from Victoria to Tower Hill via the Underground.* Purists prefer to see the use of **via** restricted to mean 'by way of' and not 'by means of': *They travelled on the Underground to Tower Hill from Victoria via the Embankment.*

viable, workable

The true meaning of **viable** (from the Latin *vita* = life) is 'the capability to maintain independent existence in life'. The word has, however, become an overworked and inaccurately used buzzword, to the extent that a doctor once claimed, '*Suicide is a viable alternative to painful terminal illness*'. Try to limit its use to mean 'capable of surviving and thriving independently': *The Channel Tunnel is expected to be operationally viable by the year 2010.* **Workable** means 'something or some plan that is practicable and can be made to work'. See **practicable, practical;** also **possible, plausible, feasible.**

Vicars and Other Men of God

The differences between **parsons, rectors** and **vicars** are largely historic. **Parsons** and **rectors** were the most fortunate because their parochial posts (called a 'living') included church property and income (called the 'benefice') and revenue from the parish (called the 'tithe'). The poor **vicar** got little or none of this, nor did the **curate**, who was an assistant to the parish priest. Their respective residences are called the **parsonage, rectory** and **vicarage.** A **curacy** is a position, not a residence. A **squarson** combined the duties of squire and parson and was usually well-off and influential.

vicious, viscous
Vicious implies a propensity for vice, hatred, spite and violence; **viscous** means 'thick and sticky', and is usually used to describe liquids.

village. See **city, town, village, hamlet**

virger. See **verger, virger**

virtually. See **practically, virtually**

virus. See **bacteria, virus, bug**

visible, visual
Visible means 'capable of being seen'; **visual** relates to anything involving the sense of sight: *visual arts, visual aids, visually handicapped, VDU (visual display unit)*, etc.

viz.
Viz. is short for the Latin adverb *videlicet*, which means 'namely' – (*He was born in the South, viz. Arkansas, but lived most of his life in Chicago* – why not simply use **namely**?

vocal cords
They are not *chords*, the musical notes, but vocal *cords* – the vibrating folds at the back of the larynx.

vocation, avocation

Although these are increasingly regarded as synonyms, they are not, and it is worthwhile preserving their separate meanings. A **vocation** is a person's regular occupation, profession or trade; an **avocation** is a diversion from a person's regular employment – a hobby or part-time job.

vomit. See **sick, sickly, ill**

von

When the name is written in full, use **von** in lower case (*Paul von Hindenburg*); where the surname only is used, omit the **von**.

voodoo, hoodoo

Voodoo is a Caribbean variety of witchcraft; a **hoodoo** is something or someone that brings bad luck: *After crashing his car, breaking an ankle and losing his girlfriend, all in one week, Peter was convinced he was the victim of a hoodoo.*

wages. See **salary, wages, renumeration**

wagon, waggon
Although **waggon** is still acceptable in British English, **wagon** is now regarded as standard.

wait. See **await, wait**

wait for, wait on, waiting for, waiting on
We'll have to wait for the next train; We've been waiting on Margaret since four o'clock; We waited on him for an hour but he never showed up. In all these usages, **wait for** is regarded as correct, and **wait on** as idiomatic but not necessarily incorrect. Careful writers will use the **wait/waiting/waited for** style.

waive, wave
These two are often confused. **Waive** means 'to relinquish, not to insist upon something': *The accused man waived his legal right to speak.*

want. See **desire, want, need**

wary, chary
There's not much between these although some writers discern a shade of difference: **wary** = watchful and wily; **chary** = careful and choosy: *In her old age Ethel had become very chary of her friends.*

was. See **were, was**

waste, wastage
Waste is the wanton, careless or useless squandering of resources, money or

time. **Wastage** is accidental or unavoidable loss through evaporation, leakage, wear or decay. The term **natural wastage** is sometimes euphemistically applied when a workforce is reduced in size by voluntary resignation, retirement, etc.

Waterloo, loo

The belief that **loo** is a truncated form of **Waterloo** seems too funny and absurd to be true. It seems academically plausible that the word is an Anglicised version of the French *lieu d'aisance* (water closet) – but it is not. Although some would still argue otherwise, **loo,** according to most learned research, derives from **Waterloo.** This however doesn't necessarily imply that *bog* comes from *Bogota,* Colombia.

way, weigh

When a ship **weighs** anchor, it then gets under **way**.

weep, cry

It used to be maintained that children cried and adults wept, but this hardly applies today as the two are almost synonymous. **Weeping**, however, suggests a deeper grief and sometimes bitterness. Mourners, for example, weep rather than cry, while a child who scratches a knee will cry – often loudly and tearfully.

well. See good, well

were, was

The use of **were/was** in sentences describing a hypothetical situation often causes hesitation: *He acted as though he were one of Bill's friends* is grammatically and stylistically correct; the informal alternative, *He acted as though he was one of Bill's friends* sounds decidedly dodgy, but many people would still use **was** rather than **were** in such instances. Remove the hypothetical situation and **was** is correct: *The man told us he was one of Bill's friends.*

West, west

When it is used adjectivally to describe a region (West Virginia, West Country, North Atlantic, the North, Middle East, etc.) the compass point is capitalised: *During the Cold War he defected to the West.* Otherwise, use lower case: *we drove north for two hours; He travelled extensively through southern Africa.*

wet, whet

Wet means 'moistened, covered or saturated with water or a liquid'; **whet** means 'to sharpen': *He whetted the knifeblade on the grindstone; the smell of cooking whetted their appetites.*

whatever, what ever, whatsoever

What ever is that funny thing over there? and *Whatever you do, don't miss the movie on Channel Five tonight* are two examples of legitimate usage of **what ever** and **whatever**. **Whatever** means 'no matter what' (*Whatever the problems, I promise to finish the job*). **What ever** is used as an interrogative: *What ever is the matter with you?* **Whatsoever** is vaguely synonymous in the context of 'at all': *Have you no manners whatsoever?* But the usage that has grown into a monster has resulted from the hijacking of **whatever** to mean 'and so on and so forth and who cares anyway?': *On Sundays I usually do some shopping, wash my hair, empty the cat litter, generally slob around and, you know, whatever…*

whet. See **wet, whet**

whether. See **if, whether**

which. See **that, which, who**

while, a while, awhile, whilst

While is a notoriously ambiguous word. In its sense of 'at the same time', there is little confusion (*You can talk to me while I iron these shirts*) but watch out for ambiguity when the meaning is 'whereas, although or but': *My wife likes a good laugh, while I watch the news; While he sleeps like a log, I like to party all night; James spent his childhood in Devon, while his parents grew up in Scotland.* **A while** is the noun and this can be tricky, too. Make sure you indicate whether it is a **long while** or a **short while.** *We only waited for a while* implies a short time and *We waited for quite a while* indicates a longer time, but both are imprecise. **A while** is the adverb which means 'a short while': *We waited awhile.* **Whilst** is an old-fashioned form of *while* and ought to be avoided.

whisky, whiskey

Traditionally, **whisky** is produced in Scotland (*Scotch whisky*), whereas **whiskey** is the equivalent Irish, American and Canadian liquor.

white paper, green paper

A **white paper** is a published report that states the [British] Government's policy on legislation that will come before Parliament. A **green paper** sets out proposals for legislation for discussion and comment by interested parties.

whither. See **wither, whither**

To Whomever It May Concern: Who and Whom

It is not easy to explain the rules governing the use of **who** and **whom**, and as a consequence popular usage has all but abandoned **whom** because of (a) the likelihood of using it incorrectly, and (b) the fear of sounding pompous. Furthermore, exclusive users of **who** are probably right 80 per cent of the time. But if you wish to retain **whom** in your vocabulary, the rough-and-ready **who/whom, he/him/ she/her** formula should help. Simply substitute **he** or **she** for **who,** and **him** or **her** for **whom**: thus *He is a man who/whom I know is honest.* He is honest? Him is honest? The answer is obviously '*he*' and therefore the correct choice in this example is **who**. To take another example: *That's the lady who/whom I spoke to about the tickets.* I spoke to she? I spoke to her? The latter is correct and therefore so is **whom**: *That's the lady to whom I spoke about the tickets.* You can remember the rules with the celebrated mnemonic derived from a John Donne sermon. Which sounds right: *For Whom the Bell Tolls* (It tolls for him/her), or *For Who the Bell Tolls* (It tolls for he/she)? Obviously the first choice is the correct one.

whoever, who ever

Whoever you are, you are not welcome uses **whoever** in its correct sense of 'no matter who you are'. The two-word version is used when **ever** is used for emphasis and usually in the interrogative: *Who ever could have done this?* This general rule of usage also applies to **whatever/ what ever, whenever/when ever,** and **wherever/where ever**.

whose, who's

Whose always relates to possession; it can ask, for example, *Whose book is this?* or it can act as a relative pronoun: *That's the man whose car was stolen.* **Who's** is an abbreviation of **who is** or **who has**: *Who's [who is] knocking at the door?; Who's [who has] been using my paint brushes?*

will, would. See shall, should, will, would

wither, withers, whither

Spelling is the problem here. **Whither** is little used today but means 'where to'; simply remember the 'wh' of **where**. **Wither** means 'wilt, decay, decline or dry up': *The entire crop was left to wither on the vine.* The **withers** are situated between the shoulder blades of a horse.

witness. See see, witness

woman. See **lady, woman**

wont, won't

Won't is a contraction of 'will not': *Young Tom simply won't do as he's told*. If you omit the apostrophe you have **wont**, either as an adjective meaning 'accustomed' (*He was wont to break into song after his fourth pint*) or as a noun meaning 'habit': *After lunch she read, pottered in the garden or dozed as was her wont*.

workable. See **viable, workable**

worthwhile, worth while

Worth while is almost always a redundancy: *Marcus said that the concert was worth while going to*. If you drop the '*while*' there is no loss of meaning, so drop it: *Marcus said that the concert was worth going to*. **Worthwhile** is an adjective meaning 'sufficiently rewarding or important': *They all agreed it was a worthwhile concert*.

would. See **shall, will, would, should**

wrack, rack

'*Wracked on the wheel of growth*' is a classic (and common) mistake. **Wrack** has the following meanings: 1. seaweed or other floating vegetation 2. wreck or piece of wreckage. **Rack** on the other hand has a plethora of meanings, not one of them having anything to do with seaweed or wreckage: a frame or framework for storing objects; an instrument of torture; mental or bodily stress; a snooker triangle for holding the balls; to rack a bottle of wine; to rack one's brain, and a dozen or so more.

wrapped, rapt

'*She was huddled by the fire, wrapped in thought*': Although one of the several meanings of **wrapped** is 'enclosed, or completely absorbed in thought', **rapt**, meaning 'engrossed, spellbound, fascinated' is probably a better choice.

wreath, wraith

A **wreath** is a circular band of flowers offered as a memorial at funerals; a **wraith** is a ghost or apparition.

write, write to

Avoid the American usage of **write**: *I'm going to write my congressman to protest*. In British English, the 'to' that follows **write** is mandatory. As a word wag once observed: *You may write the Library of Congress, but you **write** to the British Library*.

X

Xerox

It's common to hear *'Can you Xerox this for me, please?*, even though the copier may be a Canon or some other make. Like Hoover, Durex and Cellophane, **Xerox** is a trade name, not a generic name, and should be capitalised.

Xmas, xmas

Heaven forbid! Never lower case!

X-ray

X-ray is the accepted spelling of the noun although when used as a verb in a sentence it is common to use only lower case: *Tim had to have his shoulder x-rayed*.

Y

Yiddish. See **Jewish, Hebrew, Yiddish**

yoghurt, yogurt, yoghourt
All three spellings are correct somewhere in the world but in the UK **yoghurt** and **yogurt** are now standard. It is specifically fermented milk using two bacteria, *Lactobacillus bulgaricus* and *Streptococcus thermophilus*.

yoke, yolk
Both are pronounced the same and there is occasional confusion. The **yolk** is the yellow part of an egg; a **yoke** is traditionally the collar and bar worn by oxen but is now mostly used figuratively: *The peasants had suffered under the yoke for too long and were ready to revolt.*

YOKE, YOLK

you (*the reader*) and one

The use of the pronoun '**one**' to represent an indefinite person (*One doesn't do that kind of thing*) is stylish and elegant but can be regarded as affected. **You** is the democratic substitute and has the additional advantage of informally but directly addressing the reader: *You simply don't do that kind of thing*. Choose one or the other but don't mix them in mid-sentence as in this example: *Soon one phones one's publisher to see if one's year of birth can be removed from the [dust] jacket. Presumably, as one gets older, one gets asked instead whether the reason no one will touch you with a bargepole is because you keep writing books detailing the foul personal habits of your former boyfriends* (novelist Rachel Cusk in The Times).

your, yours, you're

Your means 'belonging to you or belonging to an unspecified person': *I love your house. Is this your own house? Is that your opinion?* **Yours** identifies a particular entity belonging to you: *Is this jacket yours? That son of yours is a real tearaway*. It is never spelt with an apostrophe. **You're** is frequently confused with **your** but it is a contraction of '**you are**': *You're [you are] all quite mad!*

Yours faithfully, Yours sincerely, Yours truly

Yours does not have an apostrophe. **Yours faithfully** is the traditional formal closing at the end of, say, business communications or letters to strangers, while **Yours sincerely** has been preferred when the writer is addressing a named or known person. Now the difference is smudged. If you want to indicate a degree of friendliness or closeness, use *sincerely* or *truly* or some other variation. **Yours Aye** is a charming Scottish sign-off.

Z

Zeitgeist

Zeitgeist is a word borrowed from Germany in the 19th century and used rather prolifically since. It means 'the spirit of the time or age' and should always be capitalised.